THE BARBARY COAST

AN INFORMAL HISTORY OF
THE SAN FRANCISCO
UNDERWORLD

BY

HERBERT ASBURY

BASIC
BOOKS

A MEMBER OF THE PERSEUS BOOKS GROUP
NEW YORK

To Helen

Copyright © 1933 by Alfred A. Knopf

Published in 2008 by Basic Books,
A Member of the Perseus Books Group
Previously published by Thunder's Mouth Press
Published in 1933 by Alfred A. Knopf

Books published by Basic Books are available at
special discounts for bulk purchases in the United States
by corporations, institutions, and other organizations. For more
information, please contact the Special Markets Department at
the Perseus Books Group, 2300 Chestnut Street, Suite 200,
Philadelphia, PA 19103, or call (800) 810-4145, ext. 5000,
or e-mail special.markets@perseusbooks.com.

A CIP catalog record for this book is available
from the Library of Congress.
ISBN: 978-1-56025-408-9

CONTENTS

AUTHOR'S NOTE

FOR ADVICE and assistance in gathering the material for this book I am greatly indebted to many San Franciscans, among them Idwal Jones, Edgar T. Gleeson, Fremont Older, Dean Behslich, Luke Fay, Chief of Police William J. Quinn, Lieutenant James Boland, Sergeant Patrick McGee, Thomas Crowley; Mrs. Eugene Welch and Miss Helen Hamilton of the Public Library staff; Miss Mabel R. Gilles and Miss Endora Garoutte of the State Library at Sacramento; Paul Joseph Tomanoczy of the Civic Center Book Shop and Mrs. Elspeth Sedwick, through whose courtesy I was permitted to read the manuscript reminiscences of an old-time San Franciscan which Mrs. Sedwick is preparing for publication; and many members of the Family and Bohemian clubs.

I am especially grateful to Richard Prosser, Edward F. O'Day, and William Wren, without whose aid my task would have been much more difficult.

H. A.

CHAPTER I

"THE MINERS CAME IN FORTY-NINE"

THE HISTORY of the Barbary Coast properly begins
with the gold rush to California in 1849. If the precious
yellow metal hadn't been discovered in the auriferous sands
of the Sacramento Valley, the development of San Francisco's underworld in all likelihood would have proceeded
according to the traditional pattern and would have been
indistinguishable from that of any other large American
city. Instead, owing almost entirely to the influx of gold-
seekers and the horde of gamblers, thieves, harlots, politicians and other felonious parasites who battened upon
them, there arose a unique criminal district that for almost
seventy years was the scene of more viciousness and depravity, but which at the same time possessed more glamour,
than any other area of vice and iniquity on the American
continent.

2

BEFORE the beginning of the epochal movement which
brought thousands of fortune-hunting adventurers to California within a period of half a dozen years, the cosmopolitan San Francisco of song and story didn't exist, even in the
imagination of its most optimistic and far-sighted booster.
There was simply a straggling line of tents, slab shanties,
and adobe huts stretching along the beach of Yerba Buena
Cove, a horseshoe-shaped indentation in the western shore

of the Bay of San Francisco, which has long since been filled
in and built upon. Until the gold-seekers began to swarm
through the Golden Gate and across the plains, the permanent population of the somnolent little village never exceeded a few hundred. Despite the possession of one of the
finest natural harbors in the world, it was only an occasional
port of call for whaling vessels, and a trading post of such
minor importance that the Hudson's Bay Company abandoned it after vainly striving for five years to establish a
profitable commerce.

The Franciscan monks built a Mission two and one-half
miles southwest of Yerba Buena Cove in 1776, and that
same year the Mexicans established a Presidio, or fortified
military post, near the Golden Gate. But it was not until
1835 that the first dwelling on the present site of San Francisco — a canvas tent supported by four redwood posts and
covered with a ship's foresail — was erected by Captain
W. A. Richardson, an American who had been appointed
harbor-master by the Mexican government. He called the
settlement Yerba Buena, meaning "good herb," the popular
designation of a fragrant mint which grew in great profusion throughout the Bay district, and from which the
native Californians brewed tea. The name was changed to
San Francisco by order of the Alcalde, or Mayor, on January 30, 1847, a little more than six months after the American flag had been raised in the Plaza by Captain Montgomery and a detachment of sailors from the sloop-of-war
Portsmouth. In memory of this latter historic event the
Plaza was thereafter called Portsmouth Square, and the
thoroughfare along the waterfront, now half a mile or so
inland, was renamed Montgomery Street.

According to a census taken by the Board of School
Trustees about a year and a half after the landing of Captain Montgomery, the population of San Francisco was approximately seven hundred whites, about half of whom were

Americans, and a hundred and fifty Indians, Negroes, and Sandwich Islanders. The town contained two hundred buildings, including tents, sheds, and outhouses.

3

CAPTAIN JOHN A. SUTTER, a native of Germany, but until his middle years a citizen of Switzerland, arrived in California in 1839, after an adventurous career in Missouri, Oregon, Alaska, and the Sandwich Islands. He swore fealty to the Mexican government, was granted an enormous tract of land in the Sacramento Valley, and promptly took possession of an immense adjoining area, throughout which his rule was almost absolute. He called his kingdom New Helvetia, and as a capital founded a small settlement, Sutter's Fort, which consisted of a few dwellings, a blockhouse for protection from marauding bands of Indians, and a general store operated by Samuel Brannan, a Mormon Elder who had been Brigham Young's official representative in New York. On February 15, 1846, the day that the Mormons under Young left Nauvoo, Illinois, on their long march across the plains to the promised land of Utah, Brannan and a company of Mormon immigrants set sail from New York harbor in the ship *Brooklyn*. They were bound for the Pacific Coast, where they hoped to establish a colony in a country over which the United States had no jurisdiction. But the war with Mexico was won while the *Brooklyn* was at sea, and the ship sailed through the Golden Gate only a few days after Captain Montgomery had landed his sailors from the *Portsmouth*. The first thing Brannan saw when his vessel entered the Bay of San Francisco was the American flag flying from the Presidio. According to eyewitnesses, the Elder was so enraged that he flung his hat to the deck and cried in disgust: "There's that damned rag again!"[1] Nevertheless, Brannan decided to land, partly because

---

[1] M. R. Werner's biography of *Brigham Young*, page 229.

supplies were running low, and partly because dissension had arisen among the Mormons during the long voyage. He had excommunicated four of the leading men of the company for conduct which he described as " wicked and licentious," and they in turn had accused him of improperly administering communal funds. These latter charges ultimately became the basis of a court action which was tried before the first jury ever impaneled in California. Brannan was acquitted.

Having settled his flock in tents and adobe huts near Yerba Buena Cove, Brannan hurried overland to meet Brigham Young. He tried unsuccessfully to induce the Mormon leader to abandon his plan of settling in the valley of the Great Salt Lake and urged him to lead the whole body of Mormons into California and build up a strong Mormon state in the territory surrounding the Bay of San Francisco, which he represented as possessing an incomparable climate and soil of extraordinary fertility. He thus became, perhaps, the first California booster, the founder of a long line of vociferous enthusiasts whose clamor has resounded throughout the land for more than eighty years.[1] It is interesting, but, of course, fruitless, to speculate on what might have been the fate of Mormonism had Brigham Young listened to Brannan's arguments. It is quite likely that the Church would have been disrupted by the discovery of gold and the resultant excitement and corruption, for not even a devout Mormon can always resist the temptation to lay up treasures on earth instead of in heaven.

Brigham Young had no notion that gold would ever be found along the Pacific Coast, but he shrewdly foresaw that any area with the advantages offered by California would be thickly settled. He told Brannan that it would be inad-

---

[1] Brannan also published the first booster article about the advantages of California. On April 1, 1848 he issued a special number of his newspaper, the *California Star*, which contained an article prepared by Dr. Victor J. Fourgead, entitled: "The Prospects of California." Two thousand extra copies of the issue were printed and sent to Missouri for distribution.

visable to bring the Mormons in contact with competitive peoples, and that it would be fatal for them to attempt to colonize a seaport. Brannan returned forthwith to California, where he told the Mormons who had accompanied him to San Francisco that Utah was a poor land, and advised them not to join their brethren. In January 1847 Brannan established San Francisco's first newspaper, the *California Star,* and soon thereafter opened his store at Sutter's Fort. He declined to recognize the authority of Brigham Young, although he continued for several years to collect tithes regularly from the members of his flock. During the gold rush, when many California Mormons became wealthy, these amounted to considerable sums. None of this money was ever remitted to the Church at Salt Lake City, and when Brigham Young made formal demand for "the Lord's share," and also for a share of Brannan's personal earnings, Brannan retorted that he would pay upon a written order signed by the Lord, and not otherwise. According to Asbury Harpending, an associate of Brannan's in various business enterprises, Brigham Young several times dispatched his holy gunmen, better known as Destroying Angels, to San Francisco to deal with Brannan and collect the money by force. But the Angels were invariably met in the desert, and their wings clipped, by Brannan's "exterminators," fighting men whom he is said to have employed as a bodyguard for half a dozen years.[1]

The Mormons never became powerful in San Francisco, and ultimately Brannan resigned from the Church and devoted himself successfully to his publishing, mercantile, and mining ventures. For almost twenty years he was an important figure in the growth of San Francisco, and his place in the history of the city is secure as the principal organizer

---

[1] Described in Harpending's autobiography: *The Great Diamond Hoax, and Other Stirring Episodes in the Life of Asbury Harpending,* edited by James H. Wilkins. San Francisco, 1913.

of the first Vigilance Committee and as the head of another body which performed similar functions without using the name. In time, however, he became a drunkard, dissipated his fortune, and wandered to Mexico, where he died alone and in dire poverty.

4

IN January 1848 Captain Sutter employed James W. Marshall, an itinerant contractor, to construct a mill on a fork of the American River, some sixty miles east of the present site of the city of Sacramento. Marshall found it necessary to cut a tail-race and divert a portion of the river's current. The swift flow of water soon washed away the loose gravel and exposed a substratum glistening with tiny particles of gold, which Marshall gathered from the tail-race.[1] There are innumerable accounts of what immediately followed. One story is that Captain Sutter arranged with Marshall to say nothing of the discovery until they had enriched themselves, but that they were betrayed by a female servant who overheard them discussing the find. Another has it that Samuel Brannan filled a small sack with nuggets and gold dust, and in great excitement rode through the countryside shouting: "Gold! Gold! Gold from the American River!" A third story is that Captain Sutter convinced Marshall that the gold was worthless pyrite, and for several weeks they threw away all that came into their hands, making no effort to work the deposits or in any way to develop the find. One large nugget, however, was sent to San Francisco to be exhibited as a curiosity and was examined by Isaac Humphrey, a native of Georgia, who had had considerable mining experience. Humphrey recognized the metal as gold and,

---

[1] The exact date of the find has never been known. Marshall himself, at various times, gave three different dates — the 18th, the 19th, and the 20th of January. About 1905 the California Pioneers adopted January 24 as the proper date, on the authority of an entry in a diary kept by W. H. Bigler, a Mormon who had helped construct the mill. Bigler wrote: "January 24. This day some kind of metal that looks like gold was found in the tail race."

despite the ridicule of his friends, hurried to Sutter's mill and began prospecting. He struck a rich pocket almost immediately.

This was in March 1848, but it was not until the latter part of April that the people of San Francisco, and of other settlements in California and along the Pacific Coast, were convinced that gold had actually been found. Then they deserted their homes and abandoned their occupations and almost overnight moved *en masse* to the gold-fields. By May 1, 1848 at least two thousand men were scratching like hens in the sand and gravel of the Sacramento Valley. Within a few more weeks their numbers had been tripled by the arrival of Mexicans and natives of other Central and South American countries, who were probably the first persons not residents of the territory to dig for gold in California. Once the precious metal had been found, it seemed to be everywhere, and mining operations soon spread from the American to the Yuba and Feather rivers and then to all the ravines, gulches, and streams up to the Sierra Mountains. And of all the thousands who delved in the earth for riches none fared worse than Marshall, who had discovered the gold, or Captain Sutter, who owned the land upon which gold had first been found. Neither then nor thereafter did anyone ask Captain Sutter for permission to prospect his property, and the gold-hunters only laughed when he tried to exact a levy of ten per cent of all gold mined. Moreover, the swarming miners overran his fields, destroyed his crops, razed his buildings or appropriated them to their own uses, and killed his cattle. They even ruined his garden to obtain the particles of gold which clung to the roots of vegetables and tufts of grass. Eventually Captain Sutter lost everything he had, including title to his land. He spent his declining years in Washington, trying to obtain recompense from Congress. Having no special political influence, he failed. Marshall sold his share of the mill for about two

9

thousand dollars, and it is doubtful whether he made much more during the entire gold rush. He appears to have devoted himself almost entirely to wearing his laurels as the discoverer, to quarreling with the miners over questions of landownership, and to boasting of having made new and important finds. Many thought he was withholding knowledge of richer deposits through sheer meanness, and the miners at length became so infuriated that they threatened to lynch him unless he divulged the location of the new fields. Since it was impossible for him to impart information he didn't have, he fled the district, whereupon the miners wrecked the mill with such thoroughness that the spot upon which it stood has never been found.

Late in June 1848 Thomas O. Larkin, who had been American Consul at Monterey when California was under Mexican rule, wrote an enthusiastic letter about the discovery of gold to James Buchanan, later President of the United States, but then Secretary of State. Rapid means of communication and transportation were sorely lacking in those days, and except for Larkin's report and a few private letters no word of the new Dorado reached the Atlantic seaboard until September 1848, when the Baltimore *Sun* published a short account, which was reprinted in Boston, New York, and Philadelphia. The news gradually filtered through to the middle west, and by the late autumn of 1848 several parties had started overland for California. Months were required to make the journey by wagon train, however, and before any of these companies arrived, the steamship *California*, first of the line of Pacific mail steamers, anchored in Yerba Buena Cove with the first gold-hunters from the Eastern and Southern states. This was in February 1849.

Thereafter they came in a steady stream. In less than a year after the arrival of the first shipload of immigrants, between forty thousand and fifty thousand men had passed through the Golden Gate *en route* to the gold-fields. By the middle of July 1849 Yerba Buena Cove and other anchorages in the Bay of San Francisco were crowded with useless shipping; no sooner had a vessel dropped anchor than the sailors, and frequently the officers as well, took possession of the lifeboats and started up the Sacramento River toward the mines. "For of all people," wrote a historian of the period, "sailors were the most unrestrainable in their determination to go to the diggings; and it was there a common saying, of the truth of which I myself saw many examples, that sailors, niggers and Dutchmen were the luckiest men in the mines; a very drunken old salt was always particularly lucky." [1] Entire crews deserted their ships before either the freight or the passengers had been discharged, leaving the former to the mercy of thieves, and the latter to make their way ashore as best they could. Sometimes this was a very hazardous undertaking, for San Francisco then boasted but one small wharf, and it was necessary to load and unload most of the ships by means of scows, lighters, and small boats. For these craft it was well-nigh impossible to obtain crews except at exorbitant wages, and the men who could be hired were almost invariably without experience. During the height of the gold excitement, there were at least five hundred ships stranded in the harbor, some without even a watchman on board, and none with a crew sufficiently large to work her. Many of these vessels never sailed again. Some rotted away and sank at their moorings. Others were drawn up on the beach and turned into saloons and boarding-houses, remaining in use long after the filling in of the cove had begun and buildings were being constructed around them. One, the clipper ship *Niantic,* was sunk in shallow water about where Clay and Sansome streets now intersect, and became the foundation of the Niantic Hotel, a famous hostelry of the early days.

---

[1] *The Gold Hunters,* by J. D. Borthwick; 1924 edition; page 73.

More than half of the immigrants who arrived after the first excitement of the gold rush had subsided remained in San Francisco and engaged in various businesses and speculations, many of which were infinitely more remunerative than digging for gold would have been. By the beginning of 1850 the city had a permanent population of at least twenty-five thousand, most of whom were adult males under forty, and had become the foremost American port on the Pacific, a distinction which it retained until the phenomenal rise of Los Angeles. Several streets were marked out along the foot of the sand-hills behind Yerba Buena Cove as soon as it had become evident that the town was destined to thrive like a veritable municipal mushroom, and a few were cut through the hills. But they were neither paved nor properly graded, and in consequence were extraordinarily uneven and irregular. One man's habitation might be on the same street as that of his nearest neighbor and still be twenty to fifty feet higher or lower. Or it might perch on the side of a hill nearly thirty feet above the rim of a gulch that necessity had made an important thoroughfare. The continual passage of men, animals, and wagons soon cut up these makeshift highways until they were little more than gigantic mud-holes. Several times during the rainy season of 1849–50 horses, mules, and carts were sucked down into the mud, and the animals were drowned; and many men, trying to cross the streets while drunk, narrowly escaped similar deaths.[1] In a vain attempt to improve conditions the city authorities purchased a great quantity of brushwood and dumped it into the streets, but it soon sank from sight, as did the boxes, barrels, and other refuse thrown out by the citizens. The mud at Clay and Kearny streets, in the heart of town, at length became so deep and thick that a wag posted this sign:

---

[1] Several writers have said that men were actually drowned in these quagmires, but I have been unable to verify these statements.

THIS STREET IS IMPASSABLE;
NOT EVEN JACKASSABLE.

There were not nearly enough dwellings in San Francisco to shelter even a small proportion of the new-comers, most of whom consequently were housed in leaky canvas tents or in hastily constructed board shanties with muslin or Osnaburg partitions. Many of the lodging-houses, and some of the more pretentious hotels as well, consisted simply of one or more large rooms, with bunks fastened to the walls, and rows of uncomfortable cots on the floor. To sleep in a bunk or a cot cost as high as fifteen dollars a night, although none had either springs or mattresses. Very few private rooms were available, and the cheapest rented for from two hundred to three hundred dollars a month, payable in advance. The best brought from five hundred to a thousand dollars for a similar period. Enterprising landlords also rented sleeping-space on tables, benches, and other articles of furniture at from two to ten dollars for eight hours. One man is said to have realized fifty dollars a night from the rental of half a dozen rickety old rocking-chairs. Another placed wide redwood planks on saw-horses and sold the right to sleep on them for three dollars, the occupant to furnish his own bedding. In all of these flimsy places roamed millions of flies, lice, and other noxious bugs and insects, besides the huge gray rats, which almost immediately began to infest the waterfront and the muddy streets. Many of these repulsive rodents attained such size and ferocity that they were more than a match for a terrier, and they often attacked sleeping men, biting large chunks from ears, noses, and cheeks. In several houses signs were displayed warning the guests to cover their heads. Even this didn't help much, however, for the thrifty landlord usually removed the covers from a man's body as soon as he was asleep and gave them to a late comer.

13

The cost of practically every commodity and of every sort of personal service was on a par with that of lodging. There were few men willing to perform the necessary menial tasks, and those who did condescend to undertake such work not only charged accordingly but insisted upon grandiloquent titles calculated to disguise and dignify their labors. Thus, the few washerwomen in the town put out signs announcing " Clothing Refreshed "; the porters who handled the baggage of travelers called themselves " baggage conveyors and transporters," and the waiters in the hotels and restaurants refused to respond unless addressed respectfully as " Mister Steward." Fewer than a score of cooks were in private service, but they insisted, of course, upon being called " chefs." A notable exception to this foolery was Mammy Pleasant, a gigantic Negress from New Orleans, black as the inside of a coal-pit, but with no Negroid features whatever, whose culinary exploits were famous. She said flatly that she was a cook, and would be called nothing else. She arrived in the early part of 1850, preceded by her reputation, and was besieged by a crowd of men, all anxious to employ her, before she had so much as left the wharf at which her ship had docked. She finally sold her services at auction for five hundred dollars a month, with the stipulation that she should do no washing, not even dish-washing. This was the highest wage paid to a cook, although several others received as much as three hundred dollars a month. The porters refused to lift even the smallest piece of baggage for less than two dollars, the stewards commanded a daily wage of thirty dollars, and common laborers received from one to two dollars an hour. Washing cost twenty dollars a dozen pieces, regardless of size. So unsatisfactory was the work done by the ladies of the washhouses, however, that most of the gentry, the wealthy gamblers, and the rich miners sent their linen underwear and boiled shirts by clipper ship to Honolulu or Canton to be laundered with proper care. From three to six months were required for a garment to make such a voyage, but at least it was clean and wearable when it was returned. The cost of washing remained at the twenty-dollar level until the spring of 1850, when it was reduced to eight dollars a dozen and then to five, whereupon the *Alta California* commented: "There is now no excuse for our citizens to wear soiled or colored shirts. The effect of the reduction is already manifest — tobacco-juice-bespattered bosoms are no longer the fashion."

Vegetables in early San Francisco were luxuries that only the very rich could afford, despite the enormous yield of the near-by farms and ranches, some of which produced carrots a yard long, beets the size of small hogsheads, and cabbages from fifteen to twenty inches in diameter. Apples found a ready market at one to five dollars each, and eggs varied from ten to fifty dollars a dozen. In the restaurants a boiled egg cost never less than a dollar and quite often was several times that amount. Other foods sold at equally high prices. Tea and coffee cost from three hundred to four hundred dollars a barrel, and from four to five dollars a pound in small quantities. Wheat flour and salt pork each brought forty dollars a barrel, and a small loaf of bread, such as sold in New York for four cents, cost fifty to seventy-five cents in San Francisco. The same price was paid for a pound of common cheese.

Butcher-knives were thirty dollars each, shovels from fifteen to twenty-five dollars, and a tin wash-bowl, or pan, was considered cheap at five dollars. A blanket of the commonest sort could not be obtained for less than forty dollars, and boots of good quality cost a hundred dollars a pair. Cheaper footwear, however, was on the market at thirty to fifty dollars. Any sort of medicine, even a common pill, was ten dollars a dose, and laudanum and other drugs sold for a dollar a drop. A miner who suffered from in-

15

somnia once paid fifty dollars for enough laudanum to put
him to sleep. The few doctors in the town would not write
a prescription for less than one hundred dollars, and a
quart of good whisky cost thirty dollars, which would be
an extraordinary price even in these jolly days of Prohibition. A twenty-foot plank cost twenty dollars, but lumber
in bulk was only five hundred dollars a thousand feet. The
cost of a brick house was estimated at one dollar a brick.
Common iron tacks of the smallest size, much in demand
for fastening cloth partitions, were worth their weight in
gold — a pound of gold bought a pound of tacks. Since
gold was current at sixteen dollars an ounce (the rate of
exchange established at a public meeting in September
1848), the tacks actually cost the purchaser $192 a pound.
So far as the records show, this was the top price, although
tacks seldom dropped below ten dollars an ounce for more
than a year. By that time San Francisco had begun to pass
the muslin-partition stage, and so many tacks had been
imported that they couldn't be given away. One merchandising genius is said to have brought in a whole shipload, most
of which were eventually dumped into the bay at a considerable loss.

Rentals of hotels and other business structures, whether
of boards or of canvas, reached even dizzier heights than
did commodity prices. A single small store on Portsmouth
Square, with a fifteen-foot frontage, brought $3,000 a
month, and another, half a block away, rented for $40,000
a year. The rent of a tiny cigar-store barely large enough
for one man to stand in was $4,000 a month, and the opera-
tor of a bowling-alley in the basement of the Ward House,
which was erected on the square early in 1850, paid $5,000
a month to the owners of the property. The Parker House,
a two-storey frame structure which had cost $30,000 to
build, rented for $120,000 a year. Of this amount, half
was paid by gamblers, who occupied the whole of the second

floor. El Dorado, a gambling saloon which adjoined the Parker House, at Washington and Kearny streets, on the present site of the Hall of Justice, brought $40,000 a year to its owners, although it was nothing more than a canvas tent, fifteen by twenty-five feet. A small building on another corner of the square, occupied by a brokerage firm, rented for $75,000 a year; the proprietor of the United States Hotel, the first hostelry in San Francisco, paid $36,000 a year; and the United States government paid $7,000 a month for the board shanty which housed the Customs Office.

5

THE first public entertainment in San Francisco after the beginning of the gold rush was a circus, which gave its initial performance early in the spring of 1849, in a vacant lot on Kearny Street near Clay. Another similar show was opened a year later, and soon afterwards a third. They were described by a contemporary historian as " mere tent structures, where, on rude benches, congregated crowds of easily satisfied and deeply interested spectators, and where springboards bounced men of various sizes successively over one, two, and three horses; and daring riders, on broad wooden saddles, jumped through hoops and over ropes, most fearfully to look at." To watch these exhibitions, the spectators paid three dollars for seats in the pit, five dollars for a box, and fifty-five dollars for private stalls. The first theatrical performance, a double bill presenting *The Wife* and *Charles the Second,* was given by a traveling troupe in January 1850, in Washington Hall, a flimsy board structure on Portsmouth Square which later became the town's most elegant brothel. The first actual theater was not established, however, until April of that same year, when a French vaudeville company gave several performances in a new building on Washington Street near Montgomery. A group

17

of amateurs presented various plays at a new house called
"The Dramatic Museum" during the summer of 1850, and
in September of that year the curtain rose for the first time
in the famous Jenny Lind Theatre above the Parker House
saloon, which was owned by Tom Maguire, a celebrated
gambler and sporting man of the period. The Jenny Lind
was destroyed by fire within a few months, as was the
wooden structure which replaced it. After the conflagration
of June 22, 1851 Maguire built a new theater of stone,
which was soon afterwards purchased by the municipal
authorities for two hundred thousand dollars. For several
years it was used as a City Hall.

Despite these various amusements, all of which were
well patronized, gambling remained the principal diversion
of the great mass of restless, turbulent, gold-hungry men who
almost over night had transformed the once peaceful hamlet
of San Francisco into a bawdy, bustling bedlam of mud-
holes and shanties. "While wages and profits were so high,
and there was no comfort at their sleeping quarters," wrote
the city's first historian, "men spent money freely at different places of riotous excess, and were indeed forced to
pass their hours of leisure or recreation at drinking bars,
billiard rooms and gambling saloons. Such places were
accordingly crowded with a motley crew, who drank, swore,
and gamed to their hearts' content. *Everybody did so;* and
that circumstance was a sufficient excuse, if one were needed,
to the neophyte in debauchery. . . . But of all their haunts,
the gambling saloons were the most notorious and the best
patronized. Gambling was . . . *the* amusement — *the*
grand occupation of many classes — apparently the life and
soul of the place. . . . The extensive saloons, in each of
which a dozen . . . tables might be placed, were continually
crowded, and around the tables themselves the players often
stood in lines three or four deep, every one vieing with his
neighbors for the privilege of reaching the board, and

staking his money as fast as the wheel and ball could be rolled or the card turned. . . . Judges and clergymen, physicians and advocates, merchants and clerks, tradesmen, mechanics, laborers, miners and farmers, all adventurers in their kind — every one elbowed his way to the gaming-table, and unblushingly threw down his golden or silver stake."[1]

The exact number of gambling places in early San Francisco was never determined, but there were at least several hundred; perhaps as many as a thousand. Probably no other American city of similar size ever sheltered so many games of chance in operation at one time. No effort whatever was made to suppress them, and very little to control them; until 1855 they were, indeed, licensed by the city, and any man who wished to do so might open a gambling house or set up his tables wherever he pleased, so long as he paid the regular license fees, and perhaps a bit extra for the politicians. The first state-wide anti-gambling law in California was passed by the Legislature during the winter of 1854, but its only effect was to close a few of the smaller establishments. It was never generally enforced, and the only conviction under it was that of a crooked faro dealer in Tuolumne. It was repealed in 1859, largely through the efforts of Colonel Jack Gamble, who lived up to his name by being one of San Francisco's most expert gamblers. In later years Colonel Gamble opened a road-house, with roulette-wheels and rooms for card and dice games, on the San Jose highway fourteen miles down the peninsula from San Francisco, but was compelled to abandon the resort in 1873, when the Legislature enacted another anti-gambling law which was actually enforced.[2]

---

[1] *The Annals of San Francisco*, by Frank Soulé, John H. Gihon, M.D., and James Nisbet; New York, 1855; pages 248, 249-50.

[2] On January 11, 1848, about two weeks before the discovery of gold, the San Francisco authorities enacted an ordinance providing heavy fines for card-playing, and authorizing the seizure of all moneys found on gambling

Practically all of the big games in gold-rush days were square, the gambler depending for his profits on his skill and the naturally large percentage in favor of the banker. If a sharper attempted to operate a brace game, he was fortunate if he was not killed or run out of town. In any event his tables were deserted and he was soon starved out. The most popular games were monte, faro, rondo, roulette, rouge et noir, and vingt-et-un. Poker was comparatively unknown, for the restive San Franciscans, and the miners who regularly risked the proceeds of their back-breaking toil, considered this prince of gambling games too slow. They would not sit still long enough to play it; they craved prompt and immediate action and insisted upon staking everything upon one spin of the wheel or the turn of a single card. It was not until the banking games began to decline in popularity that poker came into its own, although a few games were in operation as early as the fall of 1849, and several stiff sessions are recorded. In one, Tony Bleecker, of the mercantile firm of Bleecker, Van Dyke & Belden, is said to have lost thirty thousand dollars at a single sitting, to a syndicate of gamblers consisting of Jim Beckett, Jim McCullough, Jack Addison, and Dick Berry.[1] Next day Bleecker insisted that he had been jobbed, refused to pay, and departed for Panama.

Portsmouth Square, the old Plaza of Mexican days, was the gambling center of the town until the gamblers were eventually driven out by the encroachments of business and changes in public and political opinion. All of the eastern side of the square, three-fourths of the northern, and a large part of the southern were occupied by buildings devoted exclusively to gambling, while tables were also available for play in the saloons and in the bar-rooms of the hotels.

---

tables. The law was so unpopular, however, that it was never enforced. It was repealed at the next meeting of the Town Council.

[1] Described in the San Francisco *Call*, April 11, 1886.

All ran wide open day and night, seven days a week, as did many other establishments in the side-streets and along the waterfront. Monte and faro lay-outs and various kinds of chuck-a-luck games were also operated, in good weather, on the streets and the plank sidewalks and in the center of the square, which at that time was little more than a wind-swept stretch of sand. The western side of the square was occupied by a few hotels and small stores, and an old adobe house, from the steps of which the Reverend William Taylor, a pioneer street preacher of the gold rush, daily fulminated against gambling and its attendant evils, while all around him the square fairly swarmed with the objects of his ecclesiastical blasts. The scene was thus described by Wilson Flint, in later years a California state Senator, in a letter to the Reverend Mr. Taylor:

"It was on a Sunday morning in December, 1849, when landing from the Panama steamer I wended my way with the throng to Portsmouth Square, this being at the time the great resort of the denizens of this rising metropolis. Three sides of the Square were mostly occupied by buildings which served the double purpose of hotels and gambling houses, the latter calling being regarded at the time as a very respectable profession. On the fourth and upper side of the square was an adobe building, from the steps of which you were discoursing from the text, ' The way of the transgressor is hard.' It was a scene I shall never forget. On all sides of you were gambling houses, each with its band of music in full blast. Crowds were going in and coming out; fortunes were being lost and won; terrible imprecations and blasphemies rose amid the horrid wail, and it seemed to me pandemonium was let loose." [1]

---

[1] This letter was dated September 10, 1856, and is quoted in the introduction to the Reverend Mr. Taylor's book: *Seven Years of Street Preaching in*

The dens of iniquity against which the Reverend Mr. Taylor thundered so ineffectually on this and other occasions included such celebrated resorts as El Dorado, which is said to have been the first gambling house opened after the discovery of gold; the Parker House; Dennison's Exchange; the Empire; the Mazourka; the Arcade; the Varsouvienne; the Ward House; La Souciedad; the Fontine House; the St. Charles; the Alhambra; the Verandah; and the Aguila de Oro; all on or very near Portsmouth Square; Bill Briggs's place in Montgomery Street near Pine; and Steve Whipple's house in Commercial Street, later occupied by the Pacific Club.

Originally El Dorado was a canvas tent, but the tent was soon replaced by a large square room of rough boards, with a few small private booths partitioned off with muslin, where a man whose mind was elsewhere than on games of chance might entertain his inamorata of the moment. The walls were covered with costly paintings, extremely lascivious in character — which is to say they were principally pictures of nude women in various abandoned postures — and the furniture and fittings were of rococo elegance. At one end was a raised platform draped with bunting, flags, and colored streamers, from which an orchestra blared without cessation. At the other end was the bar, behind which were large mirrors of fine cut glass.[1] Scattered throughout the room were the gaming tables, on which were huge piles of gold dust, nuggets, and gold and silver coins. Behind

---

San Francisco; New York, 1856. The Reverend Mr. Taylor is also responsible for introducing the eucalyptus tree into California. While in Australia in 1863, he sent his wife several seedlings, which she duly planted. From them came the giants which now line the California highways.

[1] At El Dorado, in 1849, began the career of America's greatest bartender — Professor Jerry Thomas, inventor of the Blue Blazer and of Tom and Jerry. A full account of Professor Thomas's life and works may be found in the present author's introduction to Professor Thomas's book: *The Bon Vivant's Companion, or, How to Mix Drinks;* New York, Alfred A. Knopf, 1928.

each table sat the dealer, or croupier, clad in the traditional white and black of the professional gambler. If accounts of the time are to be credited, every man who operated a game of chance in early San Francisco was apparently in the last stages of tuberculosis; he is almost invariably described as tall, thin, and cadaverous, extremely saturnine of countenance and monastic of habit. He was, likewise, a killer, and when he ensconced himself at his table to deal the cards or spin the roulette-wheel, his trusty double-barreled derringer was ever at his elbow, while in his pockets reposed at least one heavy revolver and a bowie-knife, razor-sharp. In the use of these weapons he was, of course, an expert. Says Hubert Howe Bancroft, California's foremost historian:

" The character of the typical gambler of the flush times is one of the queerest mixtures in human nature. His temperament is mercurial but non-volatilized. . . . Supreme self-command is his cardinal quality; yet, except when immersed in the intricacies of a game, his actions appear to be governed only by impulse and fancy. On the other hand his swiftest vengeance and cruellest butchery seem rather the result of policy than passion. . . . He is never known to steal except at cards; and if caught cheating he either fights or blandly smiles his sin away, suffers the stakes to be raked down without a murmur, treats good-humoredly, and resumes the game unruffled. United with the coolest cunning is the coolest courage. He is as ready with his pistol as with his toothpick, but he never uses it unless he is right; then, he will kill a man as mercilessly as he would brush a fly from his immaculate linen. . . . He accustoms himself to do without sleep, and if necessary can go for several days and nights without rest. . . . He deals his game with the most perfect sang froid, and when undergoing the heaviest losses there is no trembling of fingers or change of expression. . . . He is studiously neat in his habits, and tends to foppishness. . . ."[1]

Such descriptions may be accurate enough, but at the same time it is not improbable that the tales of the death-dealing gambler which permeate the literature of early San Francisco are of a piece with accounts of the extraordinary honesty that is said to have prevailed during the first few months of the gold rush, despite the heterogeneity of the population and the fact that a large proportion of it was criminal. Among other stories difficult to believe, it is related that when the gamblers went to lunch or dinner, they left the mounds of nuggets, gold dust, and coin unguarded upon their tables; while the miner who wished to rid himself temporarily of the burden of a heavy sack of gold deposited it casually atop a hitching-post in a busy street. The historians responsible for these fairy-like tales of painful integrity, however, tell at the same time of two Chinese who passed twenty thousand dollars in counterfeit coin over the gaming tables of El Dorado and the Alhambra, and of another Chinese who snatched twenty-five thousand dollars from El Dorado and fled into a Grant Avenue cellar.[2] Since that amount in gold weighs approximately one hundred and twenty pounds, he must have been a particularly hale and hearty Celestial. In any event the capture of this Herculean desperado unearthed several other dishonest men, who were industriously digging through the back wall of a bank.

When gambling in San Francisco was in its infancy, the

---

[1] *California Inter Pocula*, by Hubert Howe Bancroft; San Francisco, 1888; pages 705–6, 707, 708.

[2] The name of this thoroughfare was originally Dupont Street. It was changed to Grant Avenue after the fire of 1906. To avoid confusion it will be called Grant Avenue throughout this book.

dealers and croupiers were all men, but one night early in 1850 Mme Simone Jules, a strikingly beautiful French-woman, with enormous black eyes and ebon hair, made her appearance at a roulette table in the Bella Union. She immediately became the center of masculine interest, and her table did such an enormous business that the other gambling houses were compelled to follow the Bella Union's example. Despite the vigorous editorial opposition of the *Alta California*, which declared indignantly that a gambling house was not a fit place for a woman, many of the games in the first-class places were thereafter operated by handsome and amiable ladies.

There was also great rivalry among the gambling houses as to which could offer its customers the best entertainment. El Dorado retained its wheezy old orchestrion to the end of its days, but also employed as many gifted soloists as could be procured. The Verandah presented a marvel who might well be called the daddy of the modern jazz trap-drummer. When equipped for a musical evening, he wore pipes tied to his chin, a drum strapped to his back, drumsticks fastened to his elbows, and cymbals attached to his wrists. All of these instruments he played more or less in unison at approximately the same time. Moreover, he patted his feet, which were encased in enormous hard-soled shoes, and with them made a tremendous clatter upon the floor. In several establishments women played harps and pianos, and each evening at the Alhambra a French-woman performed upon the violin, for which she received daily two ounces of gold dust, or about thirty-two dollars. The Aguila de Oro had a Negro chorus during the autumn of 1849, which introduced spirituals into California; and the Bella Union offered a Mexican quintet, consisting of two harps, two guitars, and a flute. The shining star of the Bella Union, however, was the singer and violinist Charley Schultze, who first played in San Francisco, and probably in the United States as well, the tune of *Aloha*. To this famous Hawaiian air he sang: "You Never Miss Your Sainted Mother Till She's Dead and Gone to Heaven."

Ordinarily the stakes even in the largest of the gold-rush gambling houses ranged from fifty cents to ten dollars, but the aggregate was enormous; in some of the more important resorts the daily turnover sometimes exceeded $200,000. Occasionally considerable sums were wagered on a single play, and fortunes were won and lost in the course of a single evening. Gold dust worth $16,000 was once laid upon a Bella Union table as a bet, and a week later a drunken miner risked $20,000 on the turn of a single card. Jim Rynders, a prosperous gambler who was noted for the dazzling whiteness of his teeth, once won $89,000 in three days' play at faro in Steve Whipple's place, and not long afterwards lost $100,000 in the same establishment in a similar length of time. While in Europe a few years later, Rynders visited the Casino at Homberg Spa and offered to bet $25,000 on the red at roulette. The bank declined to accept the wager, and when the wheel was spun, the red won. The greatest game of faro of which there is record in San Francisco, and probably in the United States also, was played by Ed Moses in the early eighteen-fifties. Moses went into an opposition gambling house one afternoon, and at his request the limit was removed. At first he won heavily, but his luck deserted him and he was soon heavily in debt to the bank. He finally drew his I O U for $60,000 and played it straight on a single card. He lost, and left the gambling house poorer by $200,000 than when he had entered.[1]

Two of the most celebrated of the early gambling-house owners were Bill Briggs, and Colonel J. J. Bryant, who

---

[1] As described by John Philip Quinn, a reformed gambler who in 1892 published a book called: *Fools of Fortune, or, Gambling and Gamblers.*

operated the game in the Ward House, which he afterwards purchased and called the Bryant House. Briggs had
what almost amounted to a mania for throwing small coins
about the streets. He used to leave his place at four o'clock
every morning with twenty-five to fifty dollars in small
change in his pockets and go to the vegetable market, where
the gamins of the town were collecting the refuse to feed
their goats and cows. Standing on the sidewalk, the gambler
tossed handfuls of coins into the street, laughing heartily as
he watched the youngsters scramble for them. Briggs was
the last of the old-time faro dealers to close his establishment; even after the enactment of the anti-gambling laws of
1873 he operated for several years behind heavily barricaded doors. About 1880, however, discouraged by repeated
raids and the frequent destruction of his tables and furniture by the police, he quit, expressing his disgust at the
reform wave which had engulfed him and declaring that San
Francisco had become little more than a municipal Sunday
school.

Colonel Bryant had political ambitions, and ran for
sheriff in 1850 as the regular nominee of the Democratic
party, at the first popular election for county officers ever
held in San Francisco. His opponents were Colonel John
E. Townes, who had been appointed Sheriff in 1849 and
was now the choice of the Whigs; and Colonel Jack Hayes,
the famous Texas ranger, who was an independent candidate. After his nomination Colonel Bryant's hotel was
decorated with flags, bunting, and streamers, while a band
of music daily played patriotic airs from the balcony and
free lunches and drinks were dispensed to all who desired
them, which was practically everyone in San Francisco. On
election day the Colonel's supporters appeared in Portsmouth Square about noon with banners and signs on which
were emblazoned the surpassing merits of their candidate.
Preceded by a company of gayly caparisoned horsemen and

27

several carriages filled with musicians, they marched noisily about the town. This display aroused so much enthusiasm among the voters that Colonel Bryant's election appeared certain, until Colonel Hayes suddenly made his appearance astride a magnificent black charger. Alone, with his long hair waving in the breeze, and handling his mount with the skill of the superb horseman, Colonel Hayes galloped back and forth, exhibiting, as the *Annals of San Francisco* puts it, "some of the finest specimens of horsemanship ever witnessed. The sight of the hero took the people by surprise and called forth the admiration and patriotism of the vast multitude of spectators. Men crowded around him on every hand, some seizing the bridle, others clinging to his clothing and stirrups, and each anxious to obtain a grasp of his hand. The noise and tumult terrified the spirited beast he strode, which reared and plunged amid the enthusiastic crowd, though so admirably managed as to do injury to none; when at length, his rider giving him the rein, he dashed into and along the adjoining street, followed and greeted by loud huzzas at every step."[1]

This theatrical demonstration turned the trick. Colonel Hayes was victorious by a tremendous majority and soon afterwards was sworn in as the first regularly elected Sheriff of San Francisco.

6

DESPITE the amazingly high cost of living and the extraordinary opportunities for frittering away money, everyone in early San Francisco was supremely confident that he would soon be able to return home with an incalculable amount of gold. Everything was conceived on a vast scale, and there was always plenty of cash available for any scheme that might be proposed, no matter how impossible or bizarre it seemed. No one hesitated to borrow money, al-

---

[1] *The Annals of San Francisco*, page 271.

though for several years the prevailing rates of interest ranged from eight to fifteen per cent a month, payable in advance, and even higher unless gilt-edged security was provided. Everyone was in such a hurry to get rich that few men were willing to bind themselves to any sort of contract for a longer period than a month, the time basis upon which nearly all business was transacted. Real estate that a few years before had brought enormous prices from speculators, fifty-vara [1] lots which had been granted by the Alcalde upon payment of twelve to sixteen dollars, sold for tens of thousands. Fortunes were made with incredible rapidity in real estate, in building, in merchandising, at the gaming table, and in every conceivable sort of business and speculation; yet little was thought of or talked about except gold mining. Any occupation, however great the stream of profit, was regarded merely as a stopgap pending a lucky strike in the gold-fields; probably the only men who devoted themselves whole-heartedly to the business at hand were the gamblers. The town was filled with tales, seldom verified, of the few fortunate miners who were gathering fortunes in the diggings at the rate of five hundred, a thousand, and, in a few cases, ten thousand dollars a day; everyone heard of the man who had picked up a chunk of pure gold weighing thirteen pounds and worth thirty-five thousand dollars, and of the two men who had discovered an even larger nugget and had immediately left for the East to exhibit it at fifty cents a look. But practically nothing was heard of the thousands of hard-working men who were on the verge of starvation in the hills, nor of the thousands of others who, discouraged and disappointed, had returned to San Francisco and were living in squalor and destitution.

Gold worth forty million dollars was extracted from the sand and gravel of California in 1849, but very little re-

---

[1] A vara is a Spanish yard, about 33.5 inches.

mained in the hands of the men who had dug it from the
earth. Thousands of miners worked only so long as they
could withstand in comfort the roaring temptations of the
brothel, the gambling houses, and the other fascinating flesh-
pots of the city. Then, with their buckskin bags crammed
with nuggets and gold dust, they hurried into San Francisco
and forthwith embarked upon an orgy of wasteful and ex-
travagant spending. Since very few had ever before possessed more than a bare living wage, they naturally had a
decided preference for ostentatious display. They discarded
their red shirts and homespun pants for broadcloth suits,
boiled shirts, and plug hats; they flung nuggets and gold
coins to the street boys and the beggars; they squandered
their hard-earned fortunes on harlots, liquor, and games of
chance; they paid hundreds of dollars for fruit, vegetables,
and game out of season; they met without a murmur of
protest the extraordinary expenses of common food and
lodging. Many, at a loss how else to exhibit their prosperity,
employed dentists to put their own gold into their teeth. If
they had no teeth that required attention, they had good
ones dug out and gold ones substituted. Scores of men had
all of their teeth extracted and solid gold plates installed.[1]
Many who didn't care for the pain which in those early
days invariably accompanied dental ministrations spent their
money instead on gold watches and diamond pins and other
showy articles of jewelry and personal wear. " Laboring
men," wrote Borthwick, " fastened their coarse, dirty shirts
with a cluster of diamonds the size of a shilling, wore colossal
gold rings on their fingers, and displayed massive gold seals

---

[1] San Francisco's pioneer dentist was Henry D. Cogswell, who arrived
in 1849 with a capital of three thousand dollars and opened an office in California Street. He eventually retired with a fortune of about two million dollars
and became the city's first active prohibitionist. His ambition was to erect a
public fountain for every one hundred saloons. He had twenty constructed, each
surmounted by a heroic statue of himself. Seven were set up in San Francisco,
but none survived more than a few years.

and chains from their watch pockets; while hardly a man of any consequence returned to the Atlantic states without receiving from some one of his friends a huge gold-headed cane, with all his virtues and good qualities engraved upon it."

Once their gold was exhausted, the spendthrift miners hurried back to the gold-fields, supported by a sublime faith that they would immediately make another rich find and so start anew the same vicious circle. Even those who hadn't enough left to furnish outfits or to pay their transportation to the diggings didn't lose hope entirely. Scorning to degrade themselves, as they thought, by performing ordinary labor, they diligently prospected the city streets, the vacant lots, and the sand-hills behind the town; many religiously panned the daily sweepings from stores, hotels, saloons, brothels, and gambling houses, which occasionally yielded a few ounces of gold dust.

7

IT is small wonder that the correspondent of the New York *Evening Post*, after judiciously surveying the scene late in 1849, reported to his journal that "the people of San Francisco are mad, stark mad."

CHAPTER II

HOUNDS AND HARLOTS

THERE WAS such a dearth of females in the San Francisco of gold-rush days that a woman was almost as rare a sight as an elephant, while a child was an even more unusual spectacle. It is doubtful if the so-called fair sex ever before or since received such adulation and homage anywhere in the United States; even prostitutes, ordinarily scorned and ostracized by their honest and respectable customers, were treated with an exaggerated deference. Men stood for hours watching the few children at play; and whenever a woman appeared on the street, business was practically suspended. She was followed through the town by an adoring crowd, while self-appointed committees marched ahead to clear the way and to protect her from the too boisterous salutations of the emotional miners.

Once while an important auction of city lots was in progress in a Montgomery Street building, a man poked his head into the auction room and shouted: "Two ladies going by on the sidewalk!" The entire crowd immediately abandoned the auction and rushed into the street to watch the women pass. It is related that they bared their heads in reverence, but that part of the story is probably the added touch of the incorrigible romancer.

According to one historian, there were only fifteen white women in San Francisco in the spring of 1849, but his estimate may be doubted, for San Franciscans were inclined to regard as white only natives of the United States and of a few European countries. In any event, however, the female population probably did not exceed three hundred for at least a year after the beginning of the gold excitement. Of this number, perhaps two-thirds were harlots from Mexico, Peru, and Chili. Together with male natives of these and other Central and South American countries, they were known in San Francisco by the generic name of Chilenos, or, contemptuously, "greasers." [1] These pioneer prostitutes occupied tents and board shanties in the vicinity of Clark's Point, about where Broadway and Pacific Street run into the Bay, and on the eastern and southern slopes of Telegraph Hill, a three-hundred-foot elevation west and north of Yerba Buena Cove, from the summit of which the arrival of ships off the Golden Gate was signaled to the town in the valley and along the beach. Sometimes as many as half a dozen Chileno women used the same rude shelter, receiving their visitors singly or *en suite,* with no regard whatever for privacy, and no furniture excepting a wash-bowl and a few dilapidated cots or straw pallets. A few made pretense of operating wash-houses, but there were scarcely any who did not devote the nights to bawdy carousal and to sexual excesses and exhibitions. And the days, also, if there was opportunity. Many of the men who had brought them to California had gone on to the gold-fields, but others had remained in San Francisco, where they dwelt promiscuously with the harlots. They lived off the earnings of the women and what they could steal from the men who frequented the district. They also operated a few small, crooked gambling houses.

During the first six months of 1850 approximately two

---

[1] According to Hubert Howe Bancroft in his *California Pastoral,* this name was first applied by the Spaniards to the American and English traders who bought hides and tallow. The traders promptly transferred the appellation to the Spaniards who sold these products, and it soon became a term of contempt applied to all Spanish-Americans, and particularly to Mexicans.

thousand women, most of whom were harlots also, arrived
in San Francisco from France and other European countries
and from the Eastern and Southern cities of the United
States, principally New York and New Orleans. Thereafter
they came on every ship, and within a few years San Francisco possessed a red-light district that was larger than those
of many cities several times its size. Moreover, it was at
least as cosmopolitan as the remainder of the population;
it has been said that by the end of 1852 there was no country
in the world that was not represented in San Francisco by
at least one prostitute. In October 1850 the *Pacific News*
announced that nine hundred more women of the French
demi-monde, carefully chosen from the bagnios of Paris and
Marseilles for their beauty, amiability, and skill, were expected, and in the same issue delicately informed its readers
that in the mines Indian women were available " at reasonable prices." Unfortunately only fifty of the French women
arrived, but that was a sufficient number to cause considerable commotion among the miners, who were naturally eager
to determine for themselves if the ladies were as adept in
the practice of their profession as was popularly supposed.
Most of these accomplished courtesans were attended by
their pimps, whom they called *macquereaux,* a designation
which the forthright San Franciscans soon shortened to
" macks." These unsavory gentry are still so called in San
Francisco, although the red-light district was officially abolished some twenty years ago, and the city now, of course,
has no prostitutes.

The lowest of the newly arrived harlots joined their
sisters in sin in the shabby dives on Telegraph Hill and along
the waterfront, but others opened, or became inmates of,
elaborate establishments around Portsmouth Square. By
close and diligent attention to business, many of these women
amassed fortunes; one popular French courtesan is said to
have banked fifty thousand dollars clear profit during her

first year of professional activity in the New World. Several married prominent men, and themselves became ladies of consequence, successfully persuading the dead past to bury its dead.[1] Because of the lack of virtuous women, the prostitutes, especially those who dwelt in the elegant bagnios on Portsmouth Square, took an active part in the social life of early San Francisco. They were in particular much sought after as partners at the fancy-dress and masquerade balls with which the frolicsome miner sought to divert himself. There, according to an early historian, " the most extraordinary scenes were exhibited, as might have been expected when the actors and dancers were chiefly hot-headed young men, flush of money and half frantic with excitement, and lewd girls, freed from the necessity of all moral restraint." [2] These functions were usually held in one of the large gambling houses, the gaming tables being temporarily moved to one side to make room for the festivities, although play never ceased. They were announced to the public by notices in the newspapers, and by placards posted in the streets and public houses, all bearing in large letters the warning: " NO WEAPONS ADMITTED."

Several men were stationed at the door, and as each prospective merry-maker entered, he was required to surrender, for the duration of the festivities, his knife, revolver, or pistol, for which he received a check. If anyone protested that he carried no weapon, the statement was considered so preposterous that he was promptly searched. Almost in-

---

[1] The tendency of the pioneers to mate with ladies of easy virtue is celebrated in a bawdy song which was very popular for many years, and which is still sung by San Franciscans who do not take their municipal glories too seriously. It begins:

> The miners came in forty-nine,
> The whores in fifty-one;
> And when they got together
> They produced the native son.

[2] *The Annals of San Francisco*, page 248.

variably a knife or a fire-arm was found secreted in some unusual part of his clothing. Music for the dancing was furnished by the regular gambling-house orchestra, but on the program of entertainment there was always a soloist who sang at least once, to the air of *O Susannah!* the miners' favorite song:[1]

> *I came from Quakerdelphia,*
> *   With my washbowl on my knee;*
> *I'm going to California,*
> *   The gold dust for to see.*
> *It rained all night the day I left,*
> *   The weather it was dry;*
> *The sun so hot I froze to death,*
> *   Oh, Anna, don't you cry.*
>
> *Oh, Ann Eliza!*
> *   Don't you cry for me.*
> *I'm going to California*
> *   With my washbowl on my knee.*
>
> *I soon shall be in Frisco,*
> *   And then I'll look around;*
> *And when I see the gold lumps there*
> *   I'll pick them off the ground.*
> *I'll scrape the mountains clean, old girl;*
> *   I'll drain the rivers dry;*
> *A pocketful of rocks bring back,*
> *   So, Anna, don't you cry.*

Sometimes the mistresses of the large harlotry establishments presided at elaborate social affairs to which they invited the most important men of the town. They cannily

---

[1] Written by Samuel C. Upham, of Philadelphia, author of *Notes of a Voyage to California via Cape Horn, Together with Scenes in El Dorado, in the Years 1849–50*; Philadelphia, 1878.

succeeded in combining pleasure with profit by introducing new girls to their guests, by presenting old favorites in new exhibitions, and by charging outrageous prices for liquor served during the function. Occasionally, however, these gatherings were almost painfully respectable. One such is thus described in *The Annals of San Francisco:*

"See yonder house. Its curtains are of the purest white lace embroidered, and crimson damask. Go in. All the fixtures are of a keeping, most expensive, most voluptuous, most gorgeous. . . . It is a *soirée* night. The 'lady' of the establishment has sent most polite invitations, got up on the finest and most beautifully embossed note paper, to all the principal gentlemen of the city, including collector of the port, mayor, aldermen, judges of the county, and members of the legislature. A splendid band of music is in attendance. Away over the Turkey or Brussels carpet whirls the politician with some sparkling beauty, as fair as frail; and the judge joins in and enjoys the dance in company with the beautiful but lost beings, whom to-morrow, he may send to the house of correction. Everything is conducted with the utmost propriety. Not an unbecoming word is heard, not an objectionable action seen. The girls are on their good behavior, and are proud once more to move and act and appear as ladies. Did you not know, you would not suspect that you were in one of those dreadful places so vividly described by Solomon. . . . But the dance is over; now for the supper table. Every thing within the bounds of the market and the skill of the cook and confectioner, is before you. Opposite and by your side, that which nor cook nor confectioner's skill have made what they are — cheeks where the ravages of dissipation have been skilfully hidden, and eyes with pristine brilliancy undimmed, or even heightened

37

by the spirit of the recent champagne. And here the illusion fades. The champagne alone is paid for. The *soirée* has cost the mistress one thousand dollars, and at the supper and during the night she sells twelve dozen of champagne at ten dollars a bottle! . . . No loafers present, but the male *ton;* vice hides itself for the occasion, and staid dignity bends from its position to twine a few flowers of social pleasure around the heads and hearts of these poor outcasts of society."[1]

2

CURIOUSLY enough, the first important outbreak of criminal violence in San Francisco did not originate in the vice-ridden areas around Clark's Point and on the slopes of Telegraph Hill, nor was it instigated by the wretched Chilenos who dwelt there in the utmost misery and degradation. On the contrary, it was to a very large extent directed against them, and the decent citizens of the town were driven into the paradoxical position of defending a colony of depraved women against the attacks of an organization of vicious men. Moreover, it was part and parcel of the systematic and heartless persecution of the Spanish-American which began in the gold-fields, soon extended to the towns and cities, and remains one of the blackest pages of California's history. The miners, particularly those from other parts of the United States, harassed the poor "greaser" in every conceivable manner, stealing and destroying his goods and mining equipment, driving him from his claims and farms, raping his women, beating his children, flogging or killing him on little or no provocation, and hanging him with elaborate pretensions to justice if he so much as attempted to defend himself or failed promptly to vacate property which an American desired. In one of the most celebrated of many such examples of brutality the miners at

---

[1] *The Annals of San Francisco*, pages 668–9.

Downieville lynched a young Mexican woman, mistress of a gambler, for stabbing to death an American miner who had broken into her cabin during the absence of her lover and assaulted her. When the mob seized her, there was a great roar of "Give her a fair trial and hang her!" which aptly expressed the sentiment that prevailed throughout California. A physician who testified that the girl was pregnant and therefore in no condition to be hanged was compelled to leave the district. Another man who tried to interfere with the lynching was dragged bodily from the platform of the scaffold and literally kicked out of the town. The miners arranged themselves in two lines and buffeted him as he ran the gantlet.

The immediate cause of the ill treatment of Spanish-Americans was probably anger and jealousy over the fact that they, being first on the ground, had naturally occupied the richest diggings. But much of it was doubtless due to the widespread and pernicious influence of the Know-Nothing or Native American party, which had already won municipal elections in Boston and New York and was waging a strong campaign for control of the national government, on a platform that was violently anti-foreign and anti-Catholic. Also, many prominent American politicians and office-holders frequently berated all foreigners as trespassers upon the public domain, and demanded their expulsion. Among them was General Persifer F. Smith of the United States Army, who announced at Panama in January 1849, while *en route* to San Francisco, that only native Americans were entitled to share in California's riches, and that he proposed to drive all foreigners from the gold-fields. Luckily, he never attempted to enforce these views, but the fact that he held and had publicly expressed them soon became widely known, and encouraged the miners and the city mobs in their brutal excesses.

Particularly susceptible to this sort of jingoism were

the fifty or sixty young thugs who comprised an organization known at first as the Hounds and later as the San Francisco Society of Regulators. Despite this high-sounding title, they were never anything more than an aggregation of thieves and ruffians, whose principal occupation was maltreating the Spanish-Americans. Under pretense of a fervent and belligerent patriotism, the Hounds beat, stabbed, and shot the helpless Chilenos whenever opportunity offered; systematically extorted gold and jewelry from the few who had acquired wealth; burned and otherwise destroyed their tents and cabins; and made frequent forays against the colony of harlots at Clark's Point and on the slopes of Telegraph Hill, where they raped the women, tore down their shelters, and carried off their meager belongings. "With the coolest impudence," wrote Bancroft, "the Hounds asserted their determination to protect American citizens against Spanish-speaking foreigners, and sometimes claimed to have instructions from the Alcalde to extirpate the Mexicans and Chileans." [1]

Practically the entire membership of the Hounds had come to San Francisco as members of Colonel Jonathan D. Stevenson's regiment of volunteers, which had been recruited in New York to fight against Mexico. The troops reached the Pacific Coast in March 1847, after the war had ended, and the regiment was immediately broken up. Detachments were stationed at San Francisco, Santa Barbara, Sonoma, and Monterey. All had been discharged from the Army by October 1848, although scores had deserted long before then to try their luck in the gold-fields. When Colonel Stevenson was organizing his command, he announced that he would accept only young men of proved good character, and that they must be willing to remain in California after their term of military service had expired and help settle the country. There were, of course, many honest and upright

---

[1] *Popular Tribunals*, by Hubert Howe Bancroft, Volume I, page 92.

young men among the thousand who followed Colonel Stevenson, but there were also many young rowdies who had been trained in fighting, stealing, and brawling as runners or members of the New York fire-engine companies; and many others who had owed allegiance to the Bowery Boys, the Dead Rabbits, the Plug Uglies, and the other great gangs of the Bowery and the Five Points. They caused trouble not only in San Francisco but in the mines and other California towns as well.

Some threescore of these youthful blackguards organized the Hounds some time in the late autumn of 1848, under the leadership of Sam Roberts, who had been a member of Company E, of Stevenson's regiment. Roberts usurped the title of Lieutenant and wore full regimentals, while his followers likewise strutted about the streets in military dress. The favorite loafing-place of the Hounds was a saloon known as the Shades, in Kearny Street, but their official headquarters was a large tent at Kearny and Commercial streets. This they called Tammany Hall, a fact which sufficiently indicated their place of origin. They made a pretense of military organization and discipline, drilling regularly with muskets and swords, while in their tent was a drum on which "assembly" was beaten whenever their chieftains desired to lead them into mischief. Each Sunday afternoon, and sometimes on week-days, they paraded the streets, with fife and drum playing and flags and banners waving. Usually they climaxed these exhibitions of strength with attacks on the Chileno quarter. For several months no one interfered with them, and at no time did the impotent authorities of San Francisco make any effort to stop their outrages. While it is probably not true that the Hounds had been definitely instructed by the Alcalde to rid the town of Spanish-Americans, it is certain that the desperadoes were encouraged by many very influential men who subscribed to the Know Nothing doctrines. In particular, they were the

pets of the politicians, most of whom had learned the arts
of chicanery as henchmen of New York's Tammany Hall
and who had already begun to despoil the city treasury.

At first the Hounds confined their attacks to the tents,
shanties, and other property of the Chilenos, but during the
early summer of 1849 they became bolder. It was about this
time that they began to call themselves Regulators and
brazenly announced that they expected the people of San
Francisco to support them, and to pay them well for protecting the city against the Spanish-Americans. Thereafter
no man's life and goods were safe. The Hounds roamed the
streets in small and large bands, robbing men and stores in
broad day, and beating and stabbing merchants and others
who ventured to dispute their right to take what they wanted
without payment. One of their favorite pastimes was to
enter a tavern or saloon, demand the best of food and drink,
and then walk out, telling the bar-tender or waiter to collect
from the city. If the landlord protested, they destroyed his
furniture or set fire to his building. On the streets men and
even women were compelled to take to the gutters when the
Hounds approached. On one occasion a Negro accidentally
touched the august person of a Hound in passing, and his
ears were promptly shorn from his head. A few days later
a Mexican's tongue was torn out by the roots because he had
replied in kind to an insult hurled at him by one of the
thugs.

Despite such atrocities as these, it was not until the
middle of the summer of 1849 that the responsible citizens
of San Francisco at length took a hand in the situation.
In July one George Frank, a storekeeper, authorized the
Hounds to collect a claim of five hundred dollars against
Pedro Cueta, a Chileno. Cueta was unable to pay and, moreover, disputed the claim. On the afternoon of Sunday,
July 15, 1849, the Hounds marched in full battle array from
their Tammany Hall and made the most violent of all their

onslaughts upon the Chileno tents and shanties. "These they violently tore down," wrote the authors of *The Annals of San Francisco,* who saw the attack, "plundering them of money and valuables, which they carried away, and totally destroying on the spot such articles as they did not think it worth while to seize. Without provocation, and in cold blood, they barbarously beat with sticks and stones, and cuffed and kicked the offending foreigners. Not content with that, they repeatedly and wantonly fired among the injured people, and amid the shrieks of terrified women and the groans of wounded men, recklessly continued their terrible course in different quarters, wherever in fact malice or thirst for plunder led them. . . . There were no individuals brave or foolhardy enough to resist the progress of such a savage mob, whose exact force was unknown, but who were believed to be both numerous and desperate."

This outrage aroused the whole town to great excitement. Next morning Samuel Brannan and Captain Bezer Simmons called upon the Alcalde, Doctor T. M. Leavenworth, and urged him to take some action against the Hounds. Leavenworth protested his inability to cope with the gang, but was at length persuaded to issue a proclamation asking the citizens to assemble in Portsmouth Square that afternoon at three o'clock. There Brannan vigorously denounced the Hounds, collected a large sum of money for the relief of the destitute Spanish-Americans whose homes had been destroyed, and suggested that the meeting appoint a committee to bring the miscreants to justice. Two hundred and thirty men promptly volunteered for duty as special deputies and were armed with muskets and pistols. They started immediately in pursuit of the Hounds, who had scattered, terrified at the turn events were taking. Some had fled into the interior, and others had taken to the Bay in small boats and were trying to reach the Sacramento River. Twenty who had delayed their start were captured within a few hours, and Roberts, the leader, was arrested on the road to Stockton by A. L. Davis, who was in command of the armed citizenry. The prisoners were lodged in the brig of the warship *Warren*, which was anchored in the Bay, and two days later their trial began before the Alcalde, two associate judges appointed by the mass meeting, and a jury of twelve prominent men. Lawyers were assigned to defend the accused men, and more than a score of witnesses testified, including several wounded Chilenos who later died. The jury found Roberts and eight others guilty of rioting, conspiracy, robbery, and assault with intent to kill. Roberts and one Saunders were each sentenced to ten years in prison at hard labor, and the others to somewhat shorter terms, while heavy fines were imposed upon all who had been convicted. None of these penalties was actually inflicted, however, for the politicians did not fail the Hounds in their hour of peril. Within a few days all of the young thugs had been released. But they were so frightened that they made no effort to reorganize, and soon afterwards most of them left San Francisco.

One of the associate judges who helped the Alcalde try the Hounds was William M. Gwin, later the first United States Senator from California, and the hero of one of San Francisco's favorite dueling stories. In 1855 Gwin met on the field of honor one Joseph McCorckle. The duel was fought on a marsh north of the Presidio, several miles from the Gwin home in Jackson Street. Relays of horses were provided, and a messenger was engaged to carry the news of the duel to Mrs. Gwin. In due time he galloped down Jackson Street, rushed into the house and shouted:

"The first fire has been exchanged and no one is hurt!"

"Thank God!" cried Mrs. Gwin, and with the other members of her family knelt in prayer.

A little later the messenger again dashed into the house, crying:

"The second fire has been exchanged and no one is hurt!"

"Praised be the Lord!" said Mrs. Gwin.

Again the messenger rode down Jackson Street. He knocked at the door, tendered his card, and was ushered into the parlor. When Mrs. Gwin appeared he said:

"The third fire has been exchanged and no one is hurt!"

"That's good," said Mrs. Gwin.

On his next appearance the messenger was invited to remain for dinner. He ate heartily, and after some casual conversation about the weather, remarked:

"Oh, by the way, the fourth fire has been exchanged and no one is hurt. What do you think of that, Mrs. Gwin?"

"I think," said Mrs. Gwin, "that there has been some mighty poor shooting!"

3

IT was the widespread persecution of the Spanish-American that produced California's most celebrated outlaw — Joaquin Murieta, who has been variously described as the Robin Hood of the Sierras and as the bloodthirstiest villain that ever prowled the Western highways. Scarcely less notorious was his chief lieutenant, Manuel Garcia, better known as Three-Fingered Jack. Murieta's real name was Joaquin Carillo. He was born in the state of Sonora, Mexico, and at the age of seventeen came to California as a horse-trainer for a traveling circus. He was accompanied by his young wife, Rosita Felix, who was later called Antonia Molinera. Attired in men's clothing, with her black hair clipped short, she rode with him as a member of his band, took an active part in many of his robberies and murders, and remained steadfastly at his side through all the vicissitudes that eventually resulted in his death.

When the gold rush began, Murieta was in San Francisco. He followed the crowd and in the spring of 1849 staked a rich claim in Stanislaus County, from which he was soon evicted by American miners, who beat him and raped his wife. A few days later he rode into the camp astride a horse which he had borrowed from his brother, to collect what remained of his scattered belongings, and was at once accused of having stolen the animal. He protested his innocence and led the miners to his brother's ranch, where they promptly hanged the brother and seized what they desired of his horses and cattle. Joaquin they stripped, tied to a tree, and flogged until he was unconscious.

Thereafter Murieta was an outlaw, and for almost three years he left a bloody trail throughout the gold country. Sometimes he was attended by as many as eighty horsemen, all of whom had sufficient cause to hate the American miners. They robbed stage-coaches and travelers and held up mining camps and small towns and generously shared the stolen gold with their persecuted countrymen. Murieta is said to have killed every one of the men who had driven him from his claim and abused his wife, and also every member of the mob which had flogged him and hanged his brother. Most of them he captured alive and dragged at the end of a rope, behind a galloping horse, until they had been beaten almost to a pulp by the rough stones of the mountain roads. One of his pleasant diversions was tying together the queues of half a dozen Chinamen and then cutting their throats. Once after a robbery he left eight Chinese thus murdered. With extraordinary courage he rode alone into the small villages and mining camps for food and other supplies. No man dared touch him, for all knew that if he was molested, or even angered, he would return with his desperadoes and torture and kill every soul in the place. In 1852 the California Legislature offered five thousand dollars for his capture, dead or alive, and Murieta rode into the town of Stockton just as a Deputy Sheriff was affixing to a tree the placard

announcing the reward. Pushing through the crowd, the outlaw wrote at the bottom of the poster: " I will pay $1,000
myself." He signed it boldly: " J. Murieta," and departed
unharmed. Soon afterwards he attacked a schooner in the
Sacramento River near Stockton, killed the crew and passengers, and stole twenty thousand dollars in nuggets and
gold dust.

Murieta's depredations finally became so numerous and
so violent that in May 1853 the Legislature authorized Captain Harry Love, a Deputy Sheriff of Los Angeles, to raise
a company of twenty-five men and hunt the bandit to the
death. Love and his men took the trail accompanied by
William Burns, a gambler who had been friendly with
Murieta, but had consented to betray him for a few hundred
dollars. On a Saturday night in July 1853 Love, Burns, and
seven of the former's rangers came upon Murieta and
Three-Fingered Jack sitting before a camp-fire near Lake
Tulare. Three-Fingered Jack died at the first fusillade, but
Murieta leaped astride his horse and fled into the darkness.
A chance shot brought the animal down, and a volley from
the rangers sent seven bullets crashing into the outlaw's
body. Murieta threw down his rifle, raised his hands, and
called to Captain Love: "Shoot no more. The work is
done."

He sank slowly to the ground, pillowed his head on his
right arm, and died. For the night's work Captain Love
received six thousand dollars from the Legislature. He was
killed not long after in a duel, and the gambler Burns was
shot to death by Murieta's friends. The head of the outlaw
chieftain, and the mutilated hand of Three-Fingered Jack,
were severed from their bodies, placed in large bottles of
spirits, and brought to San Francisco. On the 18th of August
1853 this notice appeared in the San Francisco newspapers:

JOAQUIN'S HEAD
Is to be seen at King's,
Corner of Halleck and
Sansome Streets.
ADMISSION ONE DOLLAR

Although the exhibit was fortified by affidavits from a priest who claimed to have been the outlaw's spiritual adviser, it was never satisfactorily established that the head was that of Murieta. James W. Marshall, the discoverer of gold, who had known the bandit, said it wasn't, and so did Murieta's widow, who was convinced that her husband had escaped to Mexico. Anticipating flight, she said, he had sent to his old home in Sonora a great herd of horses and fifty thousand dollars in gold. Nevertheless, the authorities were satisfied, and the gruesome trophy remained on display. Because the hair on the head continued to grow, it attracted much attention for several years, particularly among the superstitious Mexicans. Eventually it found its way into Dr. Jordon's Museum of Horrors, in Montgomery Street, on the outskirts of the Barbary Coast. It was destroyed in the earthquake and fire of 1906.

Murieta has already become a legendary figure in California, and there are innumerable tales of his appalling cruelty, and of his great kindnesses to his countrymen. But as Bancroft points out, the outlaw obviously " had higher aims than mere revenge and pillage. His continuous conflict with military and civil authorities, and with the armed populace, would in any other country in America have been dignified with the term revolution. It is easy to see that he regarded himself as the champion of his country rather than as an outlaw. He was only a few months more than twenty-one years old when he died, and his brilliant career of crime occupied him less than three years."

CHAPTER III

THE SYDNEY DUCKS

THE NUCLEUS around which the Barbary Coast developed was the colony of Chileno harlots and thieves which clustered along the waterfront at Broadway and Pacific Street, and on the slopes of Telegraph Hill. To this whorish quarter naturally gravitated the human scum and riff-raff who, once the news of the discovery of gold had gained wide circulation, poured into San Francisco from the ports of the seven seas in ever-increasing numbers. There, in particular, gathered the ruffianly larrikins from the frontier towns of Australia, and the escaped convicts and ticket-of-leave men from the British penal settlements at Sydney, in New South Wales, and on the island of Tasmania, then called Van Diemen's Land. This wave of undesirable immigration, which to all intents and purposes was one hundred per cent criminal, began to wash against the shores of California about the middle of 1849, in direct and open violation of an old Mexican statute which forbade the entry into the territory of persons who had been convicted of crime in other countries. No effort was ever made to enforce this law. By the early autumn of 1849 the arrivals from Australia had become so numerous, and so thoroughly dominated the underworld, that the district in which they congregated began to be known as Sydney-Town, and it was so called for some ten years. It was this area that later became notorious throughout the world as the Barbary Coast, although the latter designation did not come into general use until the middle eighteen-sixties.

The villainous inhabitants of Sydney-Town were popularly called Sydney Ducks or Sydney Coves, but more often the former. It was a common saying in early San Francisco, whenever a particularly atrocious crime was committed, that " the Sydney Ducks are cackling in the pond." Unquestionably, these foreign felons gave San Francisco's underworld its initial flavor; they were pioneers in the viciousness and depravity for which the Barbary Coast became famous, and the echo of their unholy cackling was not stilled for more than half a century. By the time they began swarming into the city in force, many of the tents and shanties of the Chilenos had been replaced by flimsy wooden and brick buildings, wherein the more commercial spirits among the Sydney Ducks opened lodging-houses, dance-halls, groggeries, and taverns. Their public houses bore such fanciful and typically English and Scotch names as the Magpie, the Bobby Burns, the Tam O'Shanter, the Noggin of Ale, the Hilo Johnny, the Bird-in-Hand, the Bay of Biscay, and the Jolly Waterman, but all were described by a contemporary journalist as " hives of dronish criminals, shabby little dens with rough, hangdog fellows hanging about the doorways." Drunkenness, robbery, and all manner of strife and lewdness went on in these places. Most of them had harlots regularly attached to the establishment, and these women either sold their favors for a pinch or two of gold dust, or engaged in immoral and peculiar exhibitions, admission to which ranged from fifty cents to five dollars. He was a fortunate man who could visit a resort in Sydney-Town and escape without being slugged and robbed. Said the San Francisco *Herald:*

"There are certain spots in our city, infested by the most abandoned men and women, that have acquired a reputation little better than the Five Points of

New York or St. Giles of London. The upper part of Pacific Street, after dark, is crowded by thieves, gamblers, low women, drunken sailors, and similar characters, who resort to the groggeries that line the street, and there spend the night in the most hideous orgies. Every grog shop is provided with a fiddle, from which some half-drunken creature tortures execrable sounds, called by way of compliment, music. Shortly after dark the dancing commences, and is kept up unceasingly to the sound of the fiddle, until broke up by a row or the exhaustion of those engaged in it. These ruffian resorts are the hot beds of drunkenness, and the scenes of unnumbered crimes. Unsuspecting sailors and miners are entrapped by the dexterous thieves and swindlers that are always on the lookout, into these dens, where they are filled with liquor — drugged if necessary, until insensibility coming upon them, they fall an easy victim to their tempters. In this way many robberies are committed, which are not brought to light through shame on the part of the victim. When the habitues of this quarter have reason to believe a man has money, they follow him up for days, and employ every device to get him into their clutches. . . . These dance-groggeries are outrageous nuisances and nurseries of crime. . . ."

Perhaps the lowest of all the Sydney-Town dives were the Boar's Head, where the principal attraction was a sexual exhibition in which a woman and a boar participated; the Goat and Compass and the Golden Rule, both owned by one Hell Haggerty, a ticket-of-leave man from Sydney; and the Fierce Grizzly, so called because a live female bear was kept chained beside the door. The Goat and Compass was the particular hang-out of a Sydney-Town character known as Dirty Tom McAlear, who for a few cents would eat or drink any sort of refuse offered to him. When finally arrested

51

in 1852 for "making a beast of himself," McAlear testified
that he had been drunk for at least seven years and had not
bathed for so long that he had no memory of his last ablu-
tion. He thought, however, that it was about fifteen years
before, in England. The Fierce Grizzly was especially noted
for various exhibitions in which the bear and a man took
part, and for the nectar-like quality of its milk punches,
which were heavily laced with gin or brandy, and frequently
with knock-out drops as well. Once when a San Francisco
preacher was making a shocked survey of the district, and,
of course, seeing all the sights in order to obtain material
for future sermons, he was taken into the Fierce Grizzly and
given a milk punch which had been copiously dosed with gin.

"What do you call that?" he asked, smacking his
reverend lips.

"Just milk."

"Ah!" said the preacher. "What a glorious cow!"

Little or no effort was made to check the rapidly increasing boldness of the denizens of Sydney-Town or to
regulate the dives in which they drank, robbed, and caroused
and in which innumerable criminals found refuge. During
the early period of the gold rush government in San Francisco, particularly those phases of it that had to do with law-
enforcement and the administration of justice, was in the
same chaotic condition that characterized life in general.
The transition from the Mexican to the American systems
of municipal management was not accomplished for more
than three years after California had become American territory, partly because the military authorities insisted upon
administering civil affairs, and partly because the men who
would have ordinarily been the first to demand a stable rule
were too busy making fortunes to bother with such comparatively trivial matters. Theoretically the business of the
municipality was in the hands of the Ayuntamiento, or Town
Council, but actually during this period of change the public

treasury belonged to the man who could oftenest plunge his hands into it. Consequently it was soon looted by the politicians, who not only bankrupted San Francisco but saddled the town with a debt of almost two million dollars, most of which was afterwards repudiated.

The only official with power to hold court and try either civil or criminal cases was the First Alcalde, whose duties were roughly similar to those of the American mayor. But too often this dignitary was of the type of an early Alcalde named Meade, who knew little law, but who had a violent antipathy toward Mexicans and cigarette-smokers. To admit being either or both was tantamount to conviction in his court. Once when a Mexican was arraigned before him charged with stealing a horse, he asked but two questions:

" Do you smoke cigarettes? "

" *Si, señor.* "

" Do you blow the smoke through your nose? "

" *Si, señor.* "

" Then I find you guilty as charged, and may God have mercy on your soul! Constable, take this fellow out and shoot him! He stole the horse sure enough! "

The lawyers who practiced in these early courts were for the most part on the same intellectual plane as Alcalde Meade. One of the best-known and most successful was Ben Moors. He knew no law whatever, but he had memorized three speeches by John Randolph and one by Daniel Webster. Regardless of the nature of the case upon which he chanced to be engaged, he delivered one or another with magnificent gestures and impressive oratorical effects. His chief claim to fame in California, however, probably lies in the fact that he once publicly slapped United States Senator David C. Broderick. Moors was arrested for this heinous offense and in court described himself as " a gentleman of elegant leisure."

The first attempt to bring order out of the chaos into

which San Francisco had fallen was made by John W. Geary,
later the first Mayor under the American system, who was
chosen First Alcalde in August 1849, at an election ordered
by the military authorities. Geary immediately appeared
before the Ayuntamiento and urged the Councillors to take
immediate steps for the protection of life and property.
"You are now without a single requisite," he told them,
"for the promotion of prosperity or for the maintenance
of order."

Stirred by Geary's appeal, and likewise fearful that the
people would again take matters into their own hands as
they had done in the affair of the Hounds only a month before, the Ayuntamiento appropriated sufficient money to
purchase the brig *Euphemia,* which had been abandoned in
the Bay when its crew deserted and went to the mines. For
several years the vessel was used as a prison. It was San
Francisco's first jail — and was about as useful for the purpose as a chicken-coop would have been. The Ayuntamiento
also appointed the town's first peace officers — Colonel
John E. Townes as Sheriff; and Malachi Fallon, who had
been Warden of the Tombs, a Tammany politician, and a
saloon-keeper in New York, as City Marshal. Not long
afterwards a few policemen were employed to assist Colonel
Townes and Fallon, and about a year later an ordinance
was enacted requiring the dives and dance-halls of Sydney-
Town to close at midnight.

But these were futile gestures. They made no difference
in the conduct of the criminal element; nor did Geary, an
able and upright man, succeed in checking the activities of
the thievish politicians. The latter continued to loot the city
treasury, while Sydney-Town remained a veritable cesspool
of corruption. According to the authors of *The Annals of
San Francisco,* "it was dangerous in the highest degree for
a single person to venture within its bounds. Even the police
hardly dared enter there; and if they attempted to appre-

hend some known individuals, it was always in a numerous, strongly-armed company. The lawless inhabitants of the place united to save their luckless brothers, and generally managed to drive the assailant away." From this sink of sin and bawdy carousal issued murderers, sneak-thieves, foot-pads, burglars, harlots, arsonites, and swindlers of every variety and degree of skill, who plied their vocations throughout San Francisco without let or hindrance. They were protected, and frequently incited, by greedy and un-scrupulous city officials and politicians. During the half-dozen years that followed Alcalde Geary's first attempt to form a reputable municipal government, an average of almost two murders a day were committed in San Francisco — and at no time in that period did the city have a popula-tion of more than forty thousand. Robberies, assaults, and other crimes were so numerous that no effort was ever made to determine even their approximate number. Six times in less than two years — from December 24, 1849 to June 22, 1851 — the town was devastated by great fires, each of which almost wiped it out of existence. Investigations showed clearly that at least four of the conflagrations had been started by gangs of fire-bugs led by two former convicts from Australia — Jack Edwards and Ben Lewis. But when these precious knaves were at length, after much difficulty and delay, brought to trial, they were promptly freed by venal judges under the sway of crooked politicians. Says the *Annals*:

"When the different fires took place . . . bands of plunderers issued from this great haunt of dissipa-tion, to help themselves to whatever money or valuables lay in their way, or which they could possibly secure. With these they retreated to their dens, and defied de-tection or apprehension. Many of these fires were believed to have been raised by incendiaries, solely for

55

the opportunity which they afforded for plundering. Persons were repeatedly seen in the act of kindling loose inflammable material in out-houses and secret places; while the subsequent confessions of convicted criminals left no doubt of the fact, that not only had frequent attempts been made to fire the city, but that some of these had unfortunately been successful. Fire, however, was only one means of attaining their ends. The most daring burglaries were committed, and houses and persons rifled of their valuables. Where resistance was made, the bowie-knife or the revolver settled matters, and left the robber unmolested. Midnight assaults, ending in murder, were common. And not only were these deeds perpetrated under the shade of night; but even in daylight, in the highways and byways of the country, in the streets of the town, in crowded bars, gambling saloons and lodging houses, crimes of an equally glaring character were of constant occurrence. People at that period generally carried during all hours, and wherever they happened to be, loaded firearms about their persons; but these weapons availed nothing against the sudden stroke of the ' slung shot,' the plunge and rip of the knife, or the secret aiming of the pistol. No decent man was in safety to walk the streets after dark; while at all hours, both of night and day, his property was jeopardized by incendiarism and burglary.

"All this while, the law, whose supposed ' majesty ' is so awful in other countries, was here only a matter for ridicule. The police were few in number, and poorly as well as irregularly paid. Some of them were in league with the criminals themselves, and assisted these at all times to elude justice. Subsequent confessions of criminals on the eve of execution, implicated a considerable number of people in various high and low departments of the executive. Bail was readily accepted in the most serious cases, where the security tendered was absolutely worthless; and where, whenever necessary, both principal and cautioner quietly disappeared. The prisons likewise were small and insecure; and though filled to overflowing, could no longer contain the crowds of apprehended offenders. When these were ultimately brought to trial, seldom could a conviction be obtained. From technical errors on the part of the prosecutors, laws ill understood and worse applied, false swearing of the witnesses for the prisoners, absence often of the chief evidence for the prosecution, dishonesty of jurors, incapacity, weakness, or venality of the judge, and from many other causes, the cases generally broke down and the prisoners were freed. *Not one criminal had yet been executed.* Yet it was notorious, that, at this period, at least one hundred murders had been committed within the space of a few months; while innumerable were the instances of arson, and of theft, robbery, burglary, and assault with intent to kill. It was evident that the offenders defied and laughed at all the puny efforts of the authorities to control them. The tedious processes of legal tribunals had no terrors for them." [1]

It was this condition of affairs, the nearest approach to criminal anarchy that an American city has yet experienced, that ultimately brought about the formation of the first Vigilance Committee. About four months before the actual organization of this great popular tribunal, however, San Francisco was thrown into such a furor by a particularly brutal assault upon a respected storekeeper that an excited crowd gathered in Portsmouth Square, and only an unexpected display of energy by the municipal authorities pre-

---

[1] *The Annals of San Francisco*, pages 566–7. It is interesting to note how aptly this passage describes present-day conditions in many American cities.

vented the immediate application of lynch law. Out of this assault grew one of the most amazing cases of mistaken identity in the annals of American crime. The principals were Thomas Berdue, an itinerant gambler, who had operated in a small way in the gold-fields and who twice narrowly escaped hanging for crimes he hadn't committed; and James Stuart, better known as English Jim, a ticket-of-leave convict from Australia, and one of the most infamous of the Sydney Ducks. Stuart was deported from England at the age of sixteen, following his conviction of forgery, and served about twelve years in the British penal colony at Sydney. He received a ticket-of-leave some time during the late eighteen-forties and made his way to New York, where he became associated with a famous London burglar and sharper called Bristol Bill, whose father had been a member of the British Parliament and who had himself escaped from Sydney after serving a fourteen-year sentence.[1] For several years these accomplished scoundrels operated successfully in Eastern cities, especially in Boston and New York, but eventually detectives got close upon their trail. In search of new fields for their activities, they went to Vermont in the late autumn of 1849. There, within a few weeks, they robbed half a dozen banks, floated a large quantity of counterfeit money, and swindled a score of merchants and other business men. The bucolic police, however, succeeded where their more sophisticated brethren had failed. They captured Bristol Bill, convicted him of burglary, counterfeiting, and other crimes, and sent him to state's prison for fourteen years. English Jim escaped their clutches and came to San Francisco, where he at once became one of the chief ornaments of Sydney-Town. This was early in 1850, and throughout the next year English Jim pursued an extraor-

---

[1] Bristol Bill's real name was never known in this country. The London police knew it, but refused to divulge the information to the American authorities because of the prominence of the burglar's family.

dinary career of crime, not only in San Francisco, but in the gold-fields and other parts of the state as well—during these comparatively few months he is said to have committed or assisted in more murders and burglaries than any other man in the California of his time. In December 1850 he was arrested in Sacramento for killing Sheriff Moore of Marysville and stealing four thousand dollars from the Sheriff's home, but escaped after a few days' incarceration.

At eight o'clock in the evening of February 19, 1851 two men entered the store of Jansen, Bond & Company, in Montgomery Street, knocked J. C. Jansen, senior member of the firm, unconscious with a slung shot, and fled with two thousand dollars in gold coin, which they had taken from the till. Next day the San Francisco police arrested Thomas Berdue, believing him to be James Stuart, and lodged him in the jail to await transportation to Marysville and trial there for the murder of Sheriff Moore. A man named Windred, found in Berdue's company, was also arrested, on suspicion. Berdue was recognized as English Jim by half a dozen men who had known Stuart well, and was also positively identified by Jansen as one of the two men who had assaulted him. As the other, Jansen identified Windred, though not so certainly. Berdue protested his innocence and attempted to prove that he was not Stuart, but his protestations and evidence were alike in vain against the overwhelming physical similarity between himself and the Australian convict. In weight, height, color of eyes and hair, shape of feature, and in every other general characteristic, the two men were identical. But the resemblance went even further. The notorious Sydney Duck was known to have a small scar over his left eye. So did Berdue. In English Jim's left ear was a slit where he had been cut by a knife. Such a slit was found also in Berdue's left ear. English Jim's left forefinger had been amputated at the first joint. Berdue had suffered a precisely similar injury. So far as was ever known, Berdue and English Jim were not related. Nor did they ever so much as see each other.

The examination of Berdue and Windred was begun in the City Hall by the authorities on Saturday, February 22, and within a few hours the building was surrounded by a restless crowd of more than five thousand men. The authors of *The Annals of San Francisco*, who were present, described the gathering as " not a mob, but the *people*, in the highest sense of the term. They wanted only a leader to advise and guide them to any undertaking that promised relief from the awful state of social terror and danger to which they were reduced." Because of the positive identification of the prisoners by Jansen, there was scarcely anyone in San Francisco who doubted their guilt. There was, also, scarcely anyone who was not convinced that the two men would eventually escape punishment through the connivance of politicians and crooked officials. From the moment the crowd started to assemble, the situation possessed very dangerous possibilities, which were made more acute by the circulation of several thousand copies of this handbill:

CITIZENS OF SAN FRANCISCO.

The series of murders and robberies that have been committed in this city, seems to leave us entirely in a state of anarchy. " When thieves are left without control to rob and kill, then doth the honest traveller fear each bush a thief." Law, it appears, is but a nonentity to be scoffed at; redress can be had for aggression but through the never failing remedy so admirably laid down in the code of Judge Lynch. Not that we should admire this process for redress, but that it seems to be inevitably necessary.

Are we to be robbed and assassinated in our domiciles, and the law to let our aggressors perambulate the streets because they have furnished straw bail? If so, "let each man be his own executioner." "Fie upon your laws." They have no force.

All those who would rid our city of its robbers and murderers will assemble on Sunday at two o'clock on the plaza.

This inflammatory document was unsigned, but it is believed to have been the work of Samuel Brannan, who was always willing and ready to hang every desperado who showed his head. Despite its anonymity, it was immediately effective. A great shout of "Now's the time!" arose from the outskirts of the crowd, and several hundred men rushed into the court-room, where the prisoners were being questioned by the police. They attempted to drag Berdue and Windred into the street, but were repulsed by the members of the Washington Guard, a volunteer military organization, which had been mustered by the Mayor at the first sign of trouble and had been stationed in an adjoining room. While the Guardsmen cleared City Hall of the mob, Berdue and Windred were rushed into the basement of the building and locked in cells. Although the excitement continued, no further attempt was made that day to lynch the prisoners, and about the middle of the afternoon the crowd dispersed. It began to assemble again at dusk, and after several speeches by prominent citizens a committee of fourteen men was appointed to prevent the release of the two men on nominal bail — the usual procedure in such cases — and an additional patrol of twenty men was chosen to guard them during the night. Several hours later the Committee of Fourteen met to discuss the situation and determine how best to assure a proper trial. The feeling of the town in general was epitomized by Samuel Brannan in a brief speech, which he made in response to a suggestion that a jury of prominent men be impaneled to try the prisoners. Said Brannan:

"I am very much surprised to hear people talk about grand juries, or recorders, or mayors. I'm tired of such talk. These men are murderers, I say, as well as thieves. I know it, and will die or see them hung by the neck. I'm opposed to any farce in this business. We had enough of that eighteen months ago, when we allowed ourselves to be the tools of these judges.[1] . . . We are the Mayor and the recorder, the hangman and the laws. The law and the courts never yet hung a man in California, and every morning we are reading fresh accounts of murders and robberies. I want no technicalities. Such things are devised to shield the guilty."

Brannan urged the immediate lynching of both Berdue and Windred, but the other members of the committee were unwilling to act so precipitously, and they finally adjourned without preparing a definite program. Next afternoon between eight thousand and nine thousand men gathered in Portsmouth Square, and at the suggestion of William T. Coleman, a leader in both the Vigilance movements, another committee was named to consider the matter and recommend a course of action, subject to the approval of the mass meeting. This committee advised an immediate trial, and accordingly the hearing of evidence was begun at once in the Recorder's room of City Hall, before a judge and jury chosen from among the town's leading citizens. About dusk the jury retired to find a verdict, but at midnight reported that an agreement was apparently impossible. At that time the jurors stood nine for conviction, and three doubtful, but unwilling to acquit. Cries of "Hang them anyhow! The

---

[1] Brannan referred to the affair of the Hounds, in July 1849. In his *The Beginnings of San Francisco* Zoeth Skinner Eldredge says that "in ridding San Francisco of the thieves, gamblers and desperadoes that infested it none were more active, outspoken and fearless than Brannan; and he lashed the malefactors and their official supporters with a vigor of vituperation that has rarely been equalled."

majority rules!" burst from the disappointed crowd, and it was with great difficulty that Coleman and others prevented an immediate assault upon the jail. Soon afterwards the main body of the crowd dispersed, although hundreds of excited men remained in Portsmouth Square throughout the night, and several times small bands of men tried to storm the jail and capture the prisoners. All such attempts were repulsed by a police force of two hundred and fifty men, who had been sworn in as special officers by Mayor John W. Geary. They guarded the building for several days.

The politicians and lawyers who ordinarily would probably have procured the immediate release of Berdue and Windred on small bail were apparently frightened by the temper of the people, and the two men remained in jail for a week. They were then tried according to due process of law, found guilty of assaulting and robbing Jansen, and each sentenced to fourteen years' imprisonment, the maximum penalty under the statutes. Soon afterwards Windred escaped by cutting a hole in the floor of his cell, and he was never again seen in San Francisco. Little effort was ever made to find him, for both the authorities and the Vigilantes soon learned that he had nothing whatever to do with the crime of which he had been accused. Berdue was sent to Marysville, again identified as English Jim, and convicted of the murder of Sheriff Moore. He was sentenced to be hanged, but fortunately for him the execution was postponed for several months.

2

EVEN English Jim's followers among the Sydney Ducks were convinced that Berdue was their leader, and it soon became common talk among the dives of Sydney-Town that a suitable gesture of defiance would be made in revenge for the popular demonstration against their hero. Four of San Francisco's great fires had already occurred — on December 24, 1849; May 4, 1850; June 14, 1850; and September 17, 1850. As the anniversary of the second fire approached in 1851, the city was filled with rumors, which clearly emanated from Sydney-Town, that it would be marked by an even more extensive conflagration, and several notorious Sydney Ducks openly boasted that they intended to destroy the town. Every possible precaution was taken by merchants and householders, but in vain. A few minutes before eleven o'clock on the night of May 4, 1851 a man recognized as an habitué of Sydney-Town was seen running from a paint-shop on the southern side of Portsmouth Square, and a moment later the building burst into flames. At almost the same instant other fires started at various points in the downtown business district. Within ten hours the flames had consumed two thousand buildings, occupying twenty blocks and covering an area three-fourths of a mile north and south and one-third of a mile east and west. Many ships which had been discharging or loading cargo were endangered, but gangs of volunteer firemen demolished the wharves and created a gap which the flames could not cross. There was, naturally, a shortage of water, and any sort of liquid was used that might serve to quench the fire. A large warehouse in Commercial Street, occupied by the firm of DeWitt & Harrison, was saved by the use of vinegar, eighty thousand gallons of which were splashed against the board walls or poured upon the shingle roof.

While the fire raged, bands of plunderers swarmed out of Sydney-Town and reaped a rich harvest, carrying great quantities of valuable property into their dens. Several looters were shot by enraged citizens, and at least one innocent man was killed — a sailor who was fired upon as he picked up a burning brand with which to light his pipe. As on the previous occasions when San Francisco was well-nigh destroyed by fire, the incendiaries had chosen a night on which the wind blew from the east and the north. The flames were

thus carried away from Sydney-Town, and that vicious
quarter was almost the only section of the city left intact by
the conflagration. Three-fourths of San Francisco lay in
ruins when the fire finally burned itself out, but the task of
rebuilding was begun with characteristic energy and dispatch. Within ten days the wreckage had been cleared away
and three hundred buildings erected, while hundreds more
were under construction. By June 1 business and life in
general were proceeding almost as usual.

The fire provided sufficient proof that the demonstration of February had neither terrorized the denizens of
Sydney-Town nor appreciably checked their activities; they
became, indeed, even bolder during the period of reconstruction, and murders and robberies were of nightly occurrence.
Determined to find a remedy for a situation that instead of
showing improvement was rapidly becoming unbearable,
some two hundred prominent citizens held a secret meeting
early in June 1851, in a building at Battery and Pine streets,
owned by Samuel Brannan. After many hours of discussion
they formed the first Vigilance Committee. The following
extracts from the committee's constitution sufficiently sum-
marize its avowed aims:

"WHEREAS, it has become apparent to the citizens of San Francisco, that there is no security for life
and property, either under the regulations of society
as it at present exists, or under the law as now administered:

"THEREFORE, the citizens, whose names are hereunto attached, do unite themselves into an association
for the maintenance of the peace and good order of
society, and the preservation of the lives and property
of the citizens of San Francisco, and do bind themselves, each unto the other, to do and perform every
lawful act for the maintenance of law and order, and

to sustain the laws when faithfully and properly administered; but we are determined that no thief, burglar, incendiary or assassin, shall escape punishment, either by the quibbles of the law, the insecurity of prisons, the carelessness or corruption of the police, or a laxity of those who pretend to administer justice. And to secure the objects of this association we do hereby agree:

" 1. That the name and style of the association shall be the COMMITTEE OF VIGILANCE, for the protection of the lives and property of the citizens and residents of the city of San Francisco.

" 2. That there shall be a room selected for the meeting and deliberation of the committee, at which there shall be one or more members of the committee appointed for that purpose, in constant attendance, at all hours of the day and night, to receive the report of any member of the association, or of any other person or persons whatsoever, of any act of violence done to the person or property of any citizen of San Francisco; and if in the judgment of the member or members of the committee present, it be such an act that justifies the interference of the committee, either in aiding in the execution of the laws, or the prompt and summary punishment of the offender, the committee shall be at once assembled for the purpose of taking such action as a majority of the committee when assembled shall determine upon. . . .

" 4. That when the committee have assembled for action, the decision of a majority present shall be binding upon the whole committee, and that those members of the committee whose names are hereunto attached, do pledge their honor, and hereby bind themselves to defend and sustain each other in carrying out the determined action of this committee at the hazard of their lives and their fortunes."

Within a few days after the formal organization of the Vigilance Committee the first opportunity arose for the exercise of its functions. During the late afternoon of June 10, 1851 an Australian convict named John Jenkins, who was so thoroughly criminal that even in Sydney-Town he was known as the Miscreant, stole a small safe from George W. Virgin's shipping-office on Long Wharf, at the end of Commercial Street. The theft was soon discovered, and Virgin raised the alarm. A little while afterwards Jenkins was seen hurrying along the wharf with a heavy bundle on his shoulder. Pursued by a score of citizens, he clambered into a boat and rowed into the Bay, where he threw his burden overboard. It was promptly raised from the mud and found to be the missing safe. Jenkins was thereupon taken to the rooms of the Vigilance Committee, the members of which were summoned by an arranged signal upon the bell of the Monumental Engine Company.

For several hours the full membership of the committee examined the evidence and questioned the Miscreant. There was no doubt of the man's guilt, although he offered to produce a witness who could testify that he was asleep in a Sydney-Town dive at the time of the robbery. This witness was heard, but, under questioning, at length admitted that he had not seen Jenkins for several days. He was, it appeared later, a professional alibi witness for a large group of Sydney Ducks. About midnight Samuel Brannan came out of the committee's rooms and addressed a large crowd which had assembled before the building. He reviewed the case and the evidence and said that Jenkins had been found guilty and would be hanged within two hours in Portsmouth Square. At two o'clock in the morning the members of the Vigilance Committee, heavily armed, filed out of the committee's rooms and marched in a body to the square. In their midst was Jenkins, his arms pinioned. A rope was tied around the Miscreant's neck, and the other

67

end was thrown over a wide beam which projected from the old adobe house on the western side of the square. A few policemen now appeared and demanded custody of the prisoner, but were told by the Vigilantes that they would be fired upon if they attempted to interfere with the execution. They immediately withdrew. Two men seized Jenkins by the arms and walked with him along the front of the building. When they had gone a few feet, a score of Vigilantes seized the slack end of the rope and ran backwards, quickly dragging Jenkins off the ground and raising him to the beam. There he was held until he was strangled, members of the committee taking turns at the rope, and every man holding it at least once. Until he felt himself being lifted from the ground, Jenkins was surprisingly calm; he said nothing, but chewed vigorously and with evident pleasure upon a large piece of tobacco which a Vigilante had given him. Later it was learned that he had expected the denizens of Sydney-Town to swarm into the square in overwhelming force and rescue him. However, the criminals were apparently awed by the unexpected strength of the Vigilance Committee and by the obvious approval with which the crowd viewed the execution.

Next day, June 11, the Coroner held an inquest upon the body of the Miscreant, and a verdict was returned that he "came to his death . . . at the hands of, and in pursuance of a preconcerted action on the part of an association of citizens, styling themselves the ' Committee of Vigilance.'" Samuel Brannan and eight other members of the committee were specially mentioned as having been implicated by direct testimony. Nothing more was done, or probably contemplated, but the Vigilance Committee promptly published its entire membership, numbering at that time almost two hundred prominent citizens, together with an announcement that all were equally responsible for the hanging of Jenkins. At the same time the committee took further action toward ridding San Francisco of the murderers and robbers who had several times burned the city and had committed other crimes almost without number. All known felons were waited upon and warned to leave the city within five days under penalty of forcible deportation or death, and a sub-committee of thirty was appointed to visit incoming vessels and examine all suspicious persons. Unless they could furnish proof of honesty and good character, they were to be reshipped immediately " to the places whence they came, and not be permitted to pollute our soil." Two weeks or so later the committee usurped still greater powers, announcing that "we the Vigilance Committee DO CLAIM to ourselves the right to enter any person or persons' premises where we have good reason to believe that we shall find evidence to substantiate and carry out the object of this body. And further, deeming ourselves engaged in a good and just cause — WE INTEND TO MAINTAIN IT." So far as the records show, the committee exercised this " right " with commendable restraint and discretion, and there was much less complaint about it than might naturally have been expected.

For a few days after the hanging of the Miscreant the small steamers which made frequent voyages up the Sacramento River to the gold-fields were crowded with frightened rascals. But it soon became apparent that the exodus was confined almost entirely to the small fry; the really dangerous inhabitants of Sydney-Town remained under cover in San Francisco, confident that they could still depend upon their friends the politicians. On June 22, 1851 the Sydney Ducks made their final defiant gesture — they started a fire in a vacant house at Powell and Pacific streets and once more destroyed a large portion of the city. " There was no doubt that the fire was the work of an incendiary," says the *Annals*. " No fire had been used about the house in which it started for any purpose whatever. As it progressed, the flames would suddenly start up in advance, and in one or more instances persons were detected in applying fire." [1] These scoundrels, however, escaped and were never caught. Before the conflagration was brought under control, it had burned the greater part of eighteen blocks, from Powell Street east to Sansome Street, and from Broadway south to Clay Street. As usual, the wind blew from the north and the east, and Sydney-Town was practically untouched.

3

EARLY in July 1851 the real James Stuart, for whose crimes Thomas Berdue awaited execution in Marysville, returned to San Francisco from the interior and made a bold attempt to rob an English ship anchored in the harbor. The captain and his wife awoke to find the robber ransacking their cabin, and English Jim promptly struck each of them a terrific blow with a slung shot. The captain fell unconscious, but his wife was made of sterner stuff. She clutched Stuart's coat, and although he hit her several times, she succeeded in holding him until her cries had aroused the crew of the ship. The sailors disarmed Stuart, gave him a sound beating, and then delivered the battered burglar to the Vigilance Committee, which immediately began a thorough investigation of all his activities in San Francisco.

At nine o'clock in the morning of July 11, 1851 the trial of English Jim was begun before the entire membership of the Vigilance Committee, which now numbered more than four hundred influential men. It was necessary to present very little evidence, for Stuart at once confessed to a long list of crimes, including the murder of Sheriff Moore at Auburn and the assault upon the storekeeper Jansen in the preceding February. He thus exonerated Berdue, and Windred also, for he said that his accomplice in the Jansen

---

[1] *The Annals of San Francisco*, page 612.

attack had left San Francisco soon afterwards. After English Jim's confession had been read, the committee decided, by a unanimous vote, to hang him immediately. Colonel Jonathan D. Stevenson was delegated to announce the proposed action to an enormous crowd which had gathered outside the meeting-rooms. He described what had occurred, and then asked the people whether they would confirm the sentence. A tremendous affirmative shout arose, with a few dissenting voices from the outskirts of the throng. The dissenters were recognized as Sydney Ducks, and several were severely beaten by the indignant citizens.

While preparations were being made and while Colonel Stevenson was addressing the crowd, English Jim, heavily manacled, was held under a strong guard. He appeared to be quite indifferent to his fate. When asked if he wished to make a final statement, he replied: "This is a damned tiresome business. Get it over with."

Two hours after the committee had decided to hang him, English Jim was led into the street, surrounded by armed Vigilantes. Behind this escort, in column of twos, marched the remaining members of the committee, and after them swarmed practically the entire population of San Francisco. A derrick had been erected upon the Market Street wharf, and as the procession came in sight of it, English Jim finally lost his nerve. He collapsed, and during the last few hundred feet he was supported by four of his guards. Within a few minutes a rope had been looped about his neck, and a score of men jerked him to the top of the derrick — and the earthly career of the most notorious of the Sydney Ducks was ended. The Coroner's jury returned a verdict similar to that in the case of John Jenkins, but soon afterwards a special grand jury, impaneled to report on the state of crime in San Francisco, virtually endorsed the work of the Vigilance Committee. In its presentment the jury said that in its opinion the "members of that association have been governed by a feeling of opposition to the manner in which the law has been administered and those who have administered it, rather than a determination to disregard the law itself." The jury also acknowledged that to the committee " we are indebted for much valuable information and many important witnesses."

English Jim was scarcely dead before the Vigilance Committee had taken steps to right, as far as possible, the injustice which had been done to Thomas Berdue. A special committee rode to Marysville, informed the authorities there that the real James Stuart had been hanged, and procured Berdue's release. He was at once brought to San Francisco, where the sentence of imprisonment imposed upon him for his supposed share in the assault upon Jansen was officially annulled. He was, at last, a free man. The Vigilance Committee publicly announced that Berdue was innocent of any crime and gave him a purse of several thousand dollars. An hour after he received the money, he was seen operating a monte pitch on Long Wharf. That was his last appearance in San Francisco. What ultimately became of him is unknown.

During the few weeks that followed the hanging of English Jim the Vigilance Committee arrested two more Sydney Ducks — Samuel Whittaker and Robert McKenzie — and speedily convicted them of robbery, arson, and burglary. They were sentenced to be hanged, but no date was set for the execution, although it was popularly believed that it would take place soon after the middle of August. On August 21, 1851 Governor John MacDougal issued a proclamation, addressed to the people of San Francisco, in which he denounced " the despotic control of a self-constituted association, unknown and acting in defiance of the laws." The Vigilance Committee promptly retorted with this statement, which was sworn to by several prominent members and published in all the newspapers:

"We, the undersigned, do hereby aver that the present Governor, MacDougal, asked to be introduced to the Executive Committee of the Committee of Vigilance, which was allowed, and an hour fixed. The Governor, upon being introduced, stated that he approved of the acts of the Committee, and that much good had taken place. He hoped that they would go on, and endeavor to act in concert with the authorities, and in case any judge was guilty of mal-administration, to hang him, and he would appoint others. . . ."

MacDougal made no direct reply to this accusatory document, but a few minutes before dawn on August 21 Sheriff Jack Hayes, accompanied by a large force of policemen, appeared at the headquarters of the Vigilance Committee with a writ of habeas corpus, signed by the Governor and calling for the surrender of both Whittaker and McKenzie. The Vigilantes then present were few in number, and they offered no resistance when Sheriff Hayes removed the prisoners to the town jail under City Hall. The Sheriff posted a strong guard about the prison, and the authorities announced that in due time the two Sydney Ducks would be tried by the regular courts.

For two days the Vigilance Committee made no move, but on Sunday, August 24, thirty-six heavily armed Vigilantes overpowered the Sheriff's guard and forcibly entered the jail. They seized Whittaker and McKenzie and rushed them in a carriage to the rooms of the committee, where the entire membership had assembled. Within twenty minutes after their arrival Whittaker and McKenzie were dangling from heavy redwood beams which had been run out of the windows of the main meeting-room. Outside, a crowd of several thousand citizens had gathered, and as the struggling bodies were swung from the windows, the multitude expressed its approval by a great shout of triumph and satis-

73

faction. The two Sydney Ducks remained hanging for half an hour, while the crowd was addressed by Samuel Brannan and other leading members of the committee. They declared that the Vigilantes were not to be deterred in their purpose by the opposition of the Governor, and vigorously reiterated the committee's determination to hang with scant ceremony every felon who did not leave San Francisco. During the late afternoon the crowd quietly dispersed. Next day the Coroner's jury returned the usual verdict, and, as before, nothing further was done by the authorities.

The execution of Whittaker and McKenzie was the last official action of the first Vigilance Committee, although the organization was never formally dissolved. The hanging of the two men, together with the committee's bold and successful defiance of Governor MacDougal, caused a veritable panic in Sydney-Town; its rascally inhabitants left San Francisco in droves, and within two weeks there remained in that vicious quarter only a few dance-halls, saloons, and houses of prostitution, all of which were carefully operated in strict accordance with the law.

CHAPTER IV

THE SECOND CLEANSING

DURING THE two years that followed the hanging of Whittaker and McKenzie, San Francisco was as peaceful and law-abiding a city as could be found on the American continent. The gambling houses continued to operate wide open under a strict licensing system, but their clientele was constantly decreasing, and against them was rising a strong tide of adverse public opinion. Comparatively few murders were committed, no more devastating fires occurred, and hold-ups and robberies were the exception rather than the rule. What remained of the underworld was moribund, palsied by the knowledge that for the first, and almost the last, time in an American city punishment for crime was swift, certain, and severe. The activities of the first Vigilance Committee had frightened even the judges and other officeholders; for a brief period they displayed great diligence in law-enforcement and discovered a new and absorbing interest in their proper duties.

But such social and governmental purity could not long endure in a city ruled by graduates of Tammany Hall. In October 1854 came the flight and exposure of Henry Meiggs, an Assistant Alderman, who had forged thousands of dollars' worth of city warrants to finance an ambitious scheme for the development of North Beach, where he had constructed a two-thousand-foot wharf.[1] The immediate col-

---

[1] Meiggs fled to Peru, where he became a distinguished citizen and one of the wealthiest men in South America. In later years he repaid, in part, some

lapse of Meiggs's enterprises, with losses of approximately eight hundred thousand dollars to those who had purchased the fraudulent warrants or invested in his securities, was followed early in 1855 by the failure of several important financial institutions, and a paralyzing business depression which continued for almost a year and affected practically every line of commercial activity. A situation was thus created which necessarily focused the attention of San Francisco's leading citizens — the men who had performed such valiant service in the great popular uprising of 1851 — upon their own affairs; and the politicians promptly took advantage of it to increase their dippings into the public treasury, soon driving the city into such serious financial difficulties that bankruptcy was averted only by wholesale repudiation of the municipality's bonds and warrants. The deficit for the single year ending March 12, 1855 was $840,-000, and the annual message of the Mayor on that date showed that since the middle of 1851 obligations had been incurred amounting to $1,959,000, an enormous debt for a city with a population of less than fifty thousand. Later that same year a commission, appointed under an act of Legislature to fund the floating debt, recognized as valid indebtedness only a little more than $300,000. The remainder was repudiated.

By far the most powerful politician in early San Francisco was David C. Broderick, a New York saloon-keeper and Tammany henchman who became a United States Senator and was at length killed in a duel by Judge David S. Terry of the California Supreme Court. Partly because of the spectacular manner of his death, and partly because his career typified the traditional rise of the poor laborer's son to fame and riches, Broderick became, and remains, one of

---

of his creditors and attempted to return to San Francisco. The California Legislature passed an amnesty act, but it was vetoed by the Governor, and Meiggs was compelled to remain in Peru.

the great popular heroes of the state. There exists a vast literature about him, but for the most part it is a worthless mass of fulsome panegyric. Only two California historians of importance have been able to view Broderick and his activities with proper detachment. One declares that " the truth of history demands the statement that for a long period his methods were utterly vicious, and that he shrunk from no infamy which would promote his objects." [1] The other points out that throughout his political life Broderick " looked upon the state as an oyster to be opened as one might," that he accomplished no legislative work of lasting importance either in the state Legislature or in the United States Senate, and that his leadership in the struggle to prevent the extension of slavery to the Pacific Coast was more apparent than real.[2] And not even his most adoring worshippers have been able entirely to conceal the plain fact that in the final analysis he must, more than any one man, shoulder responsibility for the municipal corruption which was the basic cause of the second uprising of a tormented and enraged citizenry. He was the one man who could have halted the thievish officials and politicians and stopped the looting of the city treasury; since he failed to do so, it is only fair to assume that he was pretty well tarred by the same brush. From the middle of 1851 to his death, in 1859, Broderick was, for all practical purposes, in absolute control of San Francisco's political machinery. No man could be elected to office or even nominated unless he possessed Broderick's consent and endorsement and unless he agreed to share with the boss the proceeds of the post to which he aspired. As Broderick's most eulogistic biographer, Jeremiah Lynch, puts it:

---

[1] *San Francisco, a History of the Pacific Coast Metropolis*, by John P. Young; Volume I, page 214.

[2] *California, from the Conquest in 1846 to the Second Vigilance Committee in San Francisco*, by Josiah Royce; page 497.

"In San Francisco he became the dictator of the municipality. His political lessons and observations in New York were priceless. He introduced a modification of the same organization in San Francisco with which Tammany has controlled New York for lo! these many years. It was briefly this. At a forthcoming election a number of offices were to be filled; those of sheriff, district attorney, alderman, and places in the legislature. Several of these positions were very lucrative, notably that of the sheriff, tax-collector, and assessor. The incumbents received no specified salaries, but were entitled to all or a certain proportion of the fees. These fees occasionally exceeded $50,000 per annum. Broderick would say to the most popular or the most desirable aspirant: 'This office is worth $50,000 a year. Keep half and give me the other half, which I require to keep up our organization in the state. Without intelligent, systematic discipline, neither you nor I can win, and our opponents will conquer, unless I have money enough to pay the men whom I may find necessary. If you agree to that arrangement, I will have you nominated when the convention assembles, and then we will all pull together until after the election.' Possibly this candidate dissented, but then someone else consented, and as the town was hugely Democratic, his selections were usually victorious. . . . When he came there was chaos, and he created order. There was no party system in the town, and he created one." [1]

Broderick's political income from these and other sources was probably several hundred thousand dollars a year, and with such sums at his disposal he not only maintained his hold upon the city but furthered his ambition to

[1] *A Senator of the Fifties, David C. Broderick of California*, by Jeremiah Lynch; pages 68–9.

be United States Senator, despite the slashing onslaughts of several of the newspapers. Particularly violent in its attacks upon Broderick and upon the corrupt political machine which Broderick had fathered was the *Bulletin,* which began publication in October 1855, under the editorship of James King of William, the martyr of the second Vigilance movement.[1] From the beginning of his journalistic career King was Broderick's implacable foe. He started his campaign against the boss in the first number of the *Bulletin,* and in subsequent issues named several men who had paid Broderick considerable sums of money in return for political nominations. He also accused Broderick of arranging the deal whereby the city purchased the old Jenny Lind Theatre at an exorbitant price, and of complicity in many other raids upon the public funds. " If we can only escape David C. Broderick's hired bullies a little longer," wrote King, " we will turn this city inside out, but what we will expose the corruption and malfeasance of her officiary." As John P. Young said in his history of California journalism, King had no fear of a libel suit, " for the object of his assault did not dare to tempt the proof which he knew would be forthcoming in a court, even one in which justice miscarried as often as it did in San Francisco about this time." [2] But the danger of physical injury to the embattled editor was very great, for enlisted under Broderick's banner were many former Tammany heelers and sluggers who successfully applied in San Francisco the same methods of intimidation, at the polls and elsewhere, which had always proved so efficacious in New York. Several of these bruisers held minor political posts, and those for whom Broderick was unable to find jobs were on his private pay-roll.

---

[1] King was born in Georgetown, Maryland, and was the son of William King. As a youth he worked in Washington, where he found thirteen other James Kings. To avoid confusion he called himself James King the son of William, which he soon shortened to James King of William.

[2] *Journalism in California,* by John P. Young; page 27.

One of Broderick's principal lieutenants was Charles P. Duane, better known as Dutch Charley, who for a brief period was Chief Engineer of the San Francisco Fire Department. A contemporary historian described Duane as " a born leader, ambitious, and a good mixer," and wrote that " he is usually to be found in one of the gambling houses. A notorious politician as well, he has one thousand votes at his command, to be disposed of at elections by the simple plan of having his adherents vote three times in different sections of the city. Although he has no visible means of support, he lives regally on credit." Duane narrowly escaped hanging by the Vigilance Committee in 1851 for shooting A. Fayole, manager of the French Theatre, because Fayole had refused to admit him free to the playhouse. Soon after the execution of James Stuart the nominal bail upon which Duane was at liberty was withdrawn at the insistence of the Vigilantes, but before he could be tried, Fayole suddenly decided to visit his old home in France — a decision which is said to have cost Broderick and other friends of Duane about fifty thousand dollars. The case against Dutch Charley was abandoned because of the absence of the prosecuting witness.

Scarcely less prominent in Broderick's political ménage were such worthies as Bill Carr, Reuben Maloney, Mart Gallagher, Bill Lewis, Yankee Sullivan, a prize-fighter and at one time owner of a famous New York saloon, the Sawdust House in Walker Street; Woolley Kearney, equally notorious as a bar-room brawler and as the ugliest man in California; and Billy Mulligan, whom Warden Sutton of the Tombs called " a professional blackleg " and " as desperate a character as could be found among the rowdy element of New York." [1] Mulligan was very thin and slight, only a little more than five feet tall and never weighing more

---

[1] *The New York Tombs, Its Secrets and Mysteries*, by Charles Sutton, Warden; edited by James B. Mix and Samuel MacKeever; page 62.

than a hundred and twenty pounds, but he was a fierce fighter, especially when drunk. Armed only with a billiard cue, he once chased John Morrissey, heavy-weight champion of the world and a two-hundred-pound giant, out of a pool-room and down a flight of stairs. In San Francisco this redoubtable little man was one of Broderick's pet sluggers and election workers, and he was amply rewarded for his services. For two years he held the lucrative job of collector for the county treasurer, and thereafter was keeper of the jail under Sheriff David S. Scannell, himself a Broderick man and another of the group of New York saloon-keepers who became prominent in early San Francisco.

Dutch Charley Duane, Kearney, Maloney, Mulligan, and Carr were among the criminals and trouble-makers expelled from San Francisco by the second Vigilance Committee, and Yankee Sullivan committed suicide while confined in the committee's headquarters, awaiting trial for various crimes. Sullivan became so panic-stricken when he heard a Vigilante say that he would probably be hanged on the morrow that he opened a vein in his wrist and bled to death before a physician could reach him. This was on May 31, 1856, four days before Duane, Mulligan, Carr, Kearney, and several others were put aboard the ship *Golden Age,* bound for New York. Within a year after his arrival in the metropolis Mulligan tried to shoot the proprietor of a Manhattan gambling house and was sentenced to two years in Sing Sing Prison. He was pardoned in three months, however, and immediately returned to San Francisco, where he was not molested, the Vigilance Committee having long since completed its work and dissolved its organization. For several years Mulligan was a familiar figure around the saloons and gambling houses and was often in trouble with the police for fighting. It was his habit to go on protracted drinking sprees, which usually ended with an attack of delirium tremens. At such times he was very dangerous, and nothing would soothe him but a dose of valerian. Finally, during one of these debauches, he escaped his friends and barricaded himself in a room in the old St. Francis Hotel on Grant Avenue, where he began shooting from the window at passing pedestrians. He killed two men — one a stranger and the other a friend who tried to quiet him — before he was himself shot through the heart by Policeman Hopkins from a room across the street.

2

WITH an almost unbelievably corrupt political machine in the ascendancy, and with honest citizens distracted by business failures and the prospective loss of their money and property, the underworld of San Francisco naturally acquired a new lease on life. Under the protection of the politicians the dives, bagnios, and hide-aways of Sydney-Town began to reopen, and the Sydney Ducks and other criminals who had been deported or frightened away by the Vigilantes of 1851 gradually returned. By the middle of 1855 San Francisco was again a hell-roaring swirl of crime and debauchery; once more the city swarmed with murderers, thieves, burglars, gamblers, prostitutes, and swindlers of every degree. And within another six months conditions were at least as bad as they had ever been at any time during the early days of the gold rush. "Assassinations, murders, and hangings constitute the leading materials of the budget of news in San Francisco," said a New York newspaper in January 1856. "The papers devote large space to the particulars of these horrors, showing a state of things, especially in San Francisco, which carries one back to the days of vigilance." A recapitulation of California's crime statistics for the year ending January 1, 1856, published by this journal, showed that 489 murders had been committed, about two-thirds of them in San Francisco. In the then largest city of California no murderer had been punished, although in other parts of the state six had been legally executed and forty-six hanged by mobs. Another writer thus described the situation in San Francisco:

" Masked men appeared openly in the streets and garrotted citizens, apparently defying law or resistance; the rough element had apparently banded together for the purpose of preying upon the wealth held by honest hands. . . . Politics was in fact accountable for this chaotic condition of city affairs. . . . Society was sore diseased. Villainy wielded the balance of power, and honesty was at a discount. ' The law's delay, the insolence of office,' became the chafing cause of much discomfort. Honest voters on election day felt that it was but ill-spent time to cast a vote. Ballot-box stuffing, not *vox populi*, placed men in office. In short, the town was ruled by gamblers, rowdies, and state-prison convicts. Sydney Ducks again were cackling in the pond." [1]

On the evening of Thursday, November 15, 1855 Charles Cora, an Italian gambler, attended the performance at the American Theatre, where the Ravels were playing in *Nicodemus, or, The Unfortunate Fisherman.* He was accompanied by his mistress, variously known as Belle Cora and Arabella Ryan, who was the daughter of a Baltimore clergyman. She had long since abandoned the habits of the parsonage, however, and was notorious in San Francisco as the proprietor of a house of prostitution in Pike Street, now Waverly Place, which offered the handsomest and most skillful girls, at the highest prices, of any bagnio in the city. Also in the audience assembled to see the play were General W. H. Richardson, United States Marshal for the Northern

---

[1] *Metropolitan Life Unveiled, or, The Mysteries and Miseries of America's Great Cities,* by J. W. Buel; pages 258–9.

District of California; his wife, and a woman friend of Mrs. Richardson. Righteously indignant that a woman of Belle Cora's character should display herself in public, General Richardson demanded that she be ejected from the theater. The manager of the house refused, and General Richardson and his party left after a heated exchange of words with Cora.

Next day the gambler and General Richardson met in the Cosmopolitan Saloon. Under the mellowing influence of good whisky they agreed to forget the incident of the theater, and left the bar-room arm-in-arm. In the street, however, they resumed the quarrel, and General Richardson told Cora that if they met again, he would slap his face. Three days after their first encounter, on November 18, Cora was drinking in the Blue Wing Saloon when General Richardson entered. As the latter approached the bar, with the evident intention of carrying out his threat, Cora drew a derringer and shot him through the heart. The Coroner's jury, impaneled next day, reported that General Richardson had been "deprived of his life by Cora, and from the facts produced, the jury believe that the said act was premeditated, and that there was nothing to mitigate the same." The gambler was immediately arrested, and Belle Cora engaged for his defense a formidable array of lawyers, his chief of counsel being Colonel E. D. Baker, an Englishman who later became a United States Senator from Oregon and was killed during the Civil War while leading a Pacific Coast regiment at the battle of Ball's Bluff. The gambler's mistress agreed to pay Colonel Baker thirty thousand dollars for defending her lover, and as a retainer gave him immediately fifteen thousand dollars in gold, which the Colonel lost at faro that same night. Later he tried to withdraw from the case because of the pressure of public opinion, but since he was unable to repay the money he had already received from Belle Cora, he was compelled to continue.

Although the killing of General Richardson aroused a storm of public indignation and resentment, it is quite likely that Cora would have gone unpunished had it not been for James King of William and his violent editorials in the *Bulletin*. No sooner had Cora been lodged in jail than King began calling for the infliction of the death-penalty, at the same time predicting that the gambler's political friends would never let him be convicted. Thereafter King daily called attention to the many wild rumors which swept through the town. It was reported that Cora was to be permitted to escape through the connivance of Billy Mulligan, then keeper of the county prison; or, if that scheme failed because of the vigilance of the people, the jury was to be bribed with a fund of forty thousand dollars which had been raised by Cora's friends. "Look well to the jury," advised the *Bulletin*. "If the jury is packed, either hang the Sheriff or drive him out of town and make him resign. If Billy Mulligan lets his friend Cora escape, hang Billy Mulligan or drive him into banishment." Again, King wrote, "If Mr. Sheriff Scannell does not remove Billy Mulligan from his present post as keeper of the county jail and Mulligan lets Cora escape, hang Billy Mulligan; and if necessary to get rid of the Sheriff, hang him — hang the Sheriff!"

Such extraordinary journalism so stirred up the town that Cora was brought to trial within two months after the murder — unprecedented speed for the San Francisco courts. The jury promptly justified King's fears, reporting a disagreement after forty-one hours of deliberation. Cora was remanded to jail to await a second trial, which no one had any idea would ever be held. Next day the *Bulletin* said:

"Men were placed upon that jury who should never have been there. They went upon it to defeat the ends of justice, in other words, to 'tie' the jury. This they effectually did. It is not pleasant for us to comment

85

upon the depravity which has been brought to light in the trial. It is not very agreeable to state that the conviction is almost universal, that crime cannot be punished in San Francisco. But it is, nevertheless, a duty which we owe to the public community, as journalists, to put the people upon their guard. It is well for every man to understand that life here is to be protected at the muzzle of the pistol. The best man in San Francisco may be shot down tomorrow by some ruffian who does not like what he has said or done; yet the chances are an hundred to one that that ruffian will escape punishment. He may go through the farce of a trial, but nothing more. Now, what is to be the end of this? Crime will become so frequent that it can no longer be endured. Then will come lynch law, then men even suspected of crime will be hung; for people cannot live as things are now running. No man's life is safe, in our opinion, for a single moment.''

One of James King's most indefatigable journalistic enemies, and by the same token one of the most rabid supporters of Broderick and the machine, was James P. Casey, editor of a weekly political paper and a member of the Board of Supervisors. Early in November 1855, at a court hearing which grew out of an election brawl the preceding August, Casey admitted that he had served eighteen months in Sing Sing Prison for larceny. All the newspapers published this admission, and the *California Chronicle* supplemented it with a denunciatory editorial accusing Casey, among other things, of having had the ballot-boxes stuffed and himself reported as elected Supervisor from a district in which he was not even a candidate. A few days later King reprinted this attack in the *Bulletin,* and thereafter for several months he and Casey took frequent editorial pot-shots at each other, Casey in particular berating King for his attitude toward Cora. Early in May 1856 Casey's paper declared that King's brother had been refused the appointment as United States Marshal to succeed General Richardson, and that King himself had tried unsuccessfully to make a deal with the political machine of which, ostensibly, he was such a bitter foe. Both King and his brother demanded a retraction, which Casey declined to make. On May 14 the *Bulletin* published the most violent of all King's onslaughts upon Casey, again referring to the latter's prison record and asserting that he deserved " having his neck stretched " for the fraudulent manner in which he had procured his post as Supervisor. Ordinarily Casey would have replied in kind even to an attack of this sort, but friends of Cora, anxious to create a diversion that would take the popular mind off the gambler, convinced him that only King's death would wipe out the affront to his honor. When King left his office to go home on the afternoon of the day upon which the editorial had appeared, Casey met him at the entrance to the *Bulletin* building, shoved a pistol against his chest, and fired the shot which precipitated the activities of the second Vigilance Committee. King fell to the sidewalk, mortally wounded, and Casey immediately surrendered to the police. He was lodged in the city prison, but two hours later was removed to the stronger county jail on Broadway.

King was not the most popular man in San Francisco, but he was easily the most forthright and the most spectacular and perhaps the best-known. He was shot at five o'clock in the afternoon, when the streets were filled with people, and within an hour the news was all over the town, arousing a sensation such as San Francisco had not experienced since the turbulent days of 1851. By seven o'clock mobs had begun to form in various parts of the city, and soon thereafter the county jail was surrounded by a restless crowd of at least ten thousand men. Throughout the night they swarmed and howled before the stone walls. Lack of a leader alone prevented the immediate storming of the jail, which was guarded by the city's entire police force and two troops of militia, hastily called into service when the attitude of the mob became threatening. About dawn word was received that King's condition had improved, and the crowd gradually dispersed.

Meanwhile a score of leading citizens, practically all of whom had been prominent in the work of the Vigilance Committee of 1851, had held a secret meeting and had decided once more to take matters into their own hands. The morning after King was shot the newspapers published a call for a mass meeting at No. 105½ Sacramento Street, in rooms previously occupied by the Native American party. There, under the leadership of William T. Coleman, the Vigilance Committee was reorganized, and a constitution adopted similar to that under which the earlier Vigilantes had operated. During the forenoon a thousand men enrolled for whatever service the committee might see fit to demand of them, and by nightfall as many more had joined the membership list. The militiamen on duty at the jail sent their resignations to the Governor, stacked their rifles in the State Armory in Grant Avenue, and marched in a body to join the committee. Horsemen carried the news into the rural and mining districts, and within a few days mass meetings at Sacramento, Placerville, Folsom, Nevada, and Marysville had denounced the shooting of King and offered to send armed assistance if the Vigilantes desired.

The vast majority of San Franciscans greeted the formation of the Vigilance Committee with rejoicing and hailed it as the only possible cure for the evils which beset the city. The politicians, naturally enough, opposed it to a man, and with great vehemence, for it threatened their very existence; while a considerable number of respectable citizens sincerely believed that such an illegal usurpation of authority was a greater source of danger than a continuation of the corruption under which San Francisco was laboring. Among the latter was William T. Sherman, then engaged in the banking business, who later became General in the United States Army. The attitude and demeanor of David C. Broderick was exactly what might have been expected of so astute a politician. He recognized immediately the potential magnitude of the movement and realized that any hindrance he might offer to its operation would, in the long run, only lessen his hold upon the city and affect adversely his campaign to become United States Senator, always the goal of his ambition.[1] Throughout the life of the committee Broderick maintained an ostensibly neutral position; he neither assisted in the cleansing of San Francisco, nor was he active in the councils of the Law and Order party, as the opponents of the Vigilantes, with unconscious irony, called themselves. From the middle of May until the middle of August 1856, while the committee was supreme in San Francisco, Broderick was rarely seen in the city; most of that period he spent in other parts of the state, busily bringing the whole of California under his domination. When the Vigilantes at length disbanded, Broderick again appeared in San Francisco, only slightly less high in the estimation of its citizens, and an even greater political force than before, for he had gained almost complete control of the state Legislature. It was not until three years later that it became known, chiefly through his own admissions, that he had given money and advice to the Law and Order element; that he had done what he could, under cover, to hamper the Vigilantes; and that he had paid the San Francisco *Herald* two hundred dollars a week to publish editorials in defense of Judge David S. Terry, then his friend, after Terry had been arrested for stabbing an agent of the committee. The

---

[1] According to Jeremiah Lynch, Broderick once said: "To sit in the Senate of the United States as a Senator for one day, I would consent to be roasted in a slow fire on the plaza."

Herald, founded by John Nugent in 1850, and for several years San Francisco's leading newspaper, was the only journal which actively and outspokenly opposed the Vigilantes, and the enraged citizens promptly wreaked vengeance upon it. A great number of copies were publicly burned in Front Street, and then the merchants and other business men withdrew their advertising, despite the protests of William T. Coleman, who insisted that freedom of the press was one of the cardinal principles of the whole Vigilance movement. Almost overnight the *Herald* shrank from forty to sixteen columns, and within a month it had suspended publication. It was revived a year or so later, and struggled valiantly to regain its former position. It failed and in 1862 finally passed from the journalistic picture.

3

FOR several days after the shooting of James King business in San Francisco was practically suspended while the entire city awaited the outcome of the editor's wounds. Great throngs continued to threaten the county jail, and thousands of men stood silent in the street before King's residence. Detachments of armed men sent out from the headquarters of the Vigilance Committee purchased every fire-arm to be found in the hardware-stores and gun-shops, and seized the rifles, pistols, and swords in the State Armory, as well as two pieces of artillery and a large quantity of ammunition. During the afternoon of the second day the Vigilante leaders began organizing their forces, appointing a special troop to handle the confiscated guns and forming the remainder of the men into cavalry and infantry companies of one hundred each. They immediately began drilling under the command of former soldiers, who had offered their services. Alarmed by the seriousness of the situation and fearful of immediate trouble, Governor J. Neely Johnson hurried to San Francisco from Sacramento, but after a brief conference with the executive committee of the Vigilance organization he instructed Sheriff Scannell to permit a small body of Vigilantes to encamp within the prison walls, to make certain that Casey was not spirited away or permitted to escape. In an effort to enlist a strong guard for the jail, Sheriff Scannell went into the streets and served upon every man he met a court order to report at the jail and assist in repelling the attack which the Vigilance Committee was obviously planning. The Sheriff summoned several hundred men, but only fifty responded. Most of them were criminal lawyers and heelers of Broderick's political machine. Such was the temper of San Francisco's citizens that they were safer in jail than out.

On the Saturday night following the shooting King's condition became worse, and his physicians said that he had no chance of recovery. The excitement engendered by this news was increased by persistent rumors that Casey was to be rescued by his political friends before the sun had set again. At nine o'clock the next morning, when it was expected that King might die any minute, a signal upon the bell of the Monumental Engine Company summoned the Vigilantes to their headquarters, where arms were distributed and each man reported to his company commander. At noon twenty-six hundred well-armed, disciplined men, led by William T. Coleman as chairman of the committee, marched through the streets and surrounded the jail. The two pieces of artillery which had been taken from the Armory were loaded with powder and ball and trained upon the stone gates of the prison. Then Coleman and several other members of the committee rode forward and formally demanded the surrender of both Casey and Cora. With fewer than forty men under his command, Sheriff Scannell wisely offered no resistance. Heavily manacled, Casey and Cora were placed in carriages and taken to the headquarters of the committee, escorted by the whole force of Vigilantes

and followed by almost the entire population of San Francisco, a howling mob which incessantly demanded that the
two men be hanged at once. At the Sacramento Street rooms
Casey and Cora were locked in hastily prepared cells, and
three hundred men were assigned to guard them and prevent the rescue which their friends certainly contemplated.

James King died on Tuesday, May 20, 1856, six days
after Casey had fired the historic shot, and Casey was immediately placed on trial by the Vigilantes. The verdict called
the shooting " premeditated and unjustifiable," and by a
unanimous vote of the committee Casey was condemned to
death. Cora was likewise tried, and sentenced to be hanged
for the murder of General Richardson. Two days later King
was buried. A vast crowd, estimated at from fifteen thousand
to twenty thousand men and women, followed the editor to
his grave, and before the last of them returned from the
cemetery at Lone Mountain both Casey and Cora had
been hanged from the windows of the Vigilante headquarters, on makeshift gallows such as had been used five years
before in the execution of Whittaker and McKenzie. An
hour before he stepped upon the beam from which he was
to plunge to his death, Cora, with the consent of the Vigilance Committee and upon the advice of the priest who
attended him in his last hours, married the woman on whose
account the quarrel with General Richardson had started.
After the gambler's death Belle Cora remained for a month
locked in her room. When she emerged, she sold her house
of prostitution and thereafter lived alone with her servants.
She became widely known for her gifts to charity and had
thus disposed of the bulk of her fortune when she died, on
February 17, 1862. Casey was buried by his friends, and
upon his tombstone in a San Francisco cemetery the curious
tourist may still read the inscription: " May God Forgive
My Persecutors."

4

ON June 3, 1856 Governor Johnson issued a proclamation declaring San Francisco to be in a state of insurrection and ordering the Vigilance Committee to surrender its arms and disband its organization. The Vigilantes met this challenge with characteristic energy and determination. They immediately removed their headquarters to a small square near the waterfront, on which were a few buildings. In these structures they established cells, guard-houses, court-rooms, and a meeting-place for the executive committee, a large room profusely decorated with bunting and American flags. A stone wall was constructed, facing the open portion of the square, and twenty feet from the wall the Vigilantes built sand breastworks, ten feet high and six feet wide, through which a narrow, winding passage led to the interior. Upon the roof of the main building were placed a large alarm-bell and the committee's two field-pieces, which were kept loaded with powder and ball and manned day and night by a volunteer gun-crew. The place was officially called Fort Vigilance, but was popularly known as Fort Gunnybags. It was strong enough to resist successfully any attack not supported by artillery — and the Vigilantes possessed the only cannon in San Francisco, excepting those in the military and naval stores at the Presidio and on Mare Island. The officers in command of these stations had already been asked for assistance by the Governor and by the leaders of the Law and Order party, but had declined to interfere in the absence of instructions from the War and Navy departments. The President, at Washington, had also refused Governor Johnson's request for advice and aid.

The Governor's proclamation had appointed William T. Sherman, who had gained considerable fame as a soldier during the Mexican War, as Major-General of militia and had commanded the members of all volunteer companies, and all other persons subject to military duty, to report to General Sherman and assist in subduing the insurgents. Fewer than a hundred men answered the summons. Equipped with whatever arms they happened to possess, they garrisoned the State Armory and other points about the city which General Sherman considered of strategic importance. In less than a week, however, General Sherman had resigned his commission and withdrawn from active participation in the fight against the Vigilantes. He was disgusted with the Governor's vacillating course, and particularly by his refusal to order companies from other parts of the state to proceed to San Francisco. To succeed him Governor Johnson appointed Volney E. Howard, a former Texas Congressman who had been in San Francisco about two years. About the middle of June 1856 the Governor sent Reuben Maloney, one of Broderick's political henchmen, from Sacramento in charge of a large quantity of arms and ammunition for the use of General Howard's troops and the adherents of the Law and Order party. The munitions were carried down the Sacramento River aboard a flat-boat, but the Vigilantes, learning of the shipment, boarded the vessel in the Bay of San Francisco and confiscated the entire cargo, which was stored in the arsenal at Fort Gunnybags. Next day the Vigilantes seized another shipment of rifles and pistols, which agents of the Governor were attempting to smuggle into San Francisco. They were found hidden beneath a cargo of bricks aboard a small schooner.

Sterling A. Hopkins, a Vigilante policeman, was ordered to arrest Maloney and bring him before the executive committee for questioning. Accompanied by two assistants, Hopkins went to the office of Doctor H. P. Ashe, United States Naval Agent, where he found Maloney, Judge David S. Terry, and Doctor Ashe. Judge Terry and Doctor Ashe told Hopkins that they would not permit him to arrest Maloney, and Hopkins returned to Fort Gunnybags for reinforcements, while Maloney, Terry, and Ashe started for the State Armory on Grant Avenue to seek the protection of the Law and Order troops. About a block away from this refuge they were overtaken by Hopkins and several other Vigilantes, and a street fight occurred, in which Judge Terry stabbed Hopkins in the throat. During the excitement Judge Terry and Maloney escaped and made their way to the Armory, while Doctor Ashe returned to his office. Hopkins was carried into a physician's residence for treatment, and the entire membership of the Vigilance Committee was immediately summoned by a signal upon the alarmbell at Fort Gunnybags. Within an hour after the stabbing several thousand Vigilantes had surrounded the Armory, which was promptly surrendered by the few Law and Order men who comprised the garrison. The arms and ammunition found in the Armory were seized, but all the captives were released excepting Maloney and Judge Terry, who were confined in Fort Gunnybags to await the outcome of the wound Judge Terry had inflicted upon Hopkins. During the same afternoon the Vigilantes captured, in rapid succession, every building in the city that housed a detachment of Law and Order adherents or state militia, and by nightfall the committee was in unquestioned control of San Francisco. Not a shot had been fired.

Maloney was deported by the Vigilance Committee within the next few days, but the trial of Judge Terry was delayed for a week, until Hopkins had recovered. Judge Terry was then accused not only of stabbing Hopkins but of participation in several other affrays. The Vigilance court continued in session for seven weeks, during which time one hundred and fifty witnesses were examined. Judge Terry was finally found guilty on three counts of the indictment, and not guilty on three, but, " the usual punishments in their power to inflict not being applicable in the present instance," the committee voted to discharge him from custody. The

Vigilantes further expressed the opinion that "the interests of the state imperatively demand that the said David S. Terry should resign his position as Judge of the Supreme Court." Not for three years, however, did Terry do so, and then only after his duel with Broderick.

During the two months that followed the hanging of Cora and Casey not a single murder was committed in San Francisco, and not more than half a dozen robberies or hold-ups of importance were reported. No action by the Vigilance Committee was necessary until July 24, when one Joseph Heatherington shot and killed Doctor Andrew Randall, who was trying to collect a court judgment for twenty thousand dollars. That same day the Vigilante police captured a man named Brace, who had killed another man two years before and escaped and who had also been involved in several other crimes. Heatherington and Brace were hanged together, after trial, on July 29, 1856, on a gallows erected in the center of Davis Street, near Sacramento Street. Heatherington tried to make a speech from the scaffold, but was constantly interrupted by Brace, who had been screaming in his cell for two days. Brace's head was at length tightly covered by a large cloth, but until the trap was sprung he continued to mutter curses and blasphemy.

The hanging of Brace and Heatherington completed the work of the second Vigilance Committee. Besides instilling a wholesome fear into the corrupt politicians and city officials, the Vigilantes had hanged four men and banished twenty-six, while the number of criminals and other undesirable characters who had been frightened away has been variously estimated at from five hundred to eight hundred. By August 12, 1856 the last captive malefactor had been placed aboard an out-bound vessel, and the cells of Fort Gunnybags were empty. With San Francisco basking in the glow of municipal righteousness, the Vigilance Committee decided to disband and transfer the command of the city to the duly elected representatives of the people. On Monday, August 18, the entire population gathered to watch the final parade of the Vigilante Army, an impressive display of preparedness and power. More than eight thousand well-equipped men marched through the city, deposited their weapons in the arsenal at Fort Gunnybags, and returned without disorder to their respective vocations. A few guards remained on duty at the Vigilance headquarters until September 1, when they were withdrawn, the flags of the committee lowered, and the sandbag breastworks removed. On November 3 the arms and ammunition which had been captured from the militia and the Law and Order party were formally surrendered to the Governor, who withdrew his proclamation of insurrection.

CHAPTER V

"WHERE NO GENTLE BREEZES BLOW"

WITH THE disbanding of the second Vigilance Committee, life in San Francisco settled into its accustomed grooves. There it moved along more or less sedately for half a dozen years, a period of extraordinary growth in population, in commercial and financial activity, and in importance as a seaport. The very factors which contributed to the city's progress, however, not only opened the Golden Gate to a new influx of criminals, but lessened the probability of another uprising of a busy and prosperous citizenry. Consequently the human flotsam of the seven seas began to wash against the shores of San Francisco for the third time in its brief but eventful history. By 1862 old Sydney-Town and its environs were once more an Alsatia of dives, dance-halls, and depravity, and the transformation of the region into the more modern Barbary Coast had begun. The identity of the nomenclatorial genius who first bestowed this savage but glamorous designation upon San Francisco's underworld has not been preserved for posterity, but in all likelihood he was a sailor who had been impressed by the similarity of the quarter, in men if not precisely in methods of murder and robbery, to the Barbary Coast of Africa. In any event, the phrase was not generally used in San Francisco until the middle eighteen-sixties. Soon afterwards the newspapers began referring to the dive-operators and the thieves and swindlers who frequented the section as Rangers, an appellation which remained in use for almost twenty years.

In later times the Barbary Coast meant only the single block on Pacific Street between Kearney and Montgomery streets, a short stretch of dangerous and disreputable thoroughfare, which was also widely known, after the middle eighteen-nineties, as Terrific Street. But originally, and until the Coast was devastated by the earthquake and fire of 1906, the term was applied to the entire area, including the red-light district, wherein criminals and prostitutes congregated.[1] Owing to periodic spasms of civic virtue, to the encroachments of residential and business developments, and to other causes, its limits naturally varied with the years. Roughly, however, it always occupied a greater or lesser portion of the territory bounded on the east by the waterfront and East Street, now the Embarcadero; on the south by Clay and Commercial streets; on the west by Grant Avenue and Chinatown; and on the north by Broadway, with occasional overflows into the region around North Beach and Telegraph Hill. During most of the long period in which the Barbary Coast was the almost universal synonym for debauchery, its most iniquitous features were confined within the rectangular district limited by Broadway and Washington, Montgomery, and Stockton streets. On November 28, 1869 the San Francisco *Call* described the Barbary Coast as commencing on Pacific Street near Montgomery and following the former through to Stockton, with " various channels " leading into it from Kearney Street, Grant Avenue, and other thoroughfares. Within this area were innumerable alleys, a few of which have since been

---

[1] But not including the Uptown Tenderloin, a colony of gambling resorts, cabarets, and houses of prostitution which in later years flourished around Mason, Powell, Eddy, and Larkin streets and other thoroughfares which lead into Market Street.

widened into streets, while others have vanished with the building up of the city. Among them were Murder Point, and Hinckley, Pinckley, Bartlett, China, Dupont, Sullivan, Bull Run, Moketown, and Dead Man's Alley. Many of these dismal little passages were *culs-de-sac,* and in all of them, as well as in the main thoroughfares from which they sprouted, were to be found what the *Call* described as "scenes of wretchedness and pollution unparalleled on this side of the great mountains." The *Call* continued, on the same high note of horror:

"The Barbary Coast! That mysterious region so much talked of; so seldom visited! Of which so much is heard, but little seen! That sink of moral pollution, whose reefs are strewn with human wrecks, and into whose vortex is constantly drifting barks of moral life, while swiftly down the whirlpool of death go the sinking hulks of the murdered and the suicide! The Barbary Coast! The stamping ground of the Ranger, the last resort of the *blasé* and ruined *nymphe du pavé*, the home of vice and harbor of destruction! The coast on which no gentle breezes blow, but where rages one wild sirocco of sin! . . . Night is the time to visit the Coast. In the daytime it is dull and unattractive, seeming but a cesspool of rottenness, the air is impregnated with smells more pungent than polite; but when night lets fall its dusky curtain, the Coast brightens into life, and becomes the wild carnival of crime that has lain in lethargy during the sunny hours of the day, and now bursts forth with energy renewed by its siesta."

Some eight years later, in 1876, an indignant local historian, who made an extensive study of the district, was able to find no improvement. He thus described it:

" The Barbary Coast is the haunt of the low and the vile of every kind. The petty thief, the house burglar, the tramp, the whoremonger, lewd women, cutthroats, murderers, all are found here. Dance-halls and concert-saloons, where blear-eyed men and faded women drink vile liquor, smoke offensive tobacco, engage in vulgar conduct, sing obscene songs and say and do everything to heap upon themselves more degradation, are numerous. Low gambling houses, thronged with riot-loving rowdies, in all stages of intoxication, are there. Opium dens, where heathen Chinese and God-forsaken men and women are sprawled in miscellaneous confusion, disgustingly drowsy or completely overcome, are there. Licentiousness, debauchery, pollution, loathsome disease, insanity from dissipation, misery, poverty, wealth, profanity, blasphemy, and death, are there. And Hell, yawning to receive the putrid mass, is there also."[1]

And in 1878 the *New Overland Tourist,* to an article giving minute directions for reaching the dens of the Barbary Coast, shudderingly added this solemn warning:

" We give the precise locality so our readers may *keep away.* Give it a *wide berth* as you value your life!"

2

THE first boat-landing on the San Francisco waterfront was at the northeast corner of Pacific and Davis streets, where a flight of slippery stone steps led downward to a rude bulkhead, at which skiffs and other small vessels were moored. During the first year or two of the gold rush, Pacific Street was thus the most important thoroughfare in San Francisco, and since it was the first street cut through the sand-hills

---

[1] *Lights and Shades of San Francisco,* by Benjamin Estelle Lloyd; San Francisco, 1876.

behind Yerba Buena Cove, it was also the main highway
to Portsmouth Square and the western part of the town.
It declined rapidly in importance, however, as other streets
were opened and wharves constructed, and soon abandoned
all pretense of respectability. It was the heart of old Sydney-
Town, and it was, likewise, the heart of the Barbary Coast
throughout the years of its existence. For more than half
a century practically the entire street was given over to vice
and crime in one form or another. Eventually a few garages
and cheap restaurants crept in between the dives and grog-
shops, but for many years, and particularly during the
eighteen-sixties and the eighteen-seventies, there were only
two types of establishment which could by any stretch of
the imagination be called legitimate enterprise. They were
the cheap John clothing-stores, which catered principally to
sailors and fleeced them unmercifully with shoddy and
worthless merchandise; and a few auction places where
goods of all sorts were disposed of at public outcry, at prices
far above their actual worth. Various articles of wearing-
apparel, called by the seamen " flags of Jerusalem," dangled
from long poles above the doorways of the clothing-
emporiums, while the sidewalks in front of them were clut-
tered with stuff of every description. One of the earliest
stores of this type, and also one of the busiest, was that
operated by Solomon Levy on the south side of Pacific
Street between Montgomery and Sansome streets. Before
Levy's door was an immense pile of old blankets, chained
and padlocked to huge staples driven into the front of the
building. Above hung his sign — an elaborate tailed over-
coat, with brass buttons and an enormous moth-eaten fur
collar. On the back and front of this impressive garment
were pinned large pieces of cardboard bearing this legend:

BOUGHT & SOLD
SOLOMON LEVY.

Every customer who bought more than a dollar's worth of goods received from Levy, with much ceremony, a card on which the storekeeper had painstakingly written a verse of his own composition. The sailors considered it very excellent poetry, and sang it to every tune to which they could fit the words:

> My name is Solomon Levy,
> And I keep a clothing store
> Away up on Pacific Street —
> A hundred and fifty-four.
> If you want to buy an overcoat,
> A pair of pants or vest,
> Step up to Solomon Levy,
> And he'll sell you all the best.

Levy's most troublesome competitor was Mrs. Dora Herz, who, with the able assistance of her son, Ittzy, ran a store half a block down the street and consistently undersold the poetic Solomon. Ittzy Herz was popularly believed to bear a charmed life. He appears to have spent at least half his time being knocked down by fire-engines, carts, and runaway horses; and when he was not thus engaged, he was falling from piers, boats, and windows. His accidents were innumerable, but he invariably emerged unscathed. The climax of his career of escape came in his twentieth year, when a Barbary Coast Ranger, to whom he had sold a pair of shoes which collapsed at the first wearing, tried to shoot him in a saloon on East Street. Although the muzzle of the pistol was within two feet of Ittzy's chest, the bullet missed him and killed a bystander. Several awed witnesses of the affray declared that an unseen force had twitched the Ranger's hand just before he pulled the trigger. Thereafter for several weeks, so many people came to see Ittzy that his mother locked him in a back room and charged ten cents to peek at him through a hole cut in the door.

The most celebrated of the auction houses was the Great Eastern Auction Mart, of which Abe Fromberg was the presiding genius. It had neither doors nor windows, but was open to the street along its entire frontage. Inside, behind the pulpit from which Abe conducted his daily sales, were shelves piled high with goods — caps, jewelry, neckties, and other articles of wear and adornment which were much in demand by the shore-going sailors and others who frequented the Barbary Coast. Above the doorway was an immense stretch of canvas, about twenty-five feet long by eight feet wide, on which was painted a picture of the steamship *Great Eastern* driving before a gale. On the sidewalk outside the Auction Mart, where it served as an effective ballyhoo, was the first lung-testing machine ever seen in San Francisco. For five cents a man might blow into it, the strength of the blow being registered on a dial in pounds. This very popular apparatus was tended by Terry Shiner, who called himself Professor and claimed the blowing-championship of the world. To prove his right to the title he wore an enormous leather belt, studded with glittering pieces of vari-colored glass. For an additional fee of five cents Professor Shiner would himself blow into the machine, which promptly shivered as if it had been struck by a cyclone, while the pointer whizzed madly around the dial.

3

EXCEPT for the clothing-stores and the auction places, Pacific Street from the waterfront westward to Kearny Street and beyond was a solid mass of dance-halls, melodeons, cheap groggeries, wine and beer dens, which were popularly known as deadfalls; and concert saloons, which offered both dancing and entertainment. Most of the dance-halls and concert saloons were in cellars, and practically all of them, so far as physical appearance was concerned, were identical — a low-ceilinged, rectangular room, with a bar along one side, in the center a cleared space for dancing, and at one end a platform whereon the performers cavorted and the musicians dispensed more or less melodious sounds. In some of the cheaper places the only music came from a piano, but the more popular resorts boasted not only a piano but a squeaky fiddle and a blaring trombone and sometimes a clarinet. The melodeons resembled the dance-halls and concert saloons except that they had no dance-floors; they offered only liquor and theatrical diversion. Originally the melodeons were so called because, when first introduced in San Francisco, each was equipped with a musical instrument bearing that name — a small reed organ worked by treadles which acted upon a suction bellows, the air being drawn in through the reeds. In time, however, the word became the common designation of a type of resort which offered entertainment for men only, no women being permitted to enter except the performers and the waitresses. The shows consisted, usually, in bawdy songs, skits, and dances, principally the cancan; and, in a few places catering principally to Mexicans and Negroes, obscene poses by " finely formed females."

Many resorts similar to those on Pacific Street were in operation on Montgomery, Kearny, and Stockton streets and on other thoroughfares within the purlieus of the Barbary Coast, while the northern limits of the quarter were marked by a row of Mexican fandango houses on Broadway opposite the County Jail. In these last-named places, which were particularly disreputable, the principal musical instrument was the guitar, and the favorite dance was a very torchy version of the fandango. From late afternoon until dawn all of the dives were thronged with a motley crew of murderers, thieves, burglars, gamblers, pimps, and degenerates of every description, practically all of whom were busily gunning for the sailors, miners, countrymen, and others who visited the district through curiosity or in search of women and liquor. Every variety of vice and crime was almost constantly on display. For many years, and especially during the eighteen-sixties and eighteen-seventies, it is doubtful if a night passed in which the Barbary Coast was not the scene of at least one murder and of innumerable robberies.

When the police patrolled the district, they went in pairs or in even greater numbers; they were no more welcome than they had been in old Sydney-Town. Nor were they any more successful in preserving order and protecting the lives and property of visitors; not only was it well-nigh impossible to obtain convincing evidence against habitués of the Coast, but the Rangers had plenty of political friends who came to their aid as promptly as earlier politicians had succored the Sydney Ducks in times of stress. The resorts ran wide open, and murders and robberies continued to occur, despite occasional regulatory statutes and frequent outbursts of journalistic horror and indignation. After an exposé of conditions in 1869, in which the Barbary Coast dives were called "pest holes of debauchery and corruption," the San Francisco *Call* compelled the enactment of an ordinance prohibiting the employment of women in melodeons, dance-halls, and concert saloons. Although the law was passed with a considerable fanfare of editorial hosannas, no effort was ever made to enforce it. Another ordinance of similar intent, enacted in 1876, suffered a like fate. Under its provisions the presence of any female in a drinking cellar or saloon between the hours of six p.m. and six a.m. was unlawful, and sufficient cause for the summary closing of the resort. The Barbary Coast, however, never even knew that such a regulation existed. Three years after this gesture, in 1879, at the behest of the San Francisco *Chronicle,* the police suddenly became greatly concerned over the horrific effects of the cancan, which was on exhibition in practically every melodeon and concert saloon on the Barbary Coast. They forbade its performance and arrested Mabel Santley, a member of the Rentz Troupe, which played an engage-

ment at the Standard, a comparatively high-class theater, in
March 1879. Miss Santley was accused of indecent exposure
after Charles Warren Stoddard, a noted San Francisco
journalist and historian then writing for the *Chronicle,* had
described her rendition of the rollicking French dance as
"immodest and indecent." His principal objection appeared
to be that although the dancer was decorously clad in long
skirts, she failed to keep them down around her ankles,
where, in his opinion, they belonged. A jury convicted Miss
Santley, largely on Stoddard's testimony, and she was fined
two hundred dollars. Satisfied with this notable victory, the
Chronicle and the police relaxed their vigilance, and the
Barbary Coast danseuses not only restored the cancan to
their repertoires, but embellished it with new gestures.

4

THE lowest type of deadfall employed only a few women,
never more than half a dozen. They were, invariably, aged
and infirm wrecks, attractive only to men of particularly
myopic vision. In varying stages of dishabille, they sat at
the tables, or on hard wooden benches placed against the
walls, and acted as decoys. To each resort which offered
dancing or entertainment, however, were attached from ten
to fifty females, the number depending upon the popularity
of the dive. Some were as young as twelve or fourteen years,
while others were toothless old hags whose lives had been
almost continuous saturnalias of vice and dissipation. At least
ninety-nine per cent of them were harlots, even the children.
Regardless of their youth or decrepitude, they were called
pretty waiter girls. They wore gaudy costumes calculated to
display or accentuate their charms, if any, and in some of
the lower dance-halls and concert saloons a free-spending
visitor who was dissatisfied with the degree of revealment
was permitted, on payment of a small fee, which rarely exceeded fifty cents, to strip any girl he desired and view her

unadorned. Many of the younger, prettier women were subjected to treatment of this sort every night, and even several times a night. During the early eighteen-seventies the manager of one of the Mexican fandango dens introduced an innovation in dress which he reasoned, and rightly, would enormously increase attendance at his resort. He clad his pretty waiter girls in short red jackets, black stockings, fancy garters, red slippers — and nothing else. From the viewpoint of the customer, this was probably the most successful costume ever worn on the Barbary Coast. It was abandoned after a few weeks, however, partly because the girls complained of the cold and dampness and partly because such crowds visited the establishment that it was impossible to maintain even a semblance of order.

As regular wages the pretty waiter girls were paid from fifteen to twenty-five dollars a week. They also received a commission on the liquor they sold, usually twenty per cent; half the proceeds of their own prostitution if carried on during their hours of employment, and half the income from dancing, the price of which varied from ten to fifty cents. Occasionally a girl earned as much as fifty dollars a week, practically all of which she gave to her pimp, who promptly spent it on another woman, as has been the custom of his kind from time immemorial. In the melodeons, as well as in the concert saloons, the female performers were paid upon practically the same basis as the pretty waiter girls. Between their appearances upon the stage they were required to sell liquor, and, in most of the resorts, to prostitute themselves to any men who desired them. Very few possessed any histrionic ability, and scarcely any could sing or dance. Sometimes, however, their lack of talent was so obvious that they were, unconsciously, very comical, and so were in great demand as entertainers. In this category were six Barbary Coast artistes of the middle eighteen-seventies, who were widely known as the Galloping Cow, the Dancing

Heifer, the Roaring Gimlet, the Waddling Duck, Lady Jane Grey, and the Little Lost Chicken. The Galloping Cow and the Dancing Heifer, two enormous women who had forsaken the wash-tub for a fling at high life in the melodeons and the concert saloons, were a sister act; they performed a classical dance, lumbering about the stage like a brace of elephants. The Roaring Gimlet was very tall and extraordinarily thin, but from her scrawny throat issued a voice which would have shamed a bull of Bashan. Lady Jane Grey was a rather handsome, sad-faced woman of middle age, who was more than half-cracked on the subject of the nobility. She confided to everyone who would listen that she was the illegitimate daughter of an English earl, and during her waking hours, on or off the stage, she wore a coronet fashioned from cardboard and embellished with bits of colored glass. The Waddling Duck was a singer, sinfully fat, who was advertised as the only female who could sing in two keys at one and the same time. As a matter of fact, she sang in none; she simply opened her mouth and screeched what she called scales, along which her voice bounded like a frightened mountain goat. She was, perhaps, the first crooner in San Francisco. The Little Lost Chicken was a tiny girl in her middle twenties. She knew but one song, a ballad which began: " The boat lies high, the boat lies low; she lies high and dry on the Ohio." This she sang in a quavering falsetto, invariably bursting into tears at the last note. She so obviously required protection against the cruel blasts of the world that many gentlemen very chivalrously offered it; but always to their financial distress, for in her artless way the Little Lost Chicken was a first-rate thief and pickpocket. All of these women were very popular for a brief period, but none made any lasting impression on the Barbary Coast except the Galloping Cow. She saved her money and, about 1878, opened a saloon on Pacific Street, in a large room shaped like a half-moon, with a balcony, in which were

tables and benches. On the day she opened her establishment, the Galloping Cow announced that she had had
enough of men during her career in the concert saloons and
melodeons, and that anyone who tried to take advantage
of the fact that she was a lone woman would rue the day he
was born. Only one man ever violated her rule against flirta-
tions. He chucked her under the chin one night when she
served him a bottle of beer, and she promptly smashed the
bottle against his head. Then she flung him over the balcony
railing and broke his back. Next day a huge sign appeared
above the bar:

NO BULLS WANTED.

THIS MEANS YOU!

(Signed) THE GALLOPING COW.

5

DURING the early days of the Barbary Coast, most of the
dance-halls and concert saloons provided, in the building
above their cellars or in a sub-cellar, a large room which had
been partitioned into tiny, stall-like cubicles, furnished only
with cots or pallets on the floor. Thither the pretty waiter
girls and female performers repaired with the men who had
succumbed to their blandishments and wished to go further
into the matter. In a few of the lowest resorts, instead of
the cubicles, which provided at least a measure of privacy,
the room upstairs contained only rows of cots placed side
by side. To give the girls plenty of time in which to sell liquor
and attend to their other duties, there was usually a fifteen-
or twenty-minute interval between dances, while the acts
presented on the stage were similarly spaced. Also, before a
man visited the cubicles or the rows of cots he paid the
manager of the resort, or the bar-tender, the seventy-five
cents or dollar which was the usual price for the woman's
services. He was likewise required, by custom, to purchase
two drinks at the bar, one for himself and another for his

partner. Usually the bar-tender made a great show of putting an aphrodisiac into the girl's glass, but in reality she was served cold tea at whisky prices.

In none of the Barbary Coast dives of this early period — or, for that matter, of any other period — was a man's life or property safe. The first duty of the girl who served drinks to a visitor or with whom he danced was to determine if he possessed any considerable amount of money. If he did, the whole machinery of the place was set in motion to despoil him. So long as he spent freely and drank heavily, he was not molested, but if he once displayed an inclination to keep his pocketbook closed, or betrayed a restlessness which might presage departure, he was immediately drugged. The usual procedure was to invite him to have a few drinks at the expense of the house. If he drank beer, a pinch of snuff was dropped into it; if whisky was his tipple, it was liberally dosed with the juice of plug tobacco; if he chose a mixed drink, the bar-tender added a little sulphate of morphine. But if a man imbibed sparingly and showed no interest in the women, experiments were made upon him with cantharides, or Spanish fly, which in those days was highly esteemed as an aphrodisiac and was much used throughout the Barbary Coast. Thereafter he was either very sick or so much putty in the pretty waiter girl's hands and willingly turned his pockets inside out to obtain her favors. If the visitor survived the drugs and was of a particularly husky build and pugnacious disposition, he was allowed to depart. But as he made his way unsteadily through the narrow passage which almost invariably was the only entrance to the den, he was knocked senseless with a hickory club. He was then robbed and rolled into the gutter.

Two handsome young girls attached to one of the Mexican fandango dives, neither of them more than twelve years old when they entered the resort, achieved considerable local renown during the late eighteen-sixties for the unvarying efficacy of their method of robbery. They always worked together, or in cahoots, as the slang phrase of the time had it, and it was their proud boast that no man had ever received from them what he had paid for. Selecting their victim, usually a sailor or a countryman, they excited him with caresses and, if necessary, a drink flavored with cantharides, and then invited him to accompany them to one of the cubicles, generously offering to halve the customary fee. Having reached one of these tiny stalls, he was invited to choose a partner for the initial flight into the delightful realms of love. Without hesitation, and also without suspicion, he clasped one of the girls in his arms, whereupon the other cracked him on the head with a slung shot. They then emptied his pockets and summoned the bouncer, who rolled the unconscious form of the victim into the alley, while the murderous little señoritas divided their loot and returned to the dance-floor, still their charming and vivacious selves. Several men are said to have died as a result of their attentions, but that, so far as anyone ever knew, worried them not at all.

6

No exact computation was ever made of the number of dance-halls, melodeons, concert saloons, and other dives which flourished during the twenty years that followed the reincarnation of the old Sydney-Town quarter as the Barbary Coast, but there must have been several hundred. Many of them, with various changes in name and ownership, maintained a continuous existence until the holocaust of 1906 devastated the entire district. They included such celebrated resorts as the Bull Run, Canterbury Hall, the Louisiana, the Thunderbolt, the Cock o' the Walk, the Opera Comique, the Dew Drop Inn, the Rosebud, Every Man Welcome, Brooks' Melodeon, the Tulip, the Occidental, the Arizona, the Montana; and the Coliseum, the management of which called it the Big Dive. During the middle eighteen-seventies there was also a particularly vicious deadfall in a cellar at Pacific and Kearny streets. It was known as the Billy Goat because of the peculiarly repulsive combination of odors, compounded of stale beer, damp sawdust, and unwashed humanity, with which its smoke-laden atmosphere was permeated. The proprietor, bouncer, and chief bar-tender of the Billy Goat was a middle-aged Irishwoman called, in the expressive nomenclature of the Barbary Coast, Pigeon-Toed Sal. She kept order in her establishment with a derringer and a hickory wagon-spoke and was very adept in the use of either. She not only encouraged but if necessary assisted in the commission of any sort of crime so long as she received half the proceeds. She sold beer at a dime for an enormous mug, and vile whisky at five cents a large glassful. When served to a man who was known to have a few dollars in his pockets, they were more likely than not to contain knock-out potions.

For several years this fragrant den vied with the Bull Run for the distinction of being the toughest place in San Francisco. The police, however, were inclined to award the palm to the latter, which was also known as Hell's Kitchen and Dance Hall. This notorious dive opened its doors in the fall of 1868 and celebrated its first Christmas with a free-for-all fight in which half a dozen men were seriously hurt. During its period of greatest popularity, in the eighteen-seventies, the Bull Run was managed by an Irishman called One Year Tim, who was master of ceremonies and chief bouncer. Its owner, however, was Ned Allen, called Bull Run Allen because he had fought in the Union Army at both the first and second battles of Manassas. Allen was a huge man who always wore a snow-white ruffled shirt, in the bosom of which sparkled an enormous cluster of diamonds. He also possessed a very large and very red nose, about which he was extremely sensitive and which might have out-

shone his gems if he hadn't kept it coated with flour. This
he dusted upon his mighty proboscis from a large salt-
shaker which he always carried in his pocket. He was at
length killed by a Barbary Coast Ranger named Bartlett
Freel, who stabbed him with a clasp-knife after Allen had
run amuck in his dive with a large ivory tusk. Freel was sent
to the penitentiary, although at his trial the judge remarked that Allen's death would work no hardship upon
the community.

Allen's resort occupied a three-storey building at Pacific
Street and Sullivan Alley, with a dance-hall and bar in the
cellar, another on the street floor, and an assignation house
upstairs. Before the main entrance stood a large screen
covered with violently colored wall-paper, which was renewed two or three times each week, so that it always appeared fresh and immaculate. But the moral tone of the establishment was anything but immaculate. Allen often said
that the motto of his place was " Anything goes here." He
employed between forty and fifty girls during the Bull Run's
period of greatest prosperity, and they were notorious as
the most brazen, hopeless, and abandoned women on the
Barbary Coast. In most of the dives the drinks served to the
pretty waiter girls and the female performers were innox-
ious, and it was considered right and proper for them to dispose of unwanted beverages by dumping them into the big
brass spittoons which were scattered about the floors. At
the Bull Run, however, the girls were given real liquor and
were compelled to drink it, as their antics when drunk were
considered an amusing feature of the resort, the more so
since Allen was very liberal in the use of cantharides to
stimulate those of his employees whom he considered slug-
gish. Practically all of the Bull Run women drank beer by
choice, having full knowledge of the dynamitic effect of the
dive's whisky and brandy. But regardless of the number of
glasses which they poured down their throats, they were not

permitted to leave the dance-floor or the stage often enough to obtain the relief which the consumption of large quantities necessitated. Consequently they wore diapers instead of the frilly undergarments which the prostitute, even more than her virtuous sister, prefers. If one of Bull Run Allen's pretty waiter girls or performers became unconscious from liquor, as frequently happened, she was carried upstairs and laid on a bed, and sexual privileges were sold to all comers while she lay helpless in a drunken stupor. The price ranged from twenty-five cents to one dollar, depending upon the age and beauty of the girl. For an additional quarter a man might watch his predecessor, an extraordinary procedure which was supposed to give an additional fillip to the senses. It was not unusual for a girl to be abused by as many as thirty or forty men in the course of a single night. She was supposed to receive half the revenue from this sort of prostitution, but she was invariably cheated.

The Opera Comique, at Jackson and Kearny streets, better known as Murderer's Corner, employed French and Spanish women, both as performers and as pretty waiter girls, and offered the bawdiest and most obscene shows of any melodeon or concert saloon on the Barbary Coast. It was owned by Happy Jack Harrington, who was considered the Beau Brummel of the Coast and was invariably attired in the height of fashion. His favorite costume consisted of a high-crowned plug hat, beneath which his hair was puffed out in curls; a frock coat, a white shirt with a ruffled bosom, a fancy waistcoat, and cream- or lavender-colored trousers so tight that he looked as though he had been melted and poured into them. His principal adornment and greatest pride, however, was his silky brown mustache, which was so long that he could tie its ends under his chin. With the aid of a woman variously known as Dutch Louise and Big Louise, Happy Jack ran the Opera Comique for several years, but he was an earnest drinker and spent all their profits on liquor. Early in 1878, while recovering from an attack of delirium tremens, Happy Jack came under the influence of the Praying Band, a temperance organization of devout women who periodically invaded the Barbary Coast and annoyed the dive-keepers with their efforts to reclaim the debauched wrecks who lurched along the dismal thoroughfares. They were not particularly efficient, as their usual procedure was to surround a drunken man and ask him with great earnestness: "Have you seen Jesus?" Few had. They caught Happy Jack as he rebounded from the fearsome realms of the pink elephant and the purple crocodile; and almost before he knew it, he had professed religion, sold his dive, received a Bible with his name in it, and been installed as manager of a little restaurant in California Street, far from the temptations of the Barbary Coast. He announced that he had forsaken his erstwhile evil ways forever, much to the disgust of Big Louise, who flatly refused to accompany him on what she considered a perilous adventure. A few weeks later she married a rich miner and left San Francisco. She always retained a measure of affection for Happy Jack, however, and frequently sent him money.

Having pointed out to Harrington the sunlit summit of the mountain of salvation, the ladies of the Praying Band left him to make his way upward as best he could. Naturally, he failed to make progress, since he was by nature a drunkard and a thief. Less than a month after his supposed regeneration he was found lying drunk in the gutter before his new restaurant, his Bible clasped to his breast. Within another few weeks he had abandoned the business, which in March 1878 was disposed of, lock, stock, and barrel, at a Sheriff's sale for less than two hundred dollars. Happy Jack returned to the Barbary Coast, where he opened a resort at Pacific and Sansome streets, and became again a shining light among the Rangers. He cherished a bitter hatred of the Praying Band, and soon after the opening of his new dive he engaged an auditorium, Platt's Hall, and announced that he would lecture on "The True Inwardness of the Gospel Temperance Movement, or, The Potato Peeled." He hired a brass band for the occasion, but when he mounted the rostrum, he found that his audience consisted of six newspaper reporters and one drunken tramp who had wandered in by mistake. Nevertheless, Happy Jack lectured, berating the Praying Band for luring him from his dive and the comforting warmth of the Barbary Coast and casting him, alone and unprotected, into the midst of comparatively honest men, among whom he knew not how to conduct himself. He complained that when he finally abandoned the restaurant project, he had not a cent in the world, and that only by putting through a little deal with marked cards had he been able to amass enough money to open another concert saloon.

"Oh, King Alcohol!" cried Happy Jack. "Great is thy sway! Thou makest meaner creatures, kings, and the unfortunate fellow of the gutter forget his miseries for a while!"

"Hooray!" applauded the drunk. "More wind to you!"

"I was proprietor of one of those popular places of amusement known as dives," continued Harrington, "and all was serene and calm and I was happy, but they came down and took from me during the night my beautiful place where fortune and comfort in this life were to be mine. My beautiful soubrettes and Spanish dancers have gone, and when I look back on the scenic effects of those beautiful melodramas and the midnight dances with lighting effects, it's no wonder that I stand before you as a frightful example of the destructive effects of temperance. But though crushed to earth, I will rise again!"

One of the favorite loafing and drinking places of the

Barbary Coast Rangers, especially those of sporting pro-
clivities, was Denny O'Brien's saloon, across the way from
the Opera Comique. In the cellar below O'Brien's resort
was a pit wherein were staged dog-fights and battles between terriers and rats, which the street boys trapped under
the wharves and sold to O'Brien at from ten to twenty-five
cents, depending upon the size and ferocity of the rodent.
On a Saturday night about a month after his appearance
upon the lecture platform Happy Jack Harrington went to
O'Brien's and began drinking steadily. During the evening
he became involved in a quarrel, over some trivial matter,
with Billy Dwyer, who had just arrived in San Francisco
from Virginia City, where he had acquired considerable renown as a prize-fighter and a rough-and-tumble brawler.
Dwyer raised his arm to strike Harrington, and Happy Jack
drew his bowie-knife, which he carried slung under his left
armpit, and stabbed the pugilist in the stomach. Dwyer died
within a few hours, and Harrington was convicted of man-
slaughter and sent to San Quentin Prison. Nothing more
was ever heard of him on the Barbary Coast.

7

ALTHOUGH Pacific Street was never actually toppled
from its proud position as the heart of the Barbary Coast,
there was a long period before the earthquake and fire of
1906 when its supremacy was seriously threatened by Kearny
Street, which runs from Market Street northward past Telegraph Hill to the waterfront. But the fact that Kearny
Street provides a direct route from the northern part of the
city to the business and financial districts prevented it from
superseding Pacific Street as the most sinful thoroughfare in
San Francisco, for it increased rapidly in commercial importance, while Pacific Street, so far as legitimate business was
concerned, declined steadily from the early days of the gold
rush. Nevertheless, for some thirty years Kearny Street

boasted many dives which were fully as low and disreputable as those for which Pacific Street was so deservedly notorious. During the middle eighteen-eighties, about a decade after the murder of Bull Run Allen and the elimination of the dashing figure of Happy Jack Harrington as a factor in underworld activities, the center of sin in San Francisco was the diagonally cut block bounded by Broadway and Kearny and Montgomery streets — a comparatively small area, but so reeking with depravity that it was known both to the police and to its habitués as the Devil's Acre. In its issue of February 28, 1886 the San Francisco *Call* described it as "the resort and abiding place of the worst criminals in town," and complained that respectable citizens could not traverse Kearny Street on their way to and from business without witnessing "the utter shamelessness of the denizens." Said the *Call*:

"The women of the locality are of the lowest class. These females air themselves with offensive publicity and boldness. There is not an hour of the day or night when the vulgarity of the females . . . is not unveiled to everybody who happens to be going past. The wonder is that such exhibitions should have so long escaped the notice of those who ought to be able to suppress them, and have the authority to do so. . . . The inhabitants sun themselves at the doors of their dens and exchange Billingsgate. Drunkenness among these low creatures is common, and when they have imbibed too much liquor they are anxious to display their fighting tendencies on the thoroughfare, and their command of vituperative language. . . . For some reason the only occasion when police restraint is imposed on the female inhabitants of the quarter are when a brawl or fight has to be checked, or some noisy one has to be arrested for continuous disturbance of the peace. . . .

119

Police officers who are acquainted with the history of
the Devil's Acre say that it is the lowest spot of its kind
in the city."

Perhaps the most disreputable resorts in the Devil's
Acre were the dozen or more bagnios, deadfalls, and cheap
dance-halls on the eastern side of Kearney Street — a line
of dens which was appropriately called Battle Row. Much
of the *Call's* indignation arose from the fact that none of
the windows in the brothels were equipped with shades or
curtains, so that whatever went on inside was visible to whoever passed in the street. Otherwise there was nothing spectacular about these dives; they catered to the lowest of the
Barbary Coast hangers-on and were chiefly remarkable for
their sordidness and viciousness. Scarcely a day ever passed
in which each of them was not the scene of at least one robbery and half a dozen brawls, many of which ended fatally;
for many years Battle Row is said to have averaged a
murder a week. Equally notorious was an underground
saloon at the southern end of the row. Originally this dive
was known as the Slaughterhouse, but later it was ceremoniously rechristened — on a night in the latter part of
1885 the proprietor served free drinks to all comers and at
the conclusion of the festivities smashed a bottle of beer
against an inebriated customer's head and announced that
thenceforth his place would be called the Morgue. It was the
particular rendezvous of the macks, or pimps, and of the
lush-workers who thronged the Devil's Acre; that is, thieves
who specialized in robbing drunken men, having first, if
necessary, knocked them unconscious with a slung shot or a
section of lead pipe. The Morgue was also headquarters for
the many drug addicts, better known in those days as hoppies, who lived in the alleys of Chinatown and the Barbary
Coast. They eked out a bare existence by panhandling, by
running errands for the brothel-keepers and inmates, and

by collecting wood and old boxes, which they sold to Chinese merchants and householders. Occasionally they earned a few pennies by showing the holes in their arms to tourists. Few of the hoppies could afford a hypodermic needle; instead, they used an ordinary medicine dropper, filling it with cocaine or morphine and forcing the point into their flesh. They obtained most of their supplies of narcotics at an all-night drug-store in Grant Avenue, where enough cocaine or morphine for an injection cost from ten to fifteen cents.

A few blocks south of the Morgue, at Kearny and California streets, was a cellar deadfall and dance-hall which was opened during the middle eighteen-eighties. It flourished for some ten years, and after the Bull Run and the Billy Goat had run their allotted courses, was described by the police as "the wickedest place in San Francisco." The resort was confined within one large rectangular room, half of which was filled with rough tables and chairs, while the remainder of the space was cleared for dancing. Against one wall was a row of hard benches, and along the other was a bar which extended the entire length of the room. Music for the dancing was provided by a pianist and a fiddler, who were enthroned upon a platform at the end opposite the entrance. Behind the platform were several curtained booths, each fitted with a table, chairs, and a dilapidated couch. A dozen pretty waiter girls were employed to serve drinks, dance with, and otherwise entertain the visitors. When the dive was first opened, these accomplished ladies were clad in short skirts and silk stockings, but wore nothing at all above the waist. After a few months, however, the police ordered them to don thin blouses, which were virtually useless for purposes of concealment, the more so since they were not required to keep them buttoned. The moral tone of this establishment is further indicated by the fact that the proprietor maintained a standing offer of five free drinks to any man who found one of his pretty waiter girls wearing undergarments.

Despite the notoriety acquired by this extraordinary dive and the dens of Battle Row, the most celebrated resorts on Kearny Street, at least during the pre-earthquake period, probably were the Eureka Music Hall, a few doors north of Pacific Street, and the Strassburg Music Hall, which was at Jackson Street, near the site of Happy Jack Harrington's old Opera Comique. The Strassburg was operated for some twenty years before the fire of 1906 by Spanish Kitty, a tall, dark, strikingly handsome woman who was also known as Kate Lombard and Kate Edington. Although her place provided liquor, dancing, and bawdy shows, much of its fame was founded on the proficiency of Spanish Kitty at fifteen-ball pool, at which she was the recognized champion of the Barbary Coast. After the great conflagration, in which the Strassburg Music Hall was destroyed, Spanish Kitty retired with a fortune. She resumed her real name, which was neither Lombard nor Edington, and built an imposing home in an exclusive residential section. Her old haunts knew her no more.

The Eureka, an enormous barn-like structure, combined the worst features of the deadfall, the dance-hall, and the concert saloon, although it never ventured so deeply into depravity as did the resorts at Kearny and California streets. Its pretty waiter girls are said to have been really pretty, and many very noted Barbary Coast artistes appeared in its shows, particularly during the late eighteen-nineties. Among them were the Four Fleet Sisters, Little Josie Dupree, Dago May, and Big Louise Marshall. The Fleet Sisters, who did a dance act, were so called because they had married four chief petty officers of the United States Navy while the fleet was in the harbor about the time of the Spanish-American War. One of the husbands finally killed three of the sisters and himself. Dago May was also given to marrying sailors,

but she had no use for the Navy. She preferred whalers or
men of the merchant marine, who were less likely to return
to San Francisco. She once boasted that she had twenty husbands scattered throughout the Seven Seas. Big Louise Marshall weighed three hundred pounds, possessed unusually
long blond hair, of which she was very proud, and sang sentimental ballads and cowboy songs. She also had an extremely
irascible disposition and was almost continuously embroiled
with the other ladies of the establishment. Her strategy was
both simple and effective — she seized her opponent, hugged
her as tightly as possible, and then fell on her. She met her
Waterloo, however, in the summer of 1899, when she attempted to chastise Little Josie Dupree, a dancing girl who
weighed but 115 pounds, but made up in agility what she
lacked in heft and strength. Big Louise seized her and toppled to the floor as usual, but Little Josie squirmed from beneath the ballad-singer's bulk. Then she clambered astride
Big Louise's back and belabored her on the head with a
heavy beer-mug. To treat the serious scalp-wounds inflicted
by Little Josie, the physician found it necessary to shave
Big Louise's head, and the loss of her blond locks broke
her proud spirit. She refused to return to the Eureka
from the hospital and was never again seen on the Barbary
Coast.

8

THE crime and debauchery of the early days of the Barbary
Coast was accompanied by the gurgle of enormous quantities of liquor, the consumption of which probably reached
its peak in 1890. In that year the city granted the right to
sell beer, whisky and other intoxicating beverages to 3,117
places, or one for every ninety-six inhabitants. And there
were at least two thousand blind pigs, or blind tigers, as
speakeasies were called in those days, which operated without licenses. The municipal authorities estimated the annual

expenditure for liquor over the legal bars at $9,124,195. Although San Francisco more than doubled its population before prohibition went into effect, some thirty years after the publication of these figures, the number of saloon licenses never again exceeded three thousand.

CHAPTER VI

THE BELLA UNION

BESIDES THE establishments which were quite frankly dives, wherein the sole purpose of every employee and hanger-on was to separate the unwary visitor from his money with the greatest possible dispatch, other resorts abounded during the early days of the Barbary Coast which were a trifle more respectable. They were also called melodeons and sometimes concert saloons, but were in reality low variety and music halls. Among them were the Bella Union, the Olympic, the Pacific, Bert's New Idea Melodeon, the Adelphi, and Gilbert's Melodeon. They catered to stag audiences only, and occasionally offered very ambitious programs, but their performances, while coarse and vulgar and presented with what the Gilbert's advertisements called "freedom from constrained etiquette," were not particularly obscene. In these places there was no dancing. They charged admission, ranging from a bit, or twelve and one-half cents, to fifty cents, and their revenue was derived solely from this source and from the sale of liquor. They employed no pretty waiter girls, and discouraged drugging and robbery upon their premises. As elsewhere on the Coast, however, the female performers were required to sell drinks between their appearances on the stage, and in the curtained boxes which were a feature of each house they were permitted to do whatever in their judgment might persuade a reluctant customer to buy.

It was seldom that a prostitute appeared in any of the resorts of this type, for with the additional income from admission fees they were able to engage entertainers of some slight professional standing. Many, indeed, who trod the boards at the Bella Union and other Barbary Coast melodeons became in later years outstanding dramatic, vaudeville, and musical comedy stars of the American stage. Such well-known players as Ned Harrigan, Lotta Crabtree, James A. Hearne, J. H. O'Neill, Maggie Brewer, Eddie Foy, Junie McCree, Pauline Markham, Jefferson de Angelis, and Flora Walsh received at least a part of their early training there. Harrigan was a ship-calker at Vallejo when he became ambitious for a career behind the footlights and obtained a job singing at Gilbert's Melodeon. He was discharged after his third performance, and it was not for several weeks that he was able to get another chance, at the Bella Union. There he was an immediate success, and within a year he was receiving fifty dollars a week, a large salary for a variety actor in those days. When he played in the East a few years later, he and Tony Hart formed a song-and-dance team which soon became the most celebrated vaudeville act in the United States.

The Bella Union, at Washington and Kearny streets, was probably the most popular resort ever operated on the Barbary Coast. It was the favorite haunt of the young bloods of the town whenever they wanted to see a bit of life in the raw, or at least what they regarded as raw, and no sailor considered his shore liberty in San Francisco complete unless it included a visit to the Bella Union. Originally the place was opened as a gambling house about the middle of 1849. It was destroyed several times by the great fires which devastated San Francisco during the reign of the Sydney Ducks. In 1868 the building which had been erected after the conflagration of June 1851 was demolished and a new one constructed which stood until the earthquake and fire of 1906. Despite these vicissitudes and many changes in name and management, the Bella Union maintained a continuous existence for almost sixty years. During most of this period it was a variety house playing to men only, but there were also times when it was a family theater presenting melodrama at fifty cents top. In its later years it was called successively the Haymarket Theatre and the Imperial Concert Hall and finally ended its days as the Eden Musee, housing a penny arcade and a waxworks exhibit.

An occasional theatrical performance was staged in the Bella Union during gold-rush days, but gambling remained the principal business of the resort until 1856.[1] It was closed after the Vigilante uprising of that year, but was soon reopened as a melodeon by Samuel Tetlow, who operated the house successfully until 1880, when he shot and killed his partner, Billy Skeantlebury. Tetlow was acquitted on a plea of self-defense. A few months later he sold the Bella Union and retired to private life, but his wife died, and he became enamored of a chorus girl, who soon reduced him to poverty. He died a pauper. Under Tetlow's management the Bella Union was advertised mainly by dodgers thrown about the streets. The beauty and shapeliness of the female performers were not mentioned, nor was the fact that the performance might be highly objectionable to the sensitive indicated in any way. A typical Tetlow dodger, issued in 1862, thus described the Bella Union's theatrical fare:

BELLA UNION MELODEON

NIGHTLY

A CONSTANTLY VARIED ENTERTAINMENT

Replete with FUN and FROLIC
Abounding in SONG and DANCE

---

[1] The first minstrel show in San Francisco was given in the Bella Union on October 22, 1849, by the Philadelphia Minstrels.

Unique for GRACE and BEAUTY
Wonderful ECCENTRICITY
And Perfect in Its Object of Affording
LAUGHTER FOR MILLIONS!
In Which
HARRY COURTAINE
Sally Thayer, Maggie Brewer, Sam Wells, J. H.
O'Neill, William Lee, J. Allen, Marian Lee,
Nellie Cole, A. C. Durand, J. H. McCabe,
C. Staderman, Amanda Lee, Ellie Martell,
H. D. Thompson, Joe Mabbot, T. M. Wells,
G. Woodhull, and a host of the Best
DRAMATIC, TERPSICHOREAN AND MUSICAL
TALENT WILL APPEAR
Emphatically the
MELODEON OF THE PEOPLE
Unapproachable and Beyond Competition.

Despite Tetlow's conservatism in advertising, the Bella
Union was crowded practically every night, and the shows
were sufficiently bawdy to cause considerable journalistic
comment. A reporter for the San Francisco *Call* visited the
resort late in 1869 and thus recorded his impressions:

"Who has not heard of the Bella Union? Go to
the farthest end of our sage brush in the mountain
country, and you will meet some antique miner of the
primeval days who will tell, with glistening eye, of the
many queer sights he enjoyed at the ancient Bella
Union. . . . We enter, and passing through a large
bar room find ourselves seated in a very pretty little
theater, surrounded by a circle of curtained boxes, that

resemble so many pigeon holes. After giving the audience time to admire a drop curtain execrably painted, it is drawn up and exposed to view is a semi-circle of male and female performers seated on the stage; the latter generally quite pretty and in no way diffident in displaying their charms to the audience. Songs and dances of licentious and profane character while away the hours of the evening, and all that can pander to that morbid desire of the rabble for obscenity is served in superior style. If you have remained long enough below we will intrust ourselves to a pigeon hole above. No sooner are you seated than the curtain drops on some broad farce and the orchestra prepares for the interlude. But what is this? Don't be alarmed, my friend; this is simply the pretty little *danseuse* who performed the evolutions in the hornpipe in the last act come to solicit the wherewithal to purchase a bottle of champagne. The request is a modest one, partaking of the character of the fair petitioner. ' Only $5, now don't be stingy.' But you are stingy, and the request drops to a bottle of claret. 'No?' Under the depressing influence of your meanness it continues to drop until it at last reaches the humble solicitation of ' at least, a whiskey straight.' In the next box are seated three or four young men of respectable family connections, said respectable connections dozing away in their residences on Rincon Hill and elsewhere, under the hallucination that their worthy scions are attending a levee of the Young Men's Christian Association. How shocked they would be could they but see them as they sit there now, 'playing particular smash,' as they are pleased to term it, with the feminine attaches of the Bella Union. Well, night gives license to many strange things; but we won't moralize, although that pretty girl with the intellectual forehead that sits near one of the centers on the stage might tell you some very queer stories about some very worthy people, but she won't."

The popularity of the Bella Union declined when Samuel Tetlow left the resort, but its ancient glories were revived for a few years by Ned Foster, an able showman who always drove a team of black Shetland ponies harnessed to a gaudy dog-cart and was invariably attended by his Negro bodyguard, called Deacon Jones. Foster assumed control of the house in July 1887 and operated it profitably until 1892, when the City Council enacted a law prohibiting the sale of liquor in theaters. Unlike most statutes directed at the Barbary Coast, it was enforced. It was a lethal blow to the Bella Union and other places of its type, and they gradually passed into oblivion, although the Bella Union survived much longer than any of the others. The shows that Foster presented were no bawdier than those offered by Tetlow had been, but he made them seem so by his advertising, which had a smirking, small-boy-writing-on-the-barn quality curiously like that of the modern motion-picture ballyhoo. All of his street dodgers, in design if not in actual wording, were similar to this one of 1890:

FULL-GROWN PEOPLE
Are Invited to Visit the

BELLA UNION

If you Want to "Make a Night of It."
The Show is Not of the Kindergarten Class,
But Just Your Size, if You are In-
Clined to be Frisky and Sporty.
It is rather Rapid, Spicy and Speedy — As
Sharp as a Razor, and as Blunt at Times
as the Back of an Axe. At the

BELLA UNION

You will Find

PLAIN TALK AND BEAUTIFUL GIRLS!

REALLY GIRLY GIRLS!

No Back Numbers, but as Sweet and Charming
Creatures As Ever Escaped a Female
Seminary.
Lovely tresses! Lovely Lips! Buxom Forms!
at the

BELLA UNION

And Such Fun!
If You Don't Want to Risk Both Optics,
SHUT ONE EYE.

As For the Program, it is Enough to Make
A Blind Man See — It Is An

EYE-OPENER!

We could Tell You More About It, but It
Wouldn't Do Here. Seeing is Be-
Lieving, and if You Want
Fiery Fun, and a
Tumultuous
Time,
Come to The

BELLA UNION THEATER.

The principal rival of the Bella Union during the Foster régime was, curiously enough, not a Barbary Coast resort, but a place on Market Street, between Third and
Fourth streets, which was opened originally as the Cremorne and later was called the Midway Plaisance. This was
the first melodeon or music hall in San Francisco to make
a special feature of hoochy-coochy dancers, or, as the the-

131

atrical weekly *Variety* calls them, "torso-tossers and hip-wavers." Some of the most noted cooch artistes of the day appeared at the Midway Plaisance, among them the Girl in Blue and the original Little Egypt, who first danced in San Francisco in 1897, a few years after her triumphs in the Streets of Cairo show at the first Chicago World's Fair. The admission charge at the Midway Plaisance was ten cents, slightly lower than at the Bella Union, and it was tougher in every way; its shows were bawdier, and virtue among its female entertainers was considered very detrimental to the best interests of the establishment. Like practically all of the other melodeons, it had a mezzanine floor cut up into booths, before which hung heavy curtains. A visitor who engaged a booth for the evening was entertained between acts by the female performers, and his conduct was not questioned so long as he continued to buy liquor.

One night early in 1890 a lumberjack who had come to San Francisco from the redwood forests to spend half a year's wages became enamored of a Midway dancer. He not only bought half a dozen bottles of champagne, on each of which she received her proper commission, but stuffed several bank-notes into her stocking, a privilege which gentlemen in those days considered quite a treat. Naturally, they became very much engrossed in each other; so much so, in fact, that the dancer failed to appear on the stage when the time came for her turn. Presently one of the resort's assistant managers rushed into the booth, threatened to discharge her for neglecting her art, and forthwith snatched her from the lumberjack's lap. Thereupon the hardy woodsman drew a revolver, fired a shot into the ceiling, and cried: "Put that back!" The frightened assistant manager quickly restored the lady to her perch, and the performance was delayed until she and the lumberjack had finished their conversation.

2

PERHAPS the most fantastic of the many queer characters who delighted audiences at the Bella Union and other Barbary Coast melodeons were Big Bertha, a sprightly lass of two hundred and eighty pounds who sang sentimental ballads in a squeaky soprano; and Oofty Goofty, a stringy little man who, for a while at least, fancied himself as a dramatic actor. So far as journalistic or public knowledge went, Oofty Goofty had no other name than this singular appellation, which he acquired during his first appearance before his San Francisco public, as a wild man in a Market Street freak-show. From crown to heel he was covered with road tar, into which were stuck great quantities of horsehair, lending him a savage and ferocious appearance. He was then installed in a heavy cage, and when a sufficiently large number of people had paid their dimes to gaze upon the wild man recently captured in the jungles of Borneo and brought to San Francisco at enormous expense, large chunks of raw meat were poked between the bars by an attendant. This provender the wild man gobbled ravenously, occasionally growling, shaking the bars, and yelping these fearsome words: "Oofty goofty! Oofty goofty!"[1]

He was, naturally, immediately christened Oofty Goofty, and as such was identified to the day of his death. For a week or so he was a veritable histrionic sensation, the wildest wild man ever exhibited on the Pacific Coast. Then, since he could not perspire through his thick covering of tar and hair, he became ill and was sent to the Receiving Hospital. There physicians vainly tried for several days to remove Oofty Goofty's costume without removing his natural

[1] San Franciscans generally believe that their Oofty Goofty originated this phrase, but, as a matter of fact, a Dutch comedian named Phillips called himself Oofty Goofty Gus long before the time of the San Francisco hero. Phillips was shot by his mistress in 1879.

epidermis as well. He was at length liberally doused with a tar solvent and laid out upon the roof of the hospital, where the sun finally did the work.

Thereafter Oofty Goofty eschewed character parts and decided to scale the heights of theatrical fame as a singer and dancer. He obtained a place on the bill at Bottle Koenig's, a Barbary Coast beer hall which also offered a low variety entertainment. There he danced once and sang one song. He was then, with great ceremony, thrown into the street. In reality this was a very fortunate experience, as it indicated his future career, or, as he termed it, his " work." Oofty Goofty was kicked with considerable force, and landed heavily upon a stone sidewalk, but to his intense surprise he discovered that he was, apparently, insensible to pain. This great gift he immediately proceeded to capitalize, and for some fifteen years, except for occasional appearances at the Bella Union as a super, and a short engagement as co-star with Big Bertha, he eked out a precarious existence simply by letting himself be kicked and pummeled for a price. Upon payment of ten cents a man might kick Oofty Goofty as hard as he pleased, and for a quarter he could hit the erstwhile wild man with a walking-stick. For fifty cents Oofty Goofty would become the willing, and even prideful, recipient of a blow with a baseball bat, which he always carried with him. He became a familiar figure in San Francisco, not only on the Barbary Coast, but in other parts of the city as well. It was his custom to approach groups of men, in the streets and in bar-rooms, and diffidently inquire: " Hit me with a bat for four bits, gents? Only four bits to hit me with this bat, gents."

Oofty Goofty was knocked off his feet more times than he could remember, but he continued to follow his peculiar vocation until John L. Sullivan hit him with a billiard cue and injured his back. Not long afterwards Sullivan's pugilistic standing was impaired by James J. Corbett, the pride of San Francisco, and Oofty Goofty always felt that Corbett had acted as his agent in the matter. Oofty Goofty never entirely recovered from his encounter with Sullivan. He walked with a limp thereafter, and the slightest blow made him whimper with pain. With his one claim to distinction gone, he soon became a nonentity. He died within a few years, but medical authorities said that Sullivan's blow had not been a contributing cause.

Big Bertha arrived in San Francisco in the middle eighteen-eighties, posing as a wealthy Jewish widow searching for a good man to take care of her money, which she described as being far more than she could count. Gentlemen by the score volunteered for this arduous service, and many strove to meet the test with which she proposed to determine their worth and financial standing. She required each suitor to transfer to her a sum of money, to be added to an equal sum of her own, the whole to be risked on an investment of which she alone knew the nature. In this extraordinary manner she collected several thousand dollars from a score of lovelorn males, not a penny of which was ever seen again by its rightful owner. She was at length arrested, but none of her victims felt inclined to brave the torrent of publicity that would result from prosecution, and she was released on nominal bail, and the case against her dropped. She then decided to ornament the stage and sought an engagement from Ned Foster of the Bella Union, and Jack Hallinan, manager of the Midway Plaisance, then the Cremorne. These far-sighted impresarios promptly took her under their joint management, rented an empty store on Market Street, and exhibited her as Big Bertha, the Queen of the Confidence Women, admission ten cents. At stated intervals during her hours of exhibition Big Bertha rose from the specially constructed chair in which she reclined, and recited the story of her career of crime in San Francisco and other cities, embellishing her account with many vivid details.

Having thus established herself as a villainess of the deepest dye, she lifted her voice in song, rendering the only two songs she ever knew: *A Flower from My Angel Mother's Grave* and *The Cabin Where the Old Folks Died.*

When the furor over Big Bertha as Queen of the Confidence Women had subsided, she played a brief engagement at Bottle Koenig's and then went to the Bella Union, where she achieved considerable renown as a singer who couldn't sing, a dancer who couldn't dance, and an actress who couldn't act. Her work in the drama, indeed, was so remarkably bad that she attracted audiences from all over San Francisco and brought to the Bella Union and the Barbary Coast hundreds of citizens who had never visited the quarter before and never did again. Her greatest triumph was achieved in *Romeo and Juliet,* in which she co-starred with Oofty Goofty. They played the balcony scene with Romeo in the balcony, and Big Bertha herself, as Juliet, standing firmly upon the stage. This was probably the most popular production that Ned Foster ever staged, but within a week he was compelled to take it off the boards, for Big Bertha complained that as a lover Oofty Goofty was entirely too rough. She flatly refused to act with him any longer. Soon thereafter Foster presented her in a condensed version of *Mazeppa,* in which she made her entrance strapped to the back of a donkey. This was also greeted with great acclaim, until one night the donkey fell over the footlights, carrying Big Bertha with him, and well-nigh exterminated the orchestra. During the excitement Big Bertha, scratched and angry, crawled from beneath the braying donkey and, in language which she had doubtless learned during her career as an adventuress, indicated that she would never again play the role of Mazeppa. Thereafter she confined her stage work to singing, with an occasional dance, and appeared at various melodeons until 1895, when she obtained control of the Bella Union. Unable to sell liquor because of the law of 1892, she couldn't make the resort pay. After a few months she quit in disgust and so passed from the Barbary Coast picture.

CHAPTER VII

THE CHINESE AND THE HOODLUMS

THE CHINESE invasion of San Francisco and California began in the summer of 1848, about five months after the discovery of gold at Sutter's Fort, when three frightened subjects of the Son of Heaven — two men and a woman — disembarked from the brig *Eagle* and vanished in the foothills behind Yerba Buena Cove. So far as the records show, they were the first of their race to pass through the Golden Gate, at least in modern times. Soon thereafter the yellow torrent was raging in full flood. According to *The Annals of San Francisco*, ten thousand Celestials landed in 1852, and that same year a committee appointed by Governor John M. Bigler to study the question of Chinese immigration estimated the Chinese population of California at 22,000. The deluge of yellow men reached its peak in 1870, when the United States census showed a total of 71,328 scattered throughout the state. More than half, however, were in San Francisco. The number began to decline immediately after the passage of the Ten-year Exclusion Act in the spring of 1882, and the influx from the Flowery Kingdom was definitely stopped by the Scott Exclusion Act of 1888, which specifically forbade the importation of Chinese laborers.[1]

---

[1] The Chinese in California are now far outnumbered by the Japanese, although until the turn of the present century the latter were so few as to attract little attention.

During the first two years of the gold rush most of the Chinese who reached the Pacific Coast made their way as quickly as possible to the mines. About the beginning of 1851, however, increasingly large groups began to settle in San Francisco and engage in various occupations, while others drifted back to the city from the gold-fields, where they had met with scant success. In the early spring of 1851 the first Chinese laundry in the United States was opened at Washington Street and Grant Avenue by one Wah Lee,[1] who leased the ground floor and basement of a building, flung out a sign bearing the legend: "Wash'ng and Iron'g," and forthwith reduced the price of washing to two dollars a dozen pieces. Wah Lee was, immediately, almost overwhelmed by the deluge of shirts, collars, and other articles of apparel which poured into his establishment. Within a week he was working twenty washermen in three shifts, and in less than three months scores of laundries had been started by other Chinese throughout the city. During the eighteen-seventies and eighteen-eighties there were at least a thousand in San Francisco, and for many years washing was, in the popular mind, the principal vocation of the Chinese everywhere in the United States. But the invention and widespread use of steam and electrically driven apparatus spelled the doom of the Chinese laundry. Today it is doubtful if forty could be found in the city of their origin.

The authors of the *Annals* estimated the Chinese population of San Francisco in 1852 as 3,000, and a similar estimate was made by the San Francisco *Herald*. "Go where he [the visitor] will," said the *Herald* on April 12 of that year, "he meets natives of the Celestial empire, and subjects of the uncle to the moon, with their long plaited queues or tails, very wide pantaloons bagging behind, and curiously formed head coverings — some resembling inverted soup

---

[1] According to Idwal Jones in the *American Mercury*, August 1926.

plates, and others fitting as close to the scalp as the scalp does to the Celestial cranium it covers. We have no means of ascertaining the exact number of Chinese in San Francisco, but we should suppose that they numbered at least three thousand. They are not confined to any particular street or locality, but are scattered over the city and suburbs." Within a few years, however, the Chinese began to gather into a distinct colony of their own, which they have since maintained. They soon occupied the upper part of Sacramento Street, which in early days was cut through only a few blocks beyond Portsmouth Square, and the whole of Dupont Street, now Grant Avenue. During the eighteen-fifties this quarter was known as Little China, and its inhabitants as China Boys; not until after 1860 did San Franciscans begin calling the district Chinatown.

The Chinese settlement has always been confined within a small sliver of territory some seven blocks long and three blocks wide, and although for almost thirty years thousands of Orientals arrived in San Francisco every year, nearly all of them managed to find both lodging and business opportunity in this restricted area. In 1885 a special committee composed of W. B. Farwell, John E. Kunkler, and E. B. Pond, appointed by the Board of Supervisors to make an exhaustive survey of conditions in Chinatown, reported that a " safe minimum estimate of the population is about 30,000 Chinese living in twelve blocks." The committee visited every room in the district and found 15,180 sleeping-bunks, each of which was occupied by at least two persons. Four years later, in 1889, another official investigation placed the number of Chinese in San Francisco at 45,000, of whom about one-third were women and children, including slaves. Of the total, 5,000 men were employed as cooks and domestic servants in white households, 4,000 in cigar-making, 5,000 in the manufacture of men's clothing and women's underwear, and only about 2,000 in laundries. For many years, until soon after the beginning of the present century, practically every business enterprise in Chinatown was dominated by an organization of merchants called the Six Companies,[1] which also exercised supervisory control over most of the Chinese in California, particularly those of the coolie or laboring class. Through their agents in China the Six Companies advanced money to emigrants who desired to come to the United States, and as early as 1852 had set aside a fund of two hundred thousand dollars which was used solely for this purpose. When the immigrant arrived in this country, the Six Companies obtained a job for him or outfitted him for the mines and then saw to it that he repaid the loan, with interest. According to various investigating committees, the organization also required him to pay into its coffers a certain proportion of his earnings as long as he remained in America.

Many of the dwellings and business houses occupied by the Chinese in early San Francisco were shipped in sections from China and erected in Chinatown by the men who had imported them. Although they were small and incommodious, an incredibly large number of Chinese managed to crowd into them and live in comparative comfort. Practically all of these structures were destroyed in the great conflagrations of 1849–51, and thereafter, until the earthquake and fire of 1906 wiped out Chinatown and compelled the erection of more modern structures, the district was crowded with flimsy shacks and odorous cellars, which lined dirty, narrow streets and alleys. For almost twenty years between four hundred and five hundred Chinese men, women, and children lived in an enormous cellar, opening on an underground court into which the denizens of the place descended from the street by means of rickety ladders, on Washington Street just north of Kearny. This extraordinary habitation,

---

[1] They were the Sam Yup, Yung Wo, Kong Chow, Wing Yung, Hop Wo, and Yan Wo companies.

which lacked even the most primitive comforts and conveniences, was called the Devil's Kitchen and Ragpicker's Alley and, by facetious journalists, the Palace Hotel. Almost as many more Orientals occupied another underground chamber, known as the Dog Kennel, on the east side of Bartlett Alley.

For several years prior to the holocaust of 1906 the Dog Kennel was the home of a Chinatown character named Lem Duck, who was better known to the tourists as Happy Hooligan. He was not so bright as he might have been and consequently was the natural target of abuse by both whites and Chinese. When Happy felt sufficiently aggrieved at his tormentors, he sought the protection of his friend Detective George McMahon, who gained considerable renown in 1910 by preventing the assassination of Prince Tsai Hsun, brother of the Emperor of China and commander of the Imperial Chinese Navy, as the Prince stepped from a train at the Oakland mole. McMahon defended Happy Hooligan against the pack of practical jokers which forever bayed at the Chinaman's heels, and the grateful Happy at length offered the detective his greatest pride and most valuable possession—a large and shiny gold tooth. McMahon agreed to accept the tooth when it fell out of its own accord, and promised to fashion from it a miniature police whistle for Happy to blow when he needed protection. One night, however, two debased Chinese crept into the Dog Kennel, and while one held Happy Hooligan, the other pulled the cherished tooth with a pair of pliers. When his assailants had fled, Happy ran through the streets, crying: "Georgie man! Georgie man! Highbinder stealum whistle!"

Although white San Franciscans regarded most of the living-quarters in Chinatown as pest holes of filth and squalor, no attempt was made to cleanse them until the bubonic-plague scare of 1901, when health officers invaded the district and fumigated it with three hundred pounds of sulphur. As a matter of fact, however, even such dismal places as the Dog Kennel and the Palace Hotel were superior to the accommodations which the same class of people would have been able to obtain in China.

2

THE Chinese ultimately found their place in the California sun, and in time were recognized as, in the main, a sober, industrious, and picturesque element of the population. But this status was not reached for many years, and then only after the Chinese had survived innumerable campaigns of persecution even more systematic and cruel than those which had been directed against the Spanish-Americans. Except for occasional outbreaks, the abuse of the " greaser " was confined almost entirely to the gold-fields, while ill treatment of the Chinese was carried on in the towns and cities as well. Throughout the state, for almost half a century, John Chinaman was buffeted from pillar to post. He was everywhere discriminated against; he was robbed, beaten, and frequently murdered, and no punishment was meted out to his assailant; he was brutally and unceremoniously ejected from whatever mining or agricultural property he had managed to acquire; in the courts he was classed lower than the Negro or the Indian; and scores of laws were enacted for the sole purpose of hampering him in his efforts to earn an honest living. As the authors of *The Annals of San Francisco* put it in 1854:

> " The manners and habits of the Chinese are very repugnant to Americans in California. Of different language, blood, religion, and character, inferior in most mental and bodily qualities, the Chinaman is looked upon by some as only a little superior to the negro, and by others as somewhat inferior. . . . In short, there is a strong feeling — prejudice it may be — existing in

California against all Chinamen, and they are nick-named, cuffed about, and treated very unceremoniously by every other class. . . . It was only in 1851 and 1852 that their rapidly increasing numbers began to attract much attention. Considerable apprehension then began to be entertained of the supposed bad effect which their presence would have on the white population. Large bands of Chinese were working at the mines upon conditions which were supposed to be closely allied to a state of slavery. Much misunderstanding arose on the subject. It was believed that the gangs were receiving only subsistence and nominal wages — some four or five dollars a month for each man — and that speculators, both yellow and white, were setting them to work on various undertakings which free white laborers conceived should be executed only by themselves. If these vast inroads of Chinese were to continue, the white miner considered that he might as well leave the country at once, since he could not pretend to compete with the poverty-stricken, meek and cheap ' coolie,' as so John Chinaman was now called by many. It was true that the latter never sought to interfere with the rich claims which the American miner wrought, while he submitted very patiently to be violently driven away from whatever neglected spot he might have occupied, but which the white man suddenly chose to fancy. It was true also that the Chinaman regularly paid, as a foreigner — and was almost the only foreigner that did so — his mining license to the state; and was a peaceable and hard-working subject. These things did not matter. . . . Angry words, much strife, and perhaps some bloodshed, were generated in the mining regions, and the hapless Chinese were driven backwards and forwards and their lives made miserable."

The persecution of the Chinese in California acquired an official tinge in 1852, when Governor Bigler, at the behest of the white miners, sent a message to the Legislature in which he characterized the Chinese as "coolies" and urged the immediate passage of laws to restrict, if not entirely to prevent, their immigration. According to the *Annals*, "the terms of this message were considered offensive and uncalled for by most of the intelligent and liberal-minded Americans." After much bombastic oratory the Legislature declined to enact the statutes demanded by Bigler; but the continued influx of Chinese during the next twenty years, and several serious riots in Shasta and other mining towns, kept the question very much alive. Various governors who followed Bigler repeated his recommendations, but an element of hypocrisy was easily discernible in the attitude of many of them, notably Leland Stanford, the founder of Stanford University, who was Governor of California from 1861 to 1863. In a message to the Legislature in January 1862, Stanford declared that Chinese immigration should be discouraged by every legitimate means, and expressed the opinion that "the presence of numbers of that degraded and distinct people would exercise a deleterious effect upon the superior race." Throughout the state Governor Stanford was acclaimed for his forthright utterances upon the most important issue of the period, but enthusiasm for him waned when it was disclosed that while he was so boldly expressing his solicitude for the welfare of the white race, the corporation of which he was president was importing thousands of Chinese laborers to build the Central Pacific railroad.[1]

A few months after Stanford retired as Governor, in

---

[1] Publicly Stanford remained violently anti-Chinese, but privately he continued to employ them. As late as 1888 *Appleton's Cyclopedia of American Biography*, describing the Stanford estate in Tehema County, said: "It is divided into 500-acre tracts, and most of the labor is performed by Chinamen."

1863, the Legislature passed a law prohibiting the giving of testimony by Chinese in any legal action in which a white man was involved, and repealed a statute, passed in 1850, which had thus discriminated against only Negroes, mulattoes, and Indians. Despite the activities of the steamship and railroad companies, the constitutional convention of 1878 was overwhelmingly anti-Chinese, and the state constitution as ratified by the voters of California in the spring of 1879 reflected the prevailing attitude. It forbade the employment of Chinese by corporations, debarred them from the suffrage, annulled all contracts for coolie labor, directed the Legislature to provide for the punishment of any company which imported Chinese, and imposed severe restrictions upon their residence in the state. The popularity of these stringent provisions was further attested in September 1879, when a secret ballot was taken at the regular election on the question of permitting the entry of the Chinese. Only 833 votes, out of a total of 155,471, were cast in favor of unlimited settlement by the Orientals.

3

FOR some fifteen years after the Chinese began coming to California the attitude of San Francisco toward the yellow man was much more tolerant than that of the remainder of the state. By the late eighteen-sixties, however, considerable anti-Chinese feeling had developed, particularly among the laborers and other members of the lower social orders, and it increased in intensity until effective exclusion laws were passed by Congress. On April 5, 1874 a gigantic mass meeting, attended by more than twenty thousand persons, was held in San Francisco, at which various city and state officials delivered violent harangues against the Chinese. The meeting also adopted resolutions demanding the immediate ejection of the Chinese from California and making very definite charges against them as a race. Copies of the resolutions and also of the speeches were sent to Congress and President Grant by a special committee. Some of the accusations were:

That not one virtuous Chinawoman had been brought to America, and that here the Chinese had no wives or children.

That the Chinese had purchased no real estate.

That the Chinese ate rice, fish, and vegetables, and that otherwise their diet differed from that of white men.

That the Chinese were of no benefit to the country.

That the Six Companies had secretly established judicial tribunals, jails, and prisons, and secretly exercised judicial authority over the Chinese.

That all Chinese laboring men were slaves.

That the Chinese brought no benefits to American bankers and importers.

Several months later the Six Companies submitted to President Grant a memorial signed by the presidents of each of the companies and by Lee Tong Hay, president of the Chinese Young Men's Christian Association. In this document the charges made by the mass meeting were categorically denied, and it was pointed out, among other things, that the Chinese owned eight hundred thousand dollars' worth of real estate in San Francisco alone, and that they paid more than two million dollars in customs duties each year, and an annual poll-tax of two hundred thousand dollars to the California state treasury, besides the foreign miners' tax and many thousands of dollars in personal-property taxes. Concerning the accusation that there were no virtuous Chinawomen in California, the memorial said:

" The fact is, that already a few hundred Chinese families have been brought here. They are all chaste, pure, keepers-at-home, not known on the public street. There are also among us a few hundred, perhaps a thousand, Chinese children born in America. The reason why so few of our families are brought to this country is because it is contrary to the custom and against the inclination of virtuous Chinese women to go so far from home, and because the frequent outbursts of popular indignation against our people have not encouraged us to bring our families with us against their will. Quite a number of Chinese prostitutes have been brought to this country by unprincipled Chinamen, but these at first were brought from China at the instigation and for the gratification of white men. And even at the present time it is commonly reported that a part of the proceeds of this villainous traffic goes to enrich a certain class of men belonging to this honourable nation — a class of men, too, who are under solemn obligations to suppress the whole vile business, and who certainly have it in their power to suppress it if they so desired. A few years ago, our Chinese merchants tried to send these prostitutes back to China, and succeeded in getting a large number on board the outgoing steamer, but a certain lawyer of your honourable nation (said to be the author and bearer of these resolutions against our people), in the employ of unprincipled Chinamen, procured a writ of habeas corpus, and the courts decided that they had a right to stay in this country if they so desired. Those women are still here, and the only remedy for this evil, and also for the evil of Chinese gambling, lies, so far as we can see, in an honest and impartial administration of municipal government, in all its details, even including the Police Department. If officers would refuse bribes, then unprincipled Chinamen could no longer purchase immunity from the punishment of their crimes." [1]

Several years before the mass meeting which called forth this protest, the city authorities of San Francisco, hearkening to the voice of the masses, began to enact laws calculated to annoy and harass the patient Celestial. Among these regulatory measures was an ordinance, adopted in 1870, which prohibited the carrying of baskets suspended from or attached to poles borne across or upon the shoulders. It was in this manner that the Chinese laundrymen transported the soiled linen of all San Francisco. Several were arrested for violating this curious statute, but in police court the charges against them were dismissed because the ordinance failed to declare the act a nuisance and had provided no penalty. Another law forbade the disinterment of bodies and was intended to prevent the Chinese from following their immemorial custom of shipping their dead to China for permanent burial. A third ordinance, passed over the veto of Mayor William Alvord, levied a special tax of fifteen dollars a quarter upon every person employed in a Chinese laundry. Still another imposed a fine of from ten to fifty dollars upon " any person found sleeping in a room containing less than five hundred cubic feet of space for each person." This law made the slumbers of practically every Chinaman in San Francisco illegal. The final ordinance of this persecutory series, adopted by the Board of Supervisors on June 14, 1876, was aimed at the Chinaman's most cherished adornment — his pigtail. It provided that the hair of every male imprisoned in the county jail be " cut or clipped to an uniform length of one inch from the scalp."

---

[1] The memorial in full may be found in *Metropolitan Life Unveiled, or, The Mysteries and Miseries of America's Great Cities*, by J. W. Buel. (San Francisco, 1882).

Soon after the passage of this statute the police arrested one Ho Ah Kow for violating the sleeping-ordinance, and Matthew Noonan, a keeper at the jail, immediately cut off his queue. Ho Ah Kow promptly brought suit against Noonan and the Supervisors for ten thousand dollars damages, alleging that the loss of his queue had exposed him to public contempt and ridicule and had irreparably injured him in the eyes of his countrymen. In 1879 the United States Circuit Court held that the queue ordinance was invalid, in that its provisions exceeded the powers of the Board of Supervisors. The claims of the victorious Ho Ah Kow were settled by the payment of a few hundred dollars, and the authorities molested no more pigtails, either in or out of prison. The Chinese retained their queues until the success of the revolt against the Manchu dynasty filled them with zeal for modernity and progress and impelled them to apply their own shears.

4

THE most industrious persecutors of the Chinese in San Francisco were the hoodlums, young thieves and brawlers who were a veritable thorn in the flesh of the police for more than a quarter of a century. They ranged in age from twelve to thirty years and operated in organized groups which, with the exception of the Sydney Ducks and the Hounds of gold-rush days, were the only criminal gangs that the San Francisco underworld has ever produced. In general characteristics, and especially in deportment and dislike of honest labor, the hoodlums were identical with the larrikins of Australia, the hooligans of London, and the roughs and bullies of the Bowery and Five Points districts of New York. But the name by which they were designated was of San Francisco coinage. It was first used by newspaper men there during the latter part of 1868, and for at least two years always appeared in print spelled with a capital H and enclosed within quotation marks. Its first appearance as a common noun was probably in 1872, when the Sacramento *Weekly Union* of February 24 asked editorially if the boys of that city were to be "trained as polite loafers, street hounds, hoodlums, or bummers?" Within five years the word was in general use throughout the United States and had taken its proper place in the American language as the peculiarly apt designation of a young rowdy of criminal tendencies. The exact derivation of "hoodlum" is unknown, and probably always will be, in common with many other words and phrases of journalistic parentage. During the autumn of 1877 various newspapers and magazines attempted to trace its origin, but none succeeded in obtaining any definite information. In its issue of September 26, 1877 the *Congregationalist* published this account:

> "A newspaper man in San Francisco, in attempting to coin a word to designate a gang of young street Arabs under the beck of one Muldoon, hit upon the idea of dubbing them 'noodlums,' that is, simply reversing the leader's name. In writing the word, the strokes of the 'n' did not correspond in height, and the compositor taking the 'n' for an 'h' printed it hoodlums." [1]

On October 27, 1877 the San Francisco *Call* contributed this bit of philological lore:

> "Before the late war there appeared in San Francisco a man whose dress was very peculiar. The boys took a fancy to it, and organizing themselves into

---

[1] This derivation is also given in *An American Glossary*, by Richard H. Thornton; *An Etymological Dictionary of Modern English*, by Ernest Weekley, M. A.; *A Dictionary of Americanisms*, by John Russell Bartlett; and similar works.

a military company adopted in part the dress of this man. The head-dress resembled the fez, from which was suspended a long tail. The gamins called it a 'hood,' and the company became known as the 'hoods.' The rowdy element of the city adopted much of the dress of the company referred to, and were soon designated as hoodlums."

A third theory, favored by the present Chief of the San Francisco Police Department, William Quinn, describes the word as a corruption of Hoodler, the family name of several boisterous brothers who were frequently the objects of police attention. Another has it that the term was first applied to girls who wore a hood-like bonnet and were called "hoodlum girlums" by the street boys, who had invented a sort of pig-Latin by adding the syllable "lum" to every word. Still another, and the most plausible of all, was thus given in the Los Angeles *Express* of August 25, 1877:

"A gang of bad boys from fourteen to nineteen years of age were associated for the purpose of stealing. These boys had a rendezvous, and when danger threatened them their words of warning were 'Huddle 'em! Huddle 'em!' An article headed 'Huddle 'Em,' describing the gang and their plans of operation, was published in the San Francisco *Times*. The name applied to them was soon contracted to hoodlum."

The man who gave this information to the *Express* had been a reporter on the staff of the *Times,* and the article referred to appeared in the latter newspaper about the middle of 1868, after the police had obtained evidence implicating the gang in more than forty robberies and had arrested several of the youngsters. The juvenile miscreants were regularly organized, and operated under the leadership of an elected captain, who planned the crimes and assigned members of the band to commit them. Their rendezvous was an abandoned shack on an old wharf, with an entrance underneath. They stole whatever they could lay their hands on and sold their loot to fences and dealers on the Barbary Coast, in the dives of which they spent their gains. The doings of the gang occupied considerable space in the newspapers for a brief period, and the boys were called, and likewise called themselves, the " Huddle 'ems." Journalists soon began referring to other youthful scoundrels as " huddle 'ems," then as huddlems and hudlems, and finally as hoodlums. The transition to hoodlum was a perfectly logical development, the more so since a majority of unlettered men are prone to lengthen their vowels, and, in particular, to pronounce the short " u " as " oo." A striking example of this tendency is the fact that the name of the former heavy-weight champion of the world is pronounced Tooney quite as often as Tunney, especially among his former associates. Another is the widespread pronunciation of " gums " as " gooms." A California writer whose memory goes back to the early days of the hoodlums and who has delved deep into the little-known phases of San Francisco life, says that he distinctly remembers the pronunciation of the word by his parents and others as " hudlem." " To my knowledge," he wrote, " it was never a police call or cry of warning, but was a password or cue for gang action — to surround, push and force the victim or victims of rowdyism into an advantageous position for mauling. I never saw a hood worn by anyone but girls and women. The appearance of a boy or man with his coat-tails turned back and up, inside out, over his head — a rough custom of the time — may account for the hood theory." [1]

---

[1] Curtis Tobey, 654 Thirteenth Street, Oakland, California, in a letter dated April 4, 1932.

5

THE memberships of many of the early hoodlum gangs included girls, and several were captained by maladjusted representatives of the so-called gentler sex. Curiously enough, or perhaps not so curiously, these girls were almost invariably more ferocious than their male companions, and their fertile minds devised most of the unpleasant methods of torture which the hoodlums employed upon their victims. One feminine rowdy who flourished during the latter part of 1878 was a thirteen-year-old girl known as Little Dick, who led a gang of more than twenty boys of about the same age. She was finally sent to a corrective institution, after she had stolen a hundred revolvers from a gun-shop, distributed some among her followers, and sold the remainder on the Barbary Coast. She said frankly that she found her greatest delight in throwing red pepper into a Chinaman's eyes or in hanging him up by his queue.

All of these hoodlums, of whatever age, possessed a violent antipathy to the Chinese and tormented them at every opportunity and in every conceivable way. A favorite pastime of the younger hoodlums was to board street cars on which Chinese were riding, tie the yellow men's queues together, and, if possible, cut off the ends. They were as proud of these bits of Oriental hair as a savage Indian was of an enemy's scalp. There was great rivalry among the gangs as to which could accumulate the greatest number of queue ends, which the hoodlums made into belts or cap tassels or used to decorate the walls of the shacks or rooms where they made their headquarters. The more mature hoodlums sometimes indulged also in these mischievous practices, but in the main their activities were much more criminal and vicious. They set fire to the laundries and wash-houses; invaded these and other Chinese business establishments and robbed and beat the proprietors; stole the earnings of the slave girls, and stormed the houses wherein the latter were on display and compelled them to submit to frightful abuses. Without provocation, they attacked every Chinese who ventured into parts of the city where the hoodlums were especially numerous and powerful, notably the waterfront, the Telegraph Hill district and the northern purlieus of the Barbary Coast, and the section known as Tar Flat, near the gas-works south of Market Street. A typical exploit of the hoodlums occurred during the summer of 1868, when a score of youthful rowdies captured a Chinese crab-catcher and dragged him beneath a wharf. There they robbed him, beat him with a hickory club, branded him in a dozen places with hot irons, and then slit his ears and tongue. "There was apparently no other motive for this atrocity," said the San Francisco *Times* of July 30, 1868, "than the brutal instincts of the young ruffians who perpetrated it. Such boys are constantly hanging about our wharves eager to glut their cruelty upon any Chinaman who may pass."

Hundreds of more or less similar attacks were reported to the police during the next twenty or thirty years, but the most serious of all the hoodlum outbreaks against the Chinese took place some nine years after the capture and torturing of the crab-catcher. Throughout the summer of 1877 San Francisco labored in the throes of a business depression that began with the closing down of several of the mines in the Comstock Lode, with resultant heavy losses to San Francisco investors and business men; and which was intensified by crop failures and the railroad strikes that were bringing riots and bloodshed to the Eastern states. Throughout the Bay district scores of factories and retail establishments closed their doors, and the streets of San Francisco were soon thronged by unemployed men, many of whom joined the ranks of the hoodlums. Although several factors had combined to cause the lull in business activity, political demagogues preached the gospel that it was due entirely to the presence of the Chinese in California, declaring that the pestiferous Orientals were filling thousands of jobs which should have gone to white men. For weeks almost every vacant lot in San Francisco was the scene of daily meetings at which irresponsible, crack-brained spellbinders denounced the Chinese and demanded that they be ejected from the sacred soil of California by fair means or foul.

Such violent harangues, delivered to audiences which were largely composed of hoodlums and restless discontented men without work, soon bore their natural fruit. On the night of July 24, 1877 a gang of several hundred hoodlums attacked Chinese laundries and wash-houses in various parts of the city, wrecking several and setting fire to a washhouse at Turk and Leavenworth streets. The police were not numerous enough to disperse the rioters, and throughout the night the hoodlums surged howling through the streets, attacking every Chinaman who hadn't barricaded himself within doors. Half a dozen were badly beaten before they could find shelter, and several Chinese prostitutes were dragged from their houses and horribly abused by large gangs of men. Next morning San Francisco awoke to face a situation very similar to those which in former years had caused the formation of the Vigilance committees, with the machinery of law-enforcement practically helpless and the city in danger of domination by the criminal element.

At the request of Mayor Edwin Bryant, the Governor ordered all members of the San Francisco companies of the National Guard to report at their armories for immediate duty, and several prominent citizens met and hurriedly formed a Committee of Safety under the leadership of William T. Coleman, who had been head of the second Vigilance organization. Mayor Bryant also issued a proclamation calling upon all San Franciscans to obey and support the law, and announcing that the National Guard would patrol the streets to protect life and property. During the early afternoon several companies of the Guard, armed with rifles and ball cartridges, marched from the armories and took up positions in various districts in which it was believed that rioting was likely to occur. A few hours later the Guardsmen were reinforced by some two hundred men who had enrolled under the standard of the Committee of Safety. This latter detachment, during the early period of the trouble with the hoodlums, was armed only with hickory pick-handles, a circumstance which caused it to be known as the Pick Handle Brigade.[1]

Despite the presence of this considerable force in the streets, the hoodlums attacked several Chinamen during the afternoon of July 25. and demolished the interiors of half a dozen Chinese stores and laundries. Soon after dusk a mob estimated at five hundred men attempted to burn the docks of the Pacific Mail Steamship Company, which operated the vessels that had brought most of the Chinese to the Pacific Coast. The company's property was vigorously defended by the police, the National Guardsmen, and the Pick Handle Brigade, and although the battle raged for several hours, they finally succeeded in driving away the hoodlums and saving the docks. More than a score of men were shot and otherwise wounded, but none seriously. That same night the hoodlums burned a lumber yard where several Chinese had been employed. Two days later a man named James Smith was arrested, accused of setting the fire, and held in twenty-thousand-dollar bail when arraigned in police court. Conclusive evidence against him could not be obtained, however, and he was released within a few days.

---

[1] One of the members of the Pick Handle Brigade was Denis Kearney, who, later in that same year, became one of the most violent of all San Francisco's agitators against the Chinese. He acquired a certain fame as the Sandlot Orator, and as the founder of the Workingmen's party, the platform of which was, principally: " The Chinese must go! " For a brief period Kearney and his party exercised considerable power in California politics. An

Next morning, July 26, hundreds of San Franciscans flocked to join the Pick Handle Brigade and enroll as members of the Committee of Safety. As soon as each man had signed, he was armed and sent out on patrol. By mid afternoon the streets of San Francisco again echoed to the tread of an embattled citizenry determined to resist the onslaughts of the rowdies. Between 3,500 and 4,000 men, including the members of the police force and the National Guard, were on duty. This display of power soon broke the backbone of the hoodlum revolt, although several small incendiary fires occurred during the next few nights, and there were a few minor skirmishes between the hoodlums and the patrolling citizens, the latter being victorious in every engagement. By July 30 San Francisco was quiet, and that afternoon the Committee of Safety disbanded its armed forces and dissolved its organization, while the companies of the National Guard stacked their rifles in the armories and returned to their vocations as private citizens.

6

THE hoodlum of the eighteen-seventies and the eighteen-eighties seldom carried a fire-arm, but depended upon his fists, a stout hickory bludgeon, a set of brass or iron knuckles, and sometimes a knife. Usually this was ample armament, for the hoodlums ran in packs and were never known to attack even inoffensive Chinamen unless they vastly outnumbered their victims. They spent their spare time in the dives and dance-halls of the Barbary Coast, and many of them were pimps, or macks, and had girls walking the streets or entertaining all comers in the lower-class bagnios. The beau ideal of the hoodlum was the Barbary Coast Ranger and, to a lesser extent, the dive-keeper. The latter, however, was a demigod who stood proudly upon an eminence of power and

extensive, though not wholly accurate, account of the Kearney movement may be found in the second volume of Lord Bryce's *American Commonwealth.*

prosperity such as the ordinary hoodlum could scarcely hope to reach. But he could aspire to notoriety and a long and sinful life as a man-about-the-Coast, and to that end he imitated the Ranger in deportment, as far as possible; and particularly in dress, to which he added various articles of personal adornment according to individual taste and fancy. The San Francisco hoodlum toiled not, neither did he spin, yet he was always attired in raiment of fashionable cut and usually of good material. His most elaborate costume burst upon a startled city during the late eighteen-eighties, when he swaggered about with his hair oiled, puffed, curled at the sides, and parted in the middle; and clad in a velvet vest, a black or olive frock coat with a peaked sleeve which rose to his ear, knee-high boots of calfskin, a sombrero, a ruffled white shirt with a low collar, a black string tie, and tight fawn-colored trousers. It might be added that the ear which appeared above the peaked sleeve of the coat was invariably dirty, for the typical hoodlum had nothing in common with the soap-maker.

These felonious dandies, as well as their more soberly attired brethren of previous decades, were very proud of the appellation by which they were popularly known. Sometimes when they sallied forth on their nefarious errands, they heralded their progress through the streets of San Francisco by cries of "The Hoodlums are coming!" and "Look out for the Hoodlums!" Many of them apparently had the curious idea that the very sound of the word "hoodlum" terrified the police, and that by so identifying themselves they automatically became immune to arrest. Of this delusion they were, in time, disabused. In June 1871, when a policeman captured one of the members of a gang which had committed twenty-two burglaries and tried to blow up a church with giant powder, all within ten days, the youthful desperado struck the officer with a slung shot and cried indignantly: "You can't arrest me! I'm a Hoodlum!" The

159

remainder of his pronunciamento would doubtless have been equally informative, but it was never known, for the policeman closed the argument with his night-stick. Such effective repartee by the police, however, was rare; usually the hoodlum was accorded comparatively gentle treatment. Not until about 1890 did the San Francisco police learn what the New York police had already known for more than fifty years — that the best cure for hoodlumism is the frequent application of locust or hickory to the hoodlum's skull. Once the police had acquired this knowledge, the power of the rowdies rapidly declined.

The most notorious hoodlums that San Francisco ever produced were Billy Smith and James Riley, who were active for a brief period during the early and middle eighteenseventies. Smith was the leader of a gang which was variously known as the Rising Star Club and the Valley Boys. His followers numbered about two hundred, all of them thugs and rowdies of the first water. Smith himself was as expert a rough-and-tumble fighter as ever gouged out an eye or chewed off an ear. He scorned to use either a club or a knife, but went into battle equipped only with his fists and a pair of corrugated iron knuckles which covered the entire back of his hands. With glancing blows from these fearsome weapons, he could rip an opponent's face to shreds. Smith led the Valley Boys on many a successful foray, but he finally met his Waterloo on the Alameda ferry-boat in the early spring of 1871. On Sunday, April 9, the Rising Star Club, with Smith in command and with several kegs of whisky and beer, went on an outing to Faskin's Park, near the Encinal station at Alameda, across the Bay of San Francisco. The Swiss Guard, a volunteer military organization, held its annual picnic at Alameda on that day, at Schuetzen's Park, a mile or so from Faskin's. The Guard mustered about two hundred members, but on the trip to Alameda they were accompanied by their wives, children, and friends, so that the party was about one thousand strong. Fortunately for themselves, they also took along their muskets and bayonets, although they had no ammunition for the former.

Both picnic parties returned to the ferry slip on the same train, and trouble threatened to develop almost as soon as the Valley Boys, most of whom were drunk, came aboard. The principal recreation of the Swiss Guards was singing, and they broke into song as soon as the train had started, to the outspoken disgust of the hoodlums. Billy Smith sent an emissary to inform William Hartmeyer, president of the Guard Glee Club, that the Guardsmen would be thrown off the train if they didn't stop. Hartmeyer paid no attention to the warning, but harsh words were exchanged between the hoodlums and several members of the Guards. There was no actual violence, however, until all of the picnickers had been transferred to the ferry-boat and the trip across the Bay had begun. The members of the Glee Club gathered in the boat's cabin and renewed their singing, whereupon Billy Smith and a score of his followers tried to stop them. Billy Smith was promptly ejected from the cabin, but returned to the assault with the entire membership of the Rising Star Club at his heels, all armed with clubs, brass knuckles, and knives. A general fight ensued, while the women and children fled to the after part of the cabin. Most of the windows were soon broken, and practically all of the furniture in the cabin was smashed. The Guardsmen finally fixed bayonets and succeeded in prodding the hoodlums out of the cabin and to the after deck, where they were surrounded. The rowdies attacked again as the ferry-boat neared its San Francisco slip, but were again driven back by the bayonets. When the boat docked, the Guardsmen massed near the bow and refused to allow anyone to go ashore until the arrival of the police. The latter arrested a dozen or more hoodlums, but most of them escaped by clambering over the boat's guards and swimming to the dock. Among

the prisoners, however, were Billy Smith and his chief lieutenant, Jimmy Collins. Several policemen had seen Smith
strike a Swiss Guardsman with his iron knuckles, and he was
locked up charged with assault with a deadly weapon. Later
he was convicted and sent to prison, and while he renewed
his activities as a hoodlum when he returned to San Francisco, he was never again a power among the rowdies. Several members of the Guard were badly cut and bruised by
the clubs and metal knuckles of the hoodlums, while many
of the latter were painfully pierced by the Guardsmen's
bayonets, which had very sharp points.

7

JAMES RILEY was better known to the San Francisco police as Butt Riley and as King of the Hoodlums. He was
born in New York about 1848, and after a thorough ground-
ing in the arts of hoodlumism as practiced in the metropolis,
he became a sailor. The work was hard, however, and one
voyage sufficed him. He landed in San Francisco in the late
summer of 1868, liked the town, and remained to become
one of its principal criminal ornaments. Thereafter, except
when he was in prison, he never performed a single stroke
of honest work. He was a much more celebrated hoodlum than even the redoubtable Billy Smith and was in
every respect a superior man. He was a little more than six
feet tall and weighed about two hundred pounds. In a
coarse fashion he was extraordinarily handsome, and he appears to have possessed to a superlative degree that elusive
quality which the moving pictures have popularized as " it."
He was eagerly sought as a lover by the inmates of the
houses of prostitution, and by the pretty waiter girls in the
dives and dance-halls of the Barbary Coast, and it was his
proud boast that whenever he granted his favors, he reversed
the usual procedure and collected a fee from the lady. In
this unique manner he received a substantial and fairly cer-

tain income, which he augmented by the sale of his photographs to the harlots for twenty-five cents each, in cash. To his particular favorites he sold, for fifty cents cash, pictures of himself in the nude. The greatest pride of scores of San Francisco's most popular and prosperous courtesans was the signed photograph of the King of the Hoodlums which hung above their beds. Riley had new photographs of himself made every Monday, and once a week he made a selling-trip throughout the red-light districts, carrying the pictorial proofs of his desirability in a small black satchel slung over his shoulder.[1]

So far as the San Francisco police ever knew, Riley was never the leader of any particular gang. But he had a widespread reputation in hoodlum circles as a fierce fighter and was a very inventive fellow in matters of torture; in fact, he gained his sobriquet as King of the Hoodlums because there wasn't a band of rowdies in the city that wouldn't flock to his support when he called upon it. Riley always carried a set of brass knuckles, a hickory bludgeon, a slung shot, and a big knife, but he seldom used any of these weapons. He depended principally upon his head, which he claimed had the thickest skull in Christendom. His method of fighting was to rush his opponent and butt him in the stomach or on the point of the chin, a procedure which soon rendered an enemy *hors de combat*. When he led hoodlums in raids upon Chinese houses or slave dens, he always demolished the doors with his head; and when his men had captured a Chinaman, it was his pleasure to see how far he could butt the poor Celestial. He was eager to establish a record in this sport, and probably did so, for with a running start he once butted a Chinaman, weighing about a hundred and sixty pounds,

---

[1] At least a dozen old-time San Franciscans, whose names cannot be published for obvious reasons, told the present author that they remembered having seen Riley's photographs in the houses of prostitution. Many also recalled Riley's black satchel and his selling-trips from house to house.

ten feet. The King of the Hoodlums also commercialized his gift, splintering doors with his head for fifty cents or a dollar, depending upon the thickness of the planks. He abandoned this particular aspect of his career, however, after he had, on a five-dollar bet, butted a hole in a door constructed of heavy oaken timbers. For the first time in his life he had a headache, and it frightened him.

For some three years the King of the Hoodlums continued to butt his way to fame, but in September 1871 he butted one man too many. During a row at Dora and Harrison streets he twice crashed his thick skull against the unprotected stomach of John Jordan, a twenty-two-year-old carriage-painter, and as he rushed forward for a third collision Jordan shot him in the breast with an English self-cocking revolver, one of the first weapons of that type ever seen in San Francisco. Riley was taken to the county hospital, where physicians said that he had been fatally wounded. But when the Coroner came to his bedside to take an ante-mortem deposition, the King of the Hoodlums said:

"By Jesus! I ain't agoin' to die. There's a chance for me yet. I know of lots of men who are alive with leaden bullets in their belly."

Riley recovered, but his health was poor, and he was never afterwards so prominent in hoodlum circles as he had been before Jordan shot him. Nor was he as popular among the prostitutes, for he no longer possessed the strength and beauty which had endeared him to them. He became, after a few years, a common house-breaker, and some five years after his encounter with the carriage-painter he was caught committing a robbery. He was convicted and sent to San Quentin Prison for fifteen years, and the reign of this human billy-goat as King of the Hoodlums and pet of the prostitutes was ended.

CHAPTER VIII

THE SLAVES OF CHINATOWN

THE UNDERWORLD which naturally developed in San Francisco's Chinese quarter was never an integral part of the Barbary Coast, but remained a separate entity throughout its existence. Nevertheless, they were so closely allied and had so much in common that it was sometimes difficult to determine where one ended and the other began. White officials and politicians protected the purveyors of sin in Chinatown, just as they surrounded the dive-keepers of the Barbary Coast with their sheltering influence, in return for a share of the proceeds. For many years the payment of graft was a recognized and accepted custom. And as the Six Companies' memorial to President Grant in 1874 had intimated, many of the white men who thus enriched themselves occupied comparatively high positions in the municipal government. As late as 1901, only a few years before Chinatown was more or less purged of evil by earthquake and fire, a Legislative Committee appointed to investigate the rumored connection between the San Francisco police and the overlords of Chinese vice reported that it was apparent that graft was being paid in large amounts. Although the committee specifically accused no one, it strongly recommended that the Mayor, the Police Commissioners, and the Chief of Police " proceed forthwith to enforce the law." It further urged the District Attorney to take immediate action to bring about proper enforcement and requested the Grand

Jury of San Francisco County to lay charges against any public official who neglected his duty. The dives and bagnios were closed for a few days while the committee was making inquiries and examining witnesses, but otherwise no attention was paid to it or to its recommendations.

The seeker after thrills or depravity found in Chinatown no melodeons, no dance-halls, no concert saloons, and only an occasional bar-room, but he did find an abundance of opium-smoking resorts, houses of prostitution, and gambling hells, which in later years were clearing-houses for the disposal of millions of Chinese lottery tickets. Although the opium dives seldom received the full measure of white political protection granted to other resorts, they flourished in considerable numbers until well after the beginning of the present century. In 1885 the special committee of the Board of Supervisors found twenty-six of these places, with 320 bunks, open to the public in Chinatown; while there were then, and for many years thereafter, at least that many more to which the ordinary man could not hope to gain admittance. They were operated for the exclusive use of white and Chinese addicts, principally the former, who were able to pay for a certain degree of privacy. Many of the places wherein opium was smoked, or was supposed to be smoked, were fakes, tourist-shockers conducted by the professional guides to the quarter, who were licensed by the city and were organized as the Chinatown Guides Association. These abodes of synthetic sin were invariably in dank and dreary cellars, and the entrances to them were so arranged as to persuade the visitor that he was traversing innumerable and, of course, dangerous underground passages. In many of these dimly lighted ways evil-looking Chinamen, in the employ of the guides, slunk back and forth, carrying knives and hatchets and providing atmosphere and local color. It was this illusion, together with the tall tales told by tourists of their experiences in San Francisco, which gave rise to the belief that Chinatown was a veritable network of subterranean galleries. This fancy persisted until the district was destroyed in 1906. While it lay in ruins, the whole area was carefully explored and mapped. Not a single underground passage was discovered, and few cellars larger or deeper than are commonly found under dwellings and business houses.

Prostitution was the principal, and by far the most remunerative, activity of Chinatown's criminal element, although gambling was the first of the popular vices to be introduced into the quarter and was, so far as the Chinese themselves were concerned, always the most liberally patronized. By the latter part of 1854, when the yellow population of San Francisco numbered only a few thousand, the upper end of Sacramento Street and the eastern side of Grant Avenue were lined with gambling houses. They were crowded both day and night, for the Chinaman is probably the most persistent and reckless gamester on earth; he will, ordinarily, bet on either side of any proposition, no matter how fantastic. Most of the Celestial gambling resorts of the early days were small and poorly furnished; in few was there room for more than three to six tables. Even fewer offered music or other entertainment. Said *The Annals of San Francisco:*

"At the innermost end of some of the principal gambling places, there is an orchestra of five or six native musicians, who produce such extraordinary sounds from their curiously shaped instruments as severely torture the white man to listen to. Occasionally a songster adds his howl or shriek to the excruciating harmony. . . . Heaven has ordered it, no doubt, for wise purposes, that the windy chaos is pleasant to the auricular nerves of the natives. Occasionally a few white men will venture into these places, and gaze with mingled contempt and wonder upon the grave, melancholy,

167

strange faces of the gamblers, and their curious mode
of playing. There seems to be only one game in vogue.
A heap of brass counters is displayed on the plain, mat-
covered table, and the banker, with a long, slender stick,
picks and counts them out one by one, while the stakers
gaze with intense interest on the process. The game
seems to be of the simplest nature, though white people
scorn to know any thing about it."

The white man may have scorned to acquire knowledge
of Chinese gambling, but he was little less than avid in his
desire to learn all there was to know about the Chinese prostitute — she was originally brought to San Francisco for his
amusement, and he remained her best customer until both
yellow and white prostitution were officially abolished by the
California Legislature in 1914. The importation of Chinese
girls for immoral purposes was begun about the middle of
1850, some two years after the arrival of the first Chinamen,
and by 1869 the trade had reached such proportions that the
San Francisco *Chronicle* referred to it as " the importation
of females in bulk " and said that " each China steamer now
brings consignments of women, destined to be placed in the
market." During the middle and late eighteen-seventies,
when Chinatown's underworld was at the peak of its activity,
the number of Chinese prostitutes in San Francisco was con-
servatively estimated at between fifteen hundred and two
thousand, while there were at least a thousand at the beginning of the present century. Until the passage of the exclusion laws in the eighteen-eighties, neither the federal nor
the city authorities attempted any effective interference with
the traffic, although occasionally, at the request of the Six
Companies or an American reform agency, the police
boarded ships from China and sent to asylums or mission
homes girls who had been destined for the bagnios of Chinatown. On one of these vessels, visited in June 1868 upon com-

plaint of the Six Companies, the police found forty-three girls, ranging from eight to thirteen years, and consigned to brothel-keepers and dealers who were described by a contemporary journalist as " notorious old harridans of this place." All of the girls were sent to the Magdalen Asylum, and the police announced that jobs would be found for them in domestic service. However, many eventually appeared in the houses of prostitution.

The various laws which forbade Chinese immigration acted as a check upon the traffic in Chinese girls, but failed to stop the shipments entirely. Thereafter they were smuggled into San Francisco, and large numbers were always available with which to replenish the stock in the bagnios. Some arrived in heavily padded crates, billed as freight, and were admitted by bribed customs and immigration officials. Others landed at Canadian ports and were brought to San Francisco by train, carriage, and, in later years, automobile. Still others, carefully coached, disembarked openly from the China steamers and succeeded in convincing state and federal inspectors that they were natives of California and had only been visiting in the land of their ancestors. When the authorities found women in the Chinese dives who had entered the country illegally, there were always plenty of Chinamen to claim them as wives; and, likewise, there were plenty of white lawyers and politicians to fight their battles in the courts. In 1901, when the United States Marshal raided the dens in Baker Court and Sullivan Alley and arrested thirty-four girls, each was claimed as wife by half a dozen Chinamen before deportation proceedings could even be begun.

Some historians appear to have taken it more or less for granted that the Six Companies were large importers of girls, and that they were also financially interested in the bagnios, the opium joints, and the gambling houses. Such accusations are clearly unjust. The fact is that the Six Companies always actively opposed anything that might hamper the commercial growth of Chinatown, which the exploitation of vice certainly did. For many years the organization attempted to procure the deportation of notorious prostitutes and dealers in women, often complained that the laws were not enforced, and furnished much of the information upon which the police and federal agents based their infrequent raids. During the late eighteen-nineties and the early years of the present century the Six Companies were joined in their fight to rid Chinatown of vice by the Chinese Society of English Education, the Chinese Students' Alliance, the Chinese Native Sons, and the Chinese Cadet Corps. The Society of English Education, composed principally of prominent Chinese merchants and teachers, was especially active and employed an American lawyer to assist them in trying to prevent the landing of Chinese prostitutes. They succeeded in having a few girls deported, and so aroused the ire of the slave-dealers that the latter announced publicly that the leading members of the society would be killed unless they ceased their interference. Several threatening letters were received at the headquarters of the society, in 709½ Commercial Street, and the final one of the series gave the names of the first victims of the slavers' fury. The missive was thus translated:

San Francisco, 7th Month, 1st Date (July 28, 1897)
To the Chinese Society of English Education:
Lately, having learned that the Chinese Society of English Education has retained an attorney to prevent girls imported for immoral purposes from landing and made efforts to deport them to China, in consequence of which there is a great loss of our blood-money. As you are all Christianized people, you should do good deeds, but if you keep on going to the Custom-house trying to deport girls brought here for immoral

purposes from China, and trying to prevent them from landing, your lives of your several people are not able to live longer than this month.

Your dying day is surely on hand.

Your dying day is surely on hand.

The dying men's names are as follows: Dear Wo, Lee Hem, Ong Lin Foon, Chin Fong, Chin Ming Sek, Hoo Yee Hin.

A few days later the slave-dealers announced, by means of placards posted upon the billboards of Chinatown, that twelve tong killers had been employed to dispose of the six members of the society. For several weeks the latter were guarded by the police and by men of their own race whom they had employed, and the murderous plans of the slavers were frustrated. Nevertheless the threatening letters accomplished their purpose, for there was a noticeable lessening of enthusiasm on the part of the Chinese Society for English Education. Thereafter this organization was content to leave the enforcement of the law to the constituted authorities, who were not particularly interested in the suppression of Chinese prostitution. Some seven years after the intimidation of the society direct action against the brothels was attempted by members of the Chinese Students' Alliance, the Native Sons, and the Cadet Corps. In September 1904, groups of earnest young crusaders invaded several houses of prostitution in Jackson Street, among them a particularly vile dive owned by an old Chinese woman called Mon Op, and succeeded in smashing the windows and wrecking the interiors before they were driven away by the police. In that same month the Chinese Consul-General formally complained about the fake opium dens and accused the white guides in Chinatown of staging immoral exhibitions in the Chinese bagnios for the delectation of the tourists. The Board of Police Commissioners, expressing great indignation at such a state of affairs, promptly adopted a resolution to revoke the license of any guide who " escorted any person to lewd, immoral or indecent practices, or to a place where opium was smoked." This gesture satisfied the Consul-General, and the guides continued to operate their bawdy shows. No licenses were revoked.

2

Two of San Francisco's golden courtesans — Ah Toy and Selina — achieved great fame in public amatory circles and made a considerable stir during their respective careers in Chinatown's underworld. Ah Toy came to San Francisco in the summer of 1850 and is said to have been the first Chinese prostitute to ply her ancient trade within the confines of Chinatown. As *The Annals of San Francisco* put it, " everybody knew that famous or infamous character, who was alternately the laughing-stock and the plague of the place." Ah Toy soon became amorously involved with several white men of more or less wealth and prominence, and as a result of their benefactions was able to buy her freedom and establish herself in business as an importer of girls for the bagnio trade. Thereafter she was known as Madame Ah Toy and for several years was one of the principal and most prosperous dealers in Chinese prostitutes in California. In addition, she operated a chain of dives in San Francisco, Sacramento, and other cities. Eventually she sold her various properties and returned to China to spend her declining years in comfort. Neither Madame Ah Toy nor the other traders who brought girls into California had any difficulty in disposing of their consignments at good prices. Said the San Francisco *Chronicle* of December 5, 1869:

" The particularly fine portions of the cargo, the fresh and pretty females who come from the interior, are used to fill special orders from wealthy merchants and prosperous tradesmen. A very considerable portion are sent into the interior under charge of special agents, in answer to demands from well-to-do miners and successful vegetable producers. Another lot of the general importation offered to the Chinese public are examined critically by those desiring to purchase, and are sold to the 'trade' or to individuals at rates ranging from $500 down to $200 per head, according to their youth, beauty and attractiveness. The refuse, consisting of 'boat-girls' and those who come from the seaboard towns, where contact with the white sailor reduces even the low standard of Chinese morals, is sold to the proprietor of the select brothels, or used in the more inferior dens of prostitution under the immediate control of the 'swell companies.' Those who are afflicted with disease, who suffer from the incurable attacks of Asiatic scrofula, or have the misfortune of possessing a bad temper, are used in this last-mentioned manner."

Selina flourished for a few years during the middle eighteen-eighties, when she was from sixteen to twenty years old, and many of San Francisco's old-time citizens still recall her as one of the most beautiful courtesans of her time. She was especially celebrated for the extraordinary symmetry of her figure, as well as for her amiability and a comprehensive knowledge of her art. She never rose from what might be called the ranks, but she did enjoy the distinction of a house of her own — a little three-room brick structure in Bartlett Alley. No Chinaman was ever admitted to her quarters; she was the particular pet of the white man, and her favors were so much in demand that during her period of greatest popularity it was customary for appointments to be made several days in advance. Her fee was one dollar, instead of the seventy-five cents which was the top price in other Chinese establishments, and her visitors always paid it without protest.

To gaze upon Selina's beautiful form, without the annoying intervention of garments, cost fifty cents, whereas other bagnio girls in Chinatown accorded the sightseer this privilege, known as a "lookee," for twenty-five cents or, in some of the lowest dens, a dime. The "lookee" was always a source of considerable revenue, because of the widespread belief, still curiously prevalent among white men, that there are important anatomical differences between the Oriental woman and her Occidental sister. For purposes of the record, this question was definitely settled in 1882 by a writer who visited the Chinese dives in Washington Street and conducted what appears to have been a very painstaking and scientific inquiry. He wrote in his book:

> "Being bent upon investigation, we enter and observe the surroundings, paying . . . for the privilege of witnessing the physical configuration of these poor, degraded creatures. . . . In order to set at rest a question which has been fiercely debated by students of nature, our investigation justifies the assertion that there are no physical differences between the Chinese and American women, their conformation being identical." [1]

There were two types of bagnio in San Francisco's Chinatown — the parlor house and the crib. The former, comparatively few in number, was to be found principally in Grant Avenue, Ross Alley, Waverly Place, and a few other important thoroughfares in or adjacent to Chinatown. Many of them were sumptuously furnished with a great clutter of teakwood and bamboo, embroidered hangings, soft couches, and cushions of embroidered silk, while exotic paintings and clouds of fragrant incense emphasized the languorous atmosphere of the Orient. The number of girls

[1] *Metropolitan Life Unveiled*, by J. W. Buel; page 276.

in each house ranged from four to twenty-five, all richly clad and seductively perfumed. Cribs existed in great profusion in Jackson and Washington streets and in China, Bartlett, Stout, Church, and other alleys throughout the quarter — they lined both sides of China Alley, a dingy, fifteen-foot passage which extended from Jackson to Washington Street. Several other alleys were likewise entirely given over to cribs. In Brooklyn Alley, off Sacramento Street near Stockton, were half a dozen cribs which during the late eighteen-nineties were occupied by Japanese girls, the first prostitutes of their race in San Francisco. In these places several ancient customs of the Yoshiwara were observed — a visitor was required to remove his shoes at the threshold; and when he departed, he received a gift, usually a good cigar, while his shoes were returned to him cleaned and polished. The Japanese cribs and the Chinese parlor houses were for white men only, but the ordinary Chinese bagnio catered to men of all races and colors. The wealthy and influential Chinaman was seldom seen in the public houses, except in a few operated for his exclusive use, the inmates of which were white women who had succumbed to the fascinations of opium. These resorts, however, were not so elegantly furnished as were the Chinese parlor houses. Most of them were one-storey buildings with long hallways, on either side of which were small cubicles with barred windows. When not otherwise engaged, the prostitute stood or sat in the center of her room, with parts of her body exposed, while Chinese in quest of amorous adventure strolled along the corridor and inspected her through the bars. Such resorts were not notably prosperous, however, as the Chinaman of means usually maintained his own harem, with from one to a dozen concubines, according to his prosperity and desires. He replenished his stock of girls whenever fresh shipments arrived from China, selling or trading those of whom he had tired or who had failed to come up to his expectations. White girls rarely became in-

mates of these establishments, partly because they lacked
sufficient docility and partly because the Chinese in general
preferred women of their own race.

The crib was exactly what its name implies — a small,
one-storey shack some twelve feet wide and fourteen feet
deep, divided into two rooms by heavy curtains of coarse
material. It was occupied by from two to six girls, each of
whom wore the traditional costume of her trade — a black
silk blouse with a narrow band of turquoise, on which flowers
had been embroidered, extending across the front and back.
In cold weather the girls were also clad in black silken
trousers, but usually their attire consisted of nothing but the
blouse. The back room of the crib was meagerly furnished
with a wash-bowl, a rickety bamboo chair or two, and hard
board shelves or bunks covered with matting. The front
room was usually carpeted, and contained a cheap bureau,
more chairs, and perhaps a wall mirror. The only entrance
to the crib was a narrow door, in which was set a small
barred window. Occupants of the den took turns standing behind the bars and striving to attract the attention of passing
men. When an interested male stopped before the crib, the
harlot displayed the upper part of her body and cajoled him
with seductive cries and motions.

" China girl nice! You come inside, please? "

She invariably added to her invitation this extraordinary information, seldom, if ever, correct:

" Your father, he just go out! " [1]

These vocal enticements she varied with a more direct
advertisement of her wares, a complete list of prices and
services. Until the late hours of the night, in all the narrow,
dirty by-ways of Chinatown, the plaintive voice of the
Chinese crib girl could be heard crying in a shrill, monoto-
nous singsong:

---

[1] Some of the Chinese considered it an honor to possess a woman whom
their fathers had also possessed.

"Two bittee lookee, flo bittee feelee, six bittee dooe!"

So far as her own person was concerned, the Chinese prostitute, even when she occupied the lowest crib, was cleanly; she shaved her entire body daily and took frequent baths. But her master always compelled her to entertain every man who applied, and in consequence at least ninety per cent of the Oriental harlots in San Francisco were diseased. Moreover, although the parlor houses refused to admit boys of sixteen or seventeen, the cribs made no such distinction. During an inquiry conducted by a special committee of the Board of Supervisors in 1885, several policemen and special watchmen testified that they had often found white boys of ten and twelve years in the cribs, and some of the youngsters regularly visited the dens two or three times a week. A member of the Board of Health, a physician, testified that he had seen white boys of eight and ten with diseases which had been contracted in the Chinese dives of Jackson Street, where prices were lower than elsewhere in Chinatown. In these cribs a man could have his choice of girls for twenty-five or fifty cents, while special rates as low as fifteen cents were offered to boys under sixteen.

"I have never seen or heard of any country in the world," this doctor said, "where there are as many children diseased as in San Francisco."[1]

Other physicians gave similar testimony, describing a situation to which the special committee, as well as city officials, pointed with horror, but which they did little or nothing to remedy.

The backbone of Chinese prostitution in San Francisco was a system of slavery under which girls were owned and bartered as if they had been so many cattle; as, indeed, they were in the eyes of their masters. Practically every inmate of the Chinese parlor houses and cribs was a slave, and many

---

[1] Report of the Special Committee of the Board of Supervisors, 1885; page 13.

had been in bondage since infancy. Usually they were owned by syndicates of Chinamen, or by women like Madame Ah Toy, who had themselves been prostitutes and had purchased their freedom. The slave holdings of some of these groups were extremely large. Four Chinamen in the middle eighteen-seventies owned eight hundred girls, ranging in age from two to sixteen years. They had been bought in China at an average price of about eighty dollars, but were worth from four hundred to a thousand dollars each in San Francisco. At late as 1895 a slave-dealer named Charley Hung, together with an old Chinese woman called Dah Pa Tsin, kept a hundred girls, all under fourteen, in pens in the rear of a building in Church Alley. This precious pair not only bought and sold, but rented girls to owners of cribs for a percentage of their earnings. Another noted slaver of this period was Suey Hin, who ordinarily kept in stock no fewer than fifty girls of various ages. Suey Hin became converted to Christianity in 1898, and in preparation for the good life sold all of her girls but seven, who were valued at about eighty-five hundred dollars. These she decided to retain for a while, in case she found the white man's religion impracticable. Eventually, however, at the behest of the Salvation Army, she gave them their freedom. One of these girls was only ten days old when Suey Hin bought her from her parents for a few coins. She was three years old when the converted slaver placed her in the Salvation Army mission, and could easily have been sold for three hundred dollars, for she was a very pretty child and free from blemishes or deformities.

3

T H E girls who filled the bagnios of Chinatown were, for the most part, bought or kidnapped in China by agents of the San Francisco dealers, although kidnapping was seldom necessary. Chinese parents, especially those in the seaports, generally regarded their daughters as nuisances and were usually willing to sell them. The girls were shipped to San Francisco in batches of from three to a hundred and, once there, were either placed in dives operated by their masters or offered for sale in the open market. Dealers and owners of cribs and parlor houses were notified when a consignment had arrived, and those who were interested assembled at an appointed place, usually a cellar or other chamber which offered comparative safety from the prying eyes of white men, and, particularly, of the white women who operated the Chinatown missions and waged unceasing warfare against the slavers. When the sale began, the girls were brought in one by one to the block. They were stripped, punched, and prodded and in some cases examined by Chinese physicians who had, more likely than not, been bribed to warrant them sound in wind and limb. A price having been agreed upon for a given girl, the amount, in gold or currency, was placed in her outstretched palms. She immediately handed it to the man who had offered her for sale. She was then required to sign a contract, in which it was set forth that she had received the money into her own hands, and that in return she agreed to serve as a prostitute for a specified number of years. During the eighteen-seventies and the eighteen-eighties this was the usual form of contract:

> For the consideration of [whatever sum had been agreed upon], paid into my hands this day, I, [name of girl], promise to prostitute my body for the term of ——— years. If, in that time, I am sick one day, two weeks shall be added to my time; and if more than one day, my term of prostitution shall continue an additional month. But if I run away, or escape from the custody of my keeper, then I am to be held as a slave for life.

(Signed) _____

Another type of contract or agreement, which was also much in use, stipulated that the girl become a prostitute to repay the money which had been advanced for passage to the United States and for other expenses. One of these documents was introduced in evidence before the Senate Committee which in 1876 investigated the whole question of Chinese immigration:

"An agreement to assist a young girl named Loi Yan, because she became indebted to her mistress for passage, board, etc., and has nothing to pay. She makes her body over to the woman Sep Sam to serve as a prostitute, to make out the sum of $503. The money shall draw no interest, and Loi Yan shall receive no wages. Loi Yan shall serve four and one-half years. . . . When the time is out Loi Yan shall be her own master and no man shall trouble her. . . . If she is sick fifteen days she shall make up one month for every ten days. If Sep Sam should go back to China Loi Yan shall serve another master until her time is out."

Under the then existing laws of California such contracts might conceivably have been held by the courts to be valid instruments. The real jokers, of course, were the clauses relating to illness. The regular physical disturbance which every woman experiences was reckoned as within the meaning of the agreement, and the prostitute was held to be incapacitated three or four days a month on that account. At least one month, therefore, was added to every month of service under the terms of the contract, so that a Chinese girl who entered a crib or a parlor house was at once caught in a vicious circle from which there was no escape.

The prices paid for prostitutes in the San Francisco market varied with the years and with the quality of the merchandise and was naturally dependent to a great extent upon supply and demand. Before the passage of the exclusion acts the prettiest Chinese girls could be purchased for a few hundred dollars each, but after about 1888, when it became necessary to smuggle them into this country, prices rose enormously. During the early eighteen-nineties they ranged from about $100 for a one-year-old girl to a maximum of $1,200 for a girl of fourteen, which was considered the best age for prostitution. Children of six to ten brought from $200 to $800. About 1897 girls of twelve to fifteen sometimes sold for as high as $2,500 each. The record price was probably $2,800 in gold, which Charley Hung and Dah Pa Tsin paid for a fourteen-year-old girl in the early part of 1898. At whatever price a sale was made, the transaction was completed in regular form, and the purchaser received a bill of sale in which the girl was usually mentioned in a list of other commodities, which may or may not have changed hands. A typical document of this sort, conveying a nine-year-old girl, came into the hands of the Salvation Army in 1898 and was published in the San Francisco *Call:*

BILL OF SALE
Loo Wong to Loo Chee

April 16 — Rice, six mats, at $2...........$ 12
April 18 — Shrimps, 50 lbs., at 10c........... 5
April 20 — Girl 250
April 21 — Salt fish, 60 lbs., at 10c.......... 6
                                         _____
                                          $273

Received payment,

LOO CHEE

Victoria, B. C., May 1, 1898

All of the Chinese slave girls in San Francisco, particularly those who occupied the cribs, were shamefully mistreated by their masters. They received no part of their earnings, and most of them never left the dens except for brief periods two or three times a week, when they were taken out under heavy guard for exercise, like dogs on a leash. For the slightest infraction of the strict rules under which they lived, or for failure to please every man who visited them, they were lashed with whips and branded with hot irons; and other tortures, at which the Chinese have always been particularly adept, were also inflicted upon them. Six years was a long time for a girl to live after being placed in a crib, and since she almost invariably began her life of misery and degradation in her early teens, a Chinese prostitute of more than twenty years was a great rarity. Moreover, she was, by that time, nothing more than a frightfully diseased old hag. In later years girls who had broken mentally and physically under the hardships to which they were subjected in the cribs, and had so lost their attractiveness and become useless for purposes of prostitution, were permitted and encouraged to escape to the missions conducted by the Salvation Army and other organizations. But in earlier times, during the eighteen-sixties and the eighteen-seventies, they were carried into small, dismal rooms in the back alleys of Chinatown, called "hospitals," and there left alone to die. One of these places, in Cooper Alley, was thus described by the San Francisco *Chronicle* in its issue of December 5, 1869:

"The place is loathsome in the extreme. On one side is a shelf four feet wide and about a yard above the dirty floor, upon which there are two old rice mats. There is not the first suggestion of furniture in the room, no table, no chairs or stools, nor any window. . . . When any of the unfortunate harlots is no longer useful and a Chinese physician passes his opinion that her disease is incurable, she is notified that she must

182

die. . . . Led by night to this hole of a 'hospital,' she is forced within the door and made to lie down upon the shelf. A cup of water, another of boiled rice, and a little metal oil lamp are placed by her side. . . . Those who have immediate charge of the establishment know how long the oil should last, and when the limit is reached they return to the 'hospital,' unbar the door and enter. . . . Generally the woman is dead, either by starvation or from her own hand; but sometimes life is not extinct; the spark yet remains when the 'doctors' enter; yet this makes little difference to them. They come for a corpse, and they never go away without it."

So far as remedying their condition was concerned, the slave girls in San Francisco's Chinatown were helpless. Few could speak more than a dozen words of English, none had any knowledge whatsoever of American law or legal procedure, and there was no one to whom they could have appealed for aid even if it had occurred to them to protest against a custom so thoroughly grounded in the traditions of their race. The infrequent attempts of the federal and city authorities to close the brothels and free the slaves were empty gestures which met with little or no success. For the most part they were made grudgingly, and only upon the insistence of respectable Chinese organizations and the white women who operated the Chinatown missions, especially Miss Donaldina Cameron. She devoted practically her entire adult life to rescue work among the Chinese prostitutes, and to her, more than to any other one person, credit is due for the final radical improvement in the moral tone of Chinatown. While the earthquake and fire of 1906 destroyed the plague spots of the district, girls continued to be held as slaves, though not in such large numbers as before, until the enactment of the Red-light Abatement Act by the California Legislature in 1914. This, at length, placed in the hands of

Miss Cameron and her associates an effective legal weapon, which was backed by the police. Within a few years slavery in San Francisco had been abolished.

4

THE most spectacular and at the same time the most powerful agencies in the underworld of Chinatown were the tongs, which were always deeply involved in every evil scheme concocted in the quarter. The complete history of these extraordinary associations probably never will be written. It is extremely doubtful if any white man has ever thoroughly understood the innumerable ramifications of tong influence or been privy to the intricacies of their organization and methods, despite the fact that they are as American as chop suey. Like that celebrated dish, they are unknown in China.[1] The first tongs — the Hop Sings and the Suey Sings — were organized about 1860 by the Chinese in the gold-fields near Marysville, California, as mutual benefit associations. There, too, occurred the first tong war, and, in common with many of the other conflicts which have since raged in American cities, it started over a woman. The mistress of a Hop Sing man was stolen by a Suey Sing Lothario, and the Hop Sings declared war to wipe out the stain upon their brother's honor. Several men on either side were killed, but the Suey Sings were defeated and compelled to restore the girl to her rightful owner.

---

[1] Chop suey is said to have been invented in 1894. At a banquet in New York, at which Li Hung Chang, the great Chinese statesman, was the guest of honor, he was asked to have his private chef contribute one dish to the feast. Fearing that the white men would not like real Chinese food, Li Hung Chang instructed the chef to prepare a stew of meat and vegetables, which the chef called " chop suey " and flavored with a pungent sauce made from the soya bean, salt, and molasses. The concoction was immediately popular, and within a few years chop-suey parlors had sprung up all over the United States. Very few Chinese will eat it. According to Webster's dictionary the name of the dish is a corruption of the Cantonese " shop sui," meaning " odds and ends."

The tongs soon spread to the railroad construction camps in which large numbers of coolies were employed, thence to the Pacific Coast cities which harbored Chinese settlements, and finally throughout the United States. They first appeared in San Francisco during the late eighteen-sixties, and within ten years at least twenty tongs were firmly entrenched in Chinatown, with large memberships and over-flowing treasure-chests. Occasionally they engaged in legitimate business, but in particular they were the lords of the underworld — they operated gambling resorts, opium dens and houses of prostitution, and exercised practical control over the slave trade, for although the actual buying and selling of girls was done by individuals, the tongs usually collected a head-tax for every slave imported for immoral purposes. Sometimes even an honest Chinaman who brought his wife to this country was compelled to pay the tongs before she was permitted to remain.

Each of these organizations employed professional murderers and also recruited a force of *boo how doy,* or fighting men, among its own members. In later years the tong warrior fought with revolvers, bombs, and even machine-guns, but in earlier times his favorite weapons were hatchets, daggers, knives, and bludgeons, which he carried in a long silken belt wrapped around his body beneath a loose blouse. When abroad on his murderous business, his queue was wound around his head, and he wore a broad-brimmed, low-crowned black slouch hat, pulled well down over his eyes. If he succeeded in dispatching an enemy, he left beside the body the weapon with which he had struck the fatal blow. The *boo how doy,* popularly known as hatchetmen or highbinders, received regular salaries, with extra pay for exceptional bravery in battle, and bonuses based on the number of men they killed. They were subjected to strict discipline and were required to obey at all times, without question, the orders of the man who had been chosen by their tong to command them in action. What was expected of them is indicated in this communication from the supreme council of the Gee Kung tong to one of its hatchetmen in 1888. A translation of the document was embodied in the report of the United States Industrial Commission, which investigated the highbinder tongs in 1901 :

To Lum Hip, Salaried Soldier:

It has been said that to plan schemes and devise methods and to hold the seal is the work of the literary class, while to oppose foes, fight battles, and plant firm government is the work of the military. Now this tong appoints salaried soldiers to be ready to protect its members and assist others. This is our object. All, therefore, who undertake the military service of this tong must obey orders, and without orders they must not dare to act. If any of our brothers are suddenly molested it will be necessary for you to act with resolute will. You will always work in the interest of the tong, and never make your office a means of private revenge. When orders are given, you shall advance valiantly to your assigned task. . . . If, in the discharge of your duty, you are slain, we will undertake to pay $500 sympathy money to your friends. If you are wounded, a doctor will be engaged to heal your wounds, and if you are laid up for any length of time, you will receive $10 a month. If you are maimed for life, and incapacitated for work, $250 shall be paid to you, and a subscription taken to defray all costs of your journey home to China. Furthermore, when you exert your strength to kill or wound enemies of this tong, and in so doing are arrested and imprisoned, $100 per year will be collected for every year in jail.

Dated this 13th day of the 5th month of the 14th year of Kwong Su.

186

In the spring of 1875 Low Sing, a member of the Suey Sing tong, then the most powerful of all these organizations, fell in love with a slave girl named Kum Ho, who was also known as the Golden Peach. He began to live frugally and save his money, so that in time he might buy her freedom and make her his wife. But the beauteous Kum Ho had also attracted the attention of the evil Ming Long of the Kwong Dock tong, a noted assassin whose hatchet had cleaved a bloody trail through the gold-fields and the railroad labor camps. Ming Long informed Low Sing that he had himself decided to buy the Golden Peach and add her to the charmers who already graced his harem, and warned the Suey Sing man to keep away from the crib wherein Kum Ho was confined. But Low Sing was too much in love to obey. He continued to visit the Golden Peach, and on an evening in May 1875, while Low Sing stood before Kum Ho's crib and held her hand through the bars, Ming Long crept up behind him and split his skull with a hatchet.

Low Sing lived long enough to tell the head men of his tong who had attacked him, and the supreme council of the Suey Sings immediately held a solemn conclave. They considered the matter at considerable length. Witnesses who were familiar with Low Sing's love-affair with the slave girl said that the Golden Peach was also in love with Low Sing, and that the Suey Sing man had succumbed to her charms long before Ming Long of the Kwong Docks had even seen her. It was clear, therefore, that Low Sing was entitled to the girl if he could, within a reasonable time, raise sufficient money to buy her. It was likewise clear that the assault upon Low Sing had been a direct blow at the honor of the Suey Sings, for the enmities of a member of a tong were also the enmities of the entire tong. Accordingly, the literary men of the Suey Sings indited a *chun hung,* or challenge to battle, painted in black letters on vermilion paper. It was posted upon the bulletin board at Grant Avenue and Clay Street:

The Kwong Dock tong is hereby sincerely and earnestly requested to send its best fighting men to Waverly Place at midnight tomorrow to meet our *boo how doy*. If this challenge is ignored, the Kwong Dock tong must admit defeat and make compensation and apologize for the assault upon Low Sing. However, we sincerely hope that the Kwong Dock tong will accept this challenge, and paste alongside of this poster its own *chun hung*.

(Signed)　　Seal of the Suey Sing Tong [1]

Within an hour there appeared on the bulletin board another strip of vermilion paper covered with black characters, signed with the seal of the Kwong Docks. The hatchetmen of both tongs immediately began sharpening their weapons and otherwise preparing for battle. Knowledge of the coming encounter soon spread throughout Chinatown, and by eleven o'clock on the appointed night, much to the amazement of the few white policemen who patrolled the district, Waverly Place was deserted, and all doors and windows on the street level were securely locked and bolted. Even the cries of the crib girls were hushed. But the upstairs windows, and the balconies which overhung the narrow thoroughfares, were crowded with Chinese, who had assembled to watch the fighting and who were excitedly laying wagers upon the result or upon the exploits of individual hatchetmen. A few minutes before twelve o'clock the warriors began to arrive, singly and in twos and threes, queues wrapped around their heads, black slouch hats drawn down over their eyes, and blouses bulging with hatchets, knives, and clubs. In silence the fighting men of the Suey Sings took up positions on one side of the street, while the *boo how doy* of the Kwong Docks confronted them from the opposite

---

[1] *Tong War*, by Eng Ying Gong and Bruce Grant; page 17.

curb. There were about twenty-five men in each detachment, all noted killers with much experience in tong warfare.

For a little while neither side seemed to be aware of the other. But promptly at midnight the leaders began screaming insults. After a moment or two of this sort of preparation, they gave the signal, and with a flash of knives and hatchets the *boo how doy* rushed forward and clashed in the center of the street. For at least fifteen minutes the hatchetmen fought with great ferocity, and the tide of battle surged back and forth while the spectators leaned over the balcony railings and the window-sills and cheered or groaned, accordingly as they had placed their bets. Then the blast of a police whistle shrilled above the roar of combat, and reserves from a dozen precincts charged into Waverly Place with drawn revolvers, swinging night-sticks. The fighting stopped immediately, and the hatchetmen vanished into the dark and dingy passages of Chinatown. None had been killed, but nine had been seriously wounded — six Kwong Docks and three Suey Sings. Of the latter, one died within a few days, and three of the former. The police made no arrests and were never able to learn the cause of the fighting nor the identity of anyone engaged in it, although for weeks little else was talked of in Chinatown. The Suey Sings considered that they had been victorious because the Kwong Docks had suffered the greater number of casualties, and next day they dispatched a truculent missive to the Kwong Docks, again demanding indemnities and apologies. After many lengthy conferences the Kwong Docks paid a small sum of money to the relatives of Low Sing and made formal apology for the assault upon him by Ming Long. A treaty of peace was signed, and the *boo how doy* of both tongs celebrated the occasion with a great love-feast, at which the men who had so recently been at each other's throats became as brothers under the mellowing influence of rice wine, bird's-nest soup and other delicacies of the Chinese cuisine. Under the code of the tongs the life of Ming Long was forfeit to the Suey Sings, and for several days he was assiduously hunted by hatchetmen eager for the distinction that would come to his slayer. But he escaped and fled to China, where he was safe from the vengeance of the Suey Sings.

This was the first of the great tong wars that shattered the peace and quiet of San Francisco's Chinatown, but it was by no means the last. For at least half a century — the power of the tongs began to decline only about half a dozen years ago — they raged with alarming frequency, although none was fought with the ferocious spectacularity that distinguished the memorable combat in Waverly Place in the spring of 1875. But from the ranks of the *boo how doy* came many killers of great renown, whose exploits entitle them to rank beside the best of the gunmen produced by the white man's gangland. There was, for example, Hong Ah Kay, in his peaceful moments a scholar and a poet of distinction, who stood against a cellar wall and with seven blows split the skulls of seven foes. For this notable feat of arms he was greatly honored by his tong, but, unfortunately, he was hanged by the white man's law before he had a chance to wear his laurels. There were, too, Sing Dock, called the Scientific Killer because he carefully planned each murder down to the minutest detail and never struck until he was certain that his schemes would not miscarry; Big Queue Wai, who induced in himself a murderous state of mind, and incidentally perfected his aim and timing, by swatting flies for several hours before he went forth to sink his hatchet into the cranium of an enemy; and Yee Toy, otherwise Girl-Face, a dandified assassin whose ferocity belied his nickname. It was Yee Toy's pleasant custom, when time permitted, to straighten the clothing of his victim and comb his hair and otherwise make him presentable. Nor did Yee Toy neglect to remove from the dead one's pockets any money or other property that might cause unseemly bulges.

5

THE greatest and most successful of Chinatown's tong chieftains was Fung Jing Toy, better known as Little Pete, who was head of the Sum Yops and in control of other tongs with which the Sum Yops were allied. For nearly ten years he was the most powerful Chinaman on the Pacific Coast, and although it is doubtful if he ever swung a hatchet or fired a pistol, he was responsible for the deaths of no fewer than fifty men. He had a fair command of English, which he acquired at American night-schools, but if the stories told about him are true, he could neither read nor speak Chinese and employed an interpreter to assist him in communicating with many of his henchmen. He lived with his wife and two children on the third floor of a three-storey building at Washington Street and Waverly Place, from the balcony of which, as a boy of ten, he had watched the great fight between the Suey Sings and the Kwong Docks in 1875. He slept in a windowless room behind a barred and bolted door, on either side of which was chained a vicious dog. During his waking hours he wore a coat of chain mail, and inside his hat was a thin sheet of steel curved to fit his head. He employed a bodyguard of three white men, and when he went abroad, one walked beside him, and another in front, while the third brought up the rear. And prowling within call were half a dozen of his own *boo how doy*, heavily armed. Also, wherever Little Pete went he was accompanied by a trusted servant bearing his jewel-case and toilet articles, for the tong leader was a great dandy, and much concerned about his appearance. He possessed many diamond rings, a dozen handsomely engraved gold watches, and half a score of gold and platinum match-boxes set with diamonds and other precious stones. He changed his jewelry several times daily and never wore a suit, though he had forty, two days in succession. Two hours each morning he spent combing, brushing, and oiling his long and glossy queue, of which he was inordinately proud. In his leisure time he played upon the zither, listened to the music of his crickets, or wrote comedies, which were translated into Chinese and performed at the Jackson Street Theatre. He owned the playhouse and never had any trouble getting his pieces produced.

Little Pete was five years old when his father, a merchant, brought him to San Francisco from Canton. He began his career as an errand-boy for a Chinese shoe-manufacturer, and during his late teens peddled slippers from house to house in Chinatown. When he was about twenty-one years old, he embarked upon the only honest business venture of his adult life — a shoe-factory under the firm name of J. C. Peters & Company. Soon afterwards, attracted by the profits in vice, he became interested in gambling houses and opium dens and also entered the slave trade in partnership with Kwan Leung and the latter's wife, Fong Suey, a noted procuress. Backed by the Sum Yop tong, of which he gained complete control before his twenty-fifth birthday, he soon enlarged his activities. Instead of buying girls, he began to steal them, particularly from dealers and crib-owners who were members of the Sue Yop tong, one of the most powerful organizations in Chinatown. He also interfered in other Sue Yop enterprises, and the two tongs were soon engaged in one of the bitterest and bloodiest of all the wars of Chinatown. During the early stages of this conflict Little Pete overreached himself. He forgot that in the final analysis vice in Chinatown existed only upon the sufferance of the white authorities. When one of his killers was arrested and placed on trial for the murder of a Sue Yop man in 1887, Little Pete boldly tried to bribe the jurors, the District Attorney, and everyone else connected with the prosecution. He was promptly clapped into jail, later convicted of attempted bribery, and sent to San Quentin Prison for five years.

When Little Pete was released, he again assumed his

position as head of the Sum Yops and fanned into flame the embers of the war with the Sue Yops, which had subsided during his incarceration. He also strengthened his position by retaining as counsel for the Sum Yops an influential criminal lawyer, Thomas D. Riordan, and by forming an alliance with Christopher A. Buckley, the famous blind political boss of San Francisco, whom Little Pete called the Blind White Devil.[1] With Buckley's support, Little Pete was soon the undisputed king of Chinatown. Every form of vice, and almost every form of legitimate business as well, paid him tribute. If the owners of gambling houses, opium dens, or brothels refused to pay, their establishments were immediately closed by the white police — and reopened a few days later with Little Pete's men in charge. The girls in all of the cribs operated by Little Pete and his associates were supplied with counterfeit half-dollars, which they gave as change to drunken men.

Little Pete's income from his various enterprises must have been enormous, but he was not satisfied. He looked around for new sources of revenue and became greatly interested in the possibilities of horse racing. Early in the spring of 1896 he became a familiar figure in the betting rings of the Bay District and Ingleside tracks and soon attracted attention by the size of his bets. He regularly wa-

---

[1] Buckley was in absolute control of San Francisco for some twenty years, probably the most corrupt period in the history of the city. He came to San Francisco in 1862, at the age of seventeen, and became a bar-tender at Duncan Nichols's Snug Café, which he later owned. He lost his eyesight through illness in his thirtieth year. He had already gained considerable influence in politics, and his career was not halted by his misfortune. Within another five years he dominated the Democratic machine and began plundering the city for the benefit of himself and his friends. He always sat in the rear of his saloon and recognized visitors by the way they shook hands. He was finally ousted from control by a group of insurgents headed by Gavin McNab and James D. Phelan, and his power declined when Phelan was elected Mayor in the middle eighteen-nineties. Buckley died in April 1922, in his seventy-seventh year.

gered eight thousand dollars a day, and he never lost. Within
two months he had won a hundred thousand dollars, and
the stewards of the Pacific Coast Jockey Club began to believe that there might be some connection between Little
Pete's streak of luck and the sudden epidemic of sick horses
and bungling rides by hitherto skillful jockeys. Private detectives followed several riders to the offices of J. C. Peters
& Company, and further investigation disclosed the fact
that Little Pete was not only paying the jockeys to lose races,
but was bribing trainers and stablemen to poison horses
against which he wished to wager. As a result of the inquiry
Jockeys Jerry Chorn and Young Chevalier were ruled off
the turf for life, while Jockey Arthur Hinrichs and Dow
Williams, who had been Lucky Baldwin's trainer, were
barred from the two tracks which Little Pete had honored
with his operations. Nothing could be done to Little Pete,
who retired to Chinatown with a substantial addition to his
fortune.

Little Pete's star, however, was setting. He had become so rapacious that the Sue Yops determined, once and
for all, to end his reign. They invited twelve other tongs, all
of which had felt the weight of Little Pete's heavy hand, to
join them in a war of extermination against the Sum Yops,
and a formidable force of *boo how doy* took the field. A
price of three thousand dollars was placed upon Little Pete's
head, probably the largest sum that the tongs have ever offered for the death of an enemy. For weeks the hatchetmen
of the allies kept close upon the trail of the chieftain of the
Sum Yops, as did many free-lance professional killers, all
eager to win the amount, which to them meant an old age of
luxury in China. But none could pierce the wall of white
bodyguards and *boo how doy* with which Little Pete had
surrounded himself.

In January 1897 there arrived in San Francisco two
young Chinamen, Lem Jung and Chew Tin Gop, who had

been prospecting in the mountains near Baker City, Oregon. They had accumulated a small fortune and had come to San Francisco to see the sights of Chinatown, after which they intended to return to China. They were members of the Suey Sing tong, now allied with the enemies of the Sum Yops, but they were men of peace. Neither had ever handled a hatchet or fired a pistol or participated in a tong fight. They knew nothing of Little Pete, and first learned of his villainies, and of the money that would be paid to his slayer, from their cousin Lem Jok Lep, who represented the Suey Sings on the board of strategy that had been created by the allied tongs to devise means of eradicating the Sum Yops. With rising indignation Lem Jung and Chew Tin Gop listened to Lem Jok Lep's recital of the many indignities which Little Pete had heaped upon the heads of their tong brothers.

"There is no reason," said Lem Jung, "why we should not earn this money. I myself shall kill this man."

With no experience in fighting, and with scarcely any plan of campaign, these young men rushed in where the bravest hatchetmen had trodden with the utmost caution. On the evening of January 23, 1897, which was the Chinese New Year's Eve, Lem Jung and Chew Tin Gop walked calmly into a barber-shop on the ground floor of Little Pete's building at Waverly Place and Washington Street. There they found Little Pete bending over with his head under a faucet, while the barber wetted his hair preparatory to plaiting it into a queue. Every circumstance favored the assassins. Little Pete had left his apartment in a hurry, accompanied by only one of his bodyguard. And this man he had sent out to buy a paper only a few minutes before Lem Jung and Chew Tin Gop entered the shop. For the moment Little Pete was defenseless. Chew Tin Gop remained near the door on guard while Lem Jung quickly stepped forward, caught Little Pete by the hair, brushed the barber aside, and shoved the muzzle of a heavy revolver down the back of the tong leader's neck, inside the coat of mail. He pulled the trigger, and Little Pete fell to the floor dead, with five bullets in his spine. The murderers escaped, received their money, and fled to Portland, where they were received as heroes. Eventually they took ship to China. The police arrested four Chinese, Chin Poy, Wing Sing, Won Lung, and Won Chung, who had been found loitering near the barbershop. On each were found revolvers, knives, and hatchets. Wing Sing and Chin Poy were brought to trial for the murder, but were acquitted.

The death of Little Pete demoralized the Sum Yops, and the *boo how doy* of the Sue Yops and their allies promptly began a slaughter, which ended only upon the intervention of the Emperor Kwang Hsu of China, to whom Thomas Riordan, attorney for Little Pete and the Sum Yops, cabled for help. The Emperor called into consultation the great Chinese statesman Li Hung Chang.

"The matter has been attended to," said Li Hung Chang. "I have cast into prison all relatives of the Sue Yops in China, and have cabled to California that their heads will be chopped off if another Sum Yop is killed in San Francisco."

And in far-away America the war ended with startling suddenness, and the Sue Yops and the Sum Yops signed a treaty of peace which has never been violated.

The spirit of Little Pete ascended to his ancestors in a blaze of magnificence, though perhaps without proper sustenance, for his funeral was probably the most spectacular ever held in San Francisco. A cortège more than a mile long followed the body to the grave, and the air rang with the report of fire-crackers, the "windy chaos" created by three Chinese bands, and the crackling of rattles swung by black-gowned priests. Scores of hacks had been rented for the occasion, and a dozen express wagons hauled the baked meats and the rice and the cases of gin and tea which had been provided that the spirit of the tong chieftain might refresh itself before beginning the long flight to heaven. But at the cemetery a company of hoodlums fell upon the cortège, routed the mourners, and feasted upon the funeral viands.

CHAPTER IX

"GOD HELP THE POOR SAILOR!"

OR HALF a century after the beginning of the gold rush one of the most dangerous areas in San Francisco was the waterfront, along the eastern and northeastern fringes of the Barbary Coast. Murderers, footpads, burglars, hoodlums, and Rangers prowled the streets in such numbers and carried on their depredations with such boldness that the police walked their beats in pairs and went in even greater force whenever they found it necessary to enter any of the dives with which the district abounded. Every policeman assigned to waterfront duty was specially chosen for strength, bravery, and huskiness. He was equipped with the regulation night-stick and pistol and also carried, in a large outside breast-pocket within easy reach of his hand, a huge knife a foot or more in length. This fearsome weapon was infinitely more effective at close quarters than a club or the cumbersome, unreliable fire-arm of the early days. Nor did the police hesitate to use it. Several battles occurred in which beleaguered policemen chopped off the hands of their assailants or inflicted other wounds equally frightful, and at least one in which an attacking hoodlum was decapitated. This latter feat was performed by Sergeant Thomas Langford, for many years one of the best-known men of the harbor precinct. Attacked in a second-hand-clothing store in Pacific Street by several men whom he had found ransacking the place, Sergeant Langford drew his knife and rushed them in the face of a heavy pistol-fire. He struck wildly in the darkness, and with his first blow neatly sheared the head of one of the thieves from his shoulders. The remainder of the gang, several of them badly wounded by the Sergeant's slashing knife, fled in terror, and thereafter Sergeant Langford was held in greater fear by the denizens of the Barbary Coast than any other policeman in San Francisco.

Innumerable alleys and many comparatively important thoroughfares on or near the waterfront, including Davis, Drum, East (now the Embarcadero), Front, and Battery streets, and the eastern ends of Pacific, Jackson, and Washington streets, were crowded with brothels, saloons, and boarding-houses catering especially to sailors, wherein the luckless seaman was invariably robbed and frequently murdered, and from which he was shanghaied aboard an outgoing ship. It was in these resorts that the word "shanghai" was probably first used as a verb. In early times there were no ships sailing directly from Shanghai to San Francisco, and a man who wanted to travel from the Chinese port to the Pacific coast of North America had to sail round the world to reach his destination. Almost as extensive a journey was required to go from San Francisco to Shanghai, which was then little more than a fishing village. Consequently, when a ship started on a long and hazardous cruise, she was said to be making a "Shanghai voyage"; and, likewise, a sailor who had been forcibly impressed into a vessel's crew was "sent to Shanghai." Later, as the expression was naturally shortened, he was said to have been shanghaied. As early as 1852 twenty-three gangs were more or less openly engaged in this nefarious trade in San Francisco, and for many years shanghaiing was one of the most lucrative activities of the boarding-house masters, or crimps, and their natural allies, the dive-keepers of the Barbary Coast.

2

UNTIL small craft driven by steam or gasoline came into general use, communication between shore and the ships anchored in the Bay of San Francisco was maintained by professional boatmen who plied back and forth in large skiffs, called Whitehall boats. They transferred pilots to and from the vessels and carried as passengers the sailors and officers who had been given shore liberty. Many of them, in later years, became important figures in San Francisco's commercial and shipping circles, but others were scoundrels and remained so throughout their lives. In this latter category were such celebrated boatmen and waterfront characters as Old Activity, so called because he was always deeply involved in some gigantic undertaking, seldom honest; a Mexican known as Red Shirt, who was at length shot by a policeman while robbing a sailor whom he had knocked unconscious with a bludgeon; Old Buzz, shrewd but illiterate, who talked almost continuously in a low, buzzing monotone; and Solly, a gigantic ruffian who carried a revolver, a slung shot, and a pair of brass knuckles, while round his neck a knife was slung on a lanyard. Solly was one of the most accomplished and successful crooks on the waterfront, and for a small fee he would do anything from scuttling a ship to cutting a throat. One of his favorite methods of acquiring wealth was to row into the middle of the Bay and threaten to throw his passenger overboard unless he were paid double or triple the fare which had been agreed upon. There was seldom any argument, for Solly's appearance was, to say the least, terrifying. Moreover, he had a well-earned reputation for carrying out his threats. He was never jailed, as he should have been, although the police always believed that he was responsible for the deaths of several men whose bodies were washed ashore soon after they had embarked in his boat. Eventually, however, Solly met his destined fate.

He was engaged to take the mate of a British schooner out to the ship, which was anchored just inside the Golden Gate, and in mid Bay made his usual demand for more money. The mate promptly shot him and rowed the boat to the schooner, where the smaller craft was cast adrift with Solly's body draped over the gunwale.

The best customers of the boatmen were the runners who worked for the sailors' boarding-houses, from one to half a dozen being attached to each place, according to the size and popularity of the resort. The principal duty of the runner was to bring seamen into the establishment of his employer, and for each man so delivered he was paid from three to five dollars, depending upon supply and demand. Whenever a ship was reported outside the Golden Gate, the Whitehall boatmen took the runners down the Bay, where they clambered over the vessel's side, sometimes while she was still under headway, and in any event soon after she had dropped her anchor. Once aboard, the runners stopped at nothing short of murder, and not always at that, to induce or compel the sailors to desert the vessel and accompany them to the boarding-houses. "They swarm over the rail like pirates," said the San Francisco *Times* of October 21, 1861, "and virtually take possession of the deck. The crew are shoved into the runners' boats, and the vessel is often left in a perilous situation, with none to manage her, the sails unfurled, and she liable to drift afoul of the shipping at anchor. In some cases not a man has been left aboard in half an hour after the anchor has been dropped."

The wages paid to sailors shipping out of San Francisco varied with the years, but from gold-rush days to the turn of the present century they probably averaged around twenty-five dollars a month and found. Occasionally a seaman of unusual sobriety and intelligence found his own berth, but the great majority of sailors, even those who were not shanghaied, were shipped through the boarding-house masters. When a man signed his name or put his mark to a ship's articles, he received, in theory at least, two months' pay in advance, so that he might outfit himself and not have to depend upon what he could purchase from the captain's slop-chest. It was seldom, however, that any of this money actually passed into the possession of the seaman; almost invariably it went into the pockets of the crimps, ostensibly in payment for lodging and other shore expenses. The balance of the sailor's wages was not paid until the ship had completed her voyage and dropped anchor in her home port, which in sailing-ship days might mean anywhere from four months to four years. If the seaman deserted, he forfeited the entire amount. During all the time he was at sea or in port he was dependent for pocket-money upon the good nature of the captain; the latter could advance funds or withhold them, as he pleased. In San Francisco some ship captains arranged with the owners of second-hand-clothing stores, where the sailors purchased most of their supplies, to pay the bills contracted by members of their crews. The storekeeper charged exorbitant prices for everything and occasionally advanced the sailor a few dollars spending money, putting double or triple the amount on the bill. Just before the ship sailed, the captain paid the amount, deducting the sum from the seaman's wages and usually receiving a share of the graft from the storekeeper.

If the captain of a ship intended to sail within a few days or a week after arrival, it was to his interest and that of his owners to keep his crew intact, since to obtain other men he would usually have to pay out, in advance wages and bonuses to the crimps and runners, more than he would save through forfeiture of wages. But if a ship was to lay up in harbor for several weeks or months, as frequently happened, the desertion of the sailors would result in a considerable saving. A skipper who thus faced the prospect of maintaining a crew in idleness usually welcomed the runners and

did whatever he could to help them get the men off the ship.
A week or ten days before the vessel made port, he and the
mates began to pave the way for the activities of the runners
by inaugurating a process called " running the men out " —
they were deliberately cruel, compelled the ship's cook to
serve rotten and scanty rations, and put the sailors at un-
necessary and back-breaking tasks, and otherwise sought to
make their lives as miserable as possible, hoping so to enrage
and disgust them that they would leave the ship at the first
opportunity. If they failed to do so, or if they resisted the
importunities of the runners, as they sometimes did when
large sums were owing to them, the captain announced that
no shore liberty would be granted so long as the ship remained in port. The prospect of spending several weeks or
months aboard the vessel while the bright lights of the Barbary Coast beckoned was usually more than a sailor could
stand. Almost invariably, no matter how their resolve, they
deserted within a few days and made their way to shore in
small boats which a falsely sympathetic ship's officer had
made available to them. They landed with no money and no
place to go and were easy prey for the crimps and runners,
who gave them drugged liquor and then lugged them off to
the boarding-houses. Quite often even a captain who intended to remain in port only a short time would run his men
out, and after they had deserted, and so forfeited their pay,
he reshipped them through arrangements previously made
with the boarding-house masters. The sailors would thus,
and sometimes within a few hours, find themselves aboard
the vessel they had just left, unable to collect the money they
had earned during the previous voyage and with their pay
for two months of the new cruise in the hands of the crimps.

3

WHEN the runners went down the Bay to board an incoming ship, their equipment was so nearly identical as to be

practically standardized. It consisted, usually, of a revolver, a knife, a blackjack or a slung shot, a pair of brass knuckles, a flask of liquid soap, obscene pictures, and as many bottles of rum and whisky, all liberally dosed with Spanish fly, as could be crowded into their pockets. And, of course, a complete assortment of lying promises. If the runner clambered over the side of a vessel about meal-time, his first care was to empty his flask of liquid soap into the kettle of soup or stew which was usually to be found simmering on the galley stove. When the resultant offensive mess was served, it naturally increased the traditional enmity between the sailor and the ship's cook and put the former in a proper frame of mind to listen to the runner's arguments, which were as often physical as vocal. He began by giving the sailors as much whisky and rum as they could drink, and when the drugged liquor began to take effect, he produced his obscene pictures and embarked upon a glowing account of the amorous pleasures which awaited them in the dives and brothels of the Barbary Coast. He offered to provide whatever money might be required, and told the sailors that the proprietor of the boarding-house of whose staff he was such an ornament had engaged the prettiest and most skillful harlots in all San Francisco for their amusement. These ladies, the runner said, were waiting impatiently. Moreover, he promised that when the seamen had caroused to their hearts' content, the generous boarding-house master would sign them for a voyage with a kind-hearted ship's captain who was going on a pleasure cruise in the South Seas. To men who had been at sea for months, or even years, this sort of talk sounded like news from heaven and was usually very effective. As soon as a sailor showed signs of wavering, the runner rushed him across the deck and shoved him into the waiting Whitehall boat. If he came willingly, the boatman gave him a drink; if he showed fight, the boatman hit him with a slung shot or club to keep him quiet. Sailors who stub-

bornly maintained their right to stay with their ship were
threatened with revolvers or knocked down and beaten and
not infrequently were carried off the vessel by main force.
The runners operated under a sort of code by which a sailor
was anybody's game until he was actually in a boat or until
he had uttered the name of a boarding-house master, whereupon he became the property of the runner representing that
particular crimp and was no longer molested by the others.
It was not uncommon for two opposing runners to seize a
sailor's ears between their teeth and hang on, biting hard,
until the bewildered and frightened seaman cried out the
name of the boarding-house master which had been most
forcibly impressed upon his mind.

Honest shipmasters, especially those in command of
foreign vessels, were frequently warned by " certain interested parties," as the San Francisco *Times* put it in 1861,
meaning politicians and lesser city officials, that if they interfered with the runners they would not be permitted to
ship crews when they were ready to sail. Nevertheless,
many tried to keep the rascals off their vessels, although they
were seldom successful, because they were helpless against
the rush of a dozen or more heavily armed thugs. Usually
the officers of a ship were sufficiently cowed by a display of
force and the brandishing of fire-arms, but if they persisted
in their opposition, the runners sometimes drove them to
their quarters and compelled them to remain there until the
sailors had been rushed overside and were on their way to
San Francisco and the boarding-houses. The boarding of the
British ship *Loch Err* in September 1870 by runners who
ignored the captain's protests was thus described by one of
her passengers:

" I had noticed several small boats containing two
or three men in each, who with boat hooks and ropes
attached had made fast and were being dragged along-

side of our ship, which was now proceeding slowly into the harbour of San Francisco, and who had been told once or twice to let go and leave the ship. But they flatly refused to do so. . . . Whilst the crew was busy furling the sails, the men not only climbed on deck but mounted the rigging, and were soon seen very assiduously to importune, and at the same time hand bottles from which the sailors took long draughts. At first the sailors evaded them, but as the liquor began to work its effect, they gradually gave way, and allowed themselves to be cajoled. The captain several times called them down and threatened to have them arrested if they did not leave the ship. Two of them not only refused, but actually pointed a revolver at him, and told him that he was not in a ' B— Lime Juice ' country, but in God's own free land, where one man was as good as another. The captain appeared to be cowed, and did not interfere with them again. . . . At short intervals I noticed that the sailors climbed over the side and lowered themselves into the boats, accompanied by the villains, and were being rowed ashore. . . . I arose earlier than usual the next morning to pack my baggage preparatory to going ashore. Whilst partaking of coffee I heard the second officer calling all hands on deck, but receiving no response except from Dick [the oldest member of the crew, fifty of whose seventy years had been spent at sea] and the apprentices, he looked into the forecastle and found all the berths empty. I told him that the crew had been taken ashore by those who had boarded us. . . . After partaking of breakfast I was about to leave, when I saw two men drag old Dick towards the companion ladder. I attempted to stop them, but received curses and several blows on my face. I returned the insult, and letting go of old Dick we engaged in a close contest, during which I knocked him down. Meanwhile, Dick was not idle, but fought with his man in order to free himself. I was about to spring to his assistance, but on account of the hatch which was close behind him, the impetus in trying to free himself caused him to reel backwards, and before I could grasp him poor old Dick fell headlong down, striking his head against the keel of the ship. I called for assistance, and after securing the two men, we descended and found poor Dick quite dead, his head and body being frightfully mangled. The captain at once hoisted a police flag, which was quickly responded to by two water-policemen, who took the two villains in custody. I was requested to appear as a witness at the trial, which took place three days afterward. . . . The two culprits being well represented by counsel, got off with a light sentence of six months hard labour." [1]

Most of the seamen who succumbed to the blows or blandishments of the runners were taken immediately to the boarding-houses by which the runners were employed, although, as the San Francisco *Times* pointed out in 1861, " in more than one instance the crew of a newly arrived foreign vessel have actually been driven like slaves over the ship's side, stupefied with drugged liquor, and taken on board some other vessel and sent to sea, fit subjects for scurvy, without putting their feet upon land." Ordinarily the work of the runner was completed when the sailors stepped across the threshold of the boarding-house. Thereafter they were handled by the crimp, and if they proved intractable, by strong-arm bruisers who beat them into submission with slung shots and bludgeons. Once a sailor was actually in the clutches of a boarding-house master, he hadn't even the proverbial Chinaman's chance of regaining

---

[1] *Through the Golden Gate*, by Charles Ridgway, pages 7–10.

his liberty. As soon as he arrived, the bag containing his few possessions was taken from him and locked up. He was then given a bunk and as much cheap, vile whisky as he could drink. The liquor was usually dosed with laudanum or opium, Spanish fly having already served its purpose. On rare occasions women were brought in from the houses of prostitution to entertain the sailors, but more often the captives, if they had any money, were escorted by the crimp's strong-arm men to the dives and brothels of the Barbary Coast, where they were promptly robbed by the harlots and other attachés of the resorts. The crimp always received a share of the spoil and was thus relieved of the trouble, and sometimes the danger, of himself robbing the sailor.

While a seaman remained in the boarding-house, which was seldom longer than twenty-four hours, he was kept as drunk as possible. In due course a shipmaster appeared to engage a crew. As many men as he desired were produced by the crimp and were told that a ship had at last been found for them. If they were sober enough, they were permitted to sign their names to the articles and also, though they seldom knew it at the time, to a document which assigned their two months' advance pay to the crimp. If they were drunk or semi-conscious from drink, the boarding-house master signed for them. Occasionally a sailor objected to being shipped aboard a vessel of which he knew nothing for a voyage he didn't want to make, whereupon the crimp's thugs dragged him into another room and beat him until he was willing to do anything to escape further punishment. The formality of signing the articles having been completed, the captain returned to his ship, while the sailors were given more liquor, so heavily drugged that they were soon in a sodden daze. They were then carefully searched, and all valuables found were appropriated by the crimp and his hirelings. If any of the seamen wore good clothing, it was stripped from their bodies, and they were dressed in shoddy, worthless cast-offs or wrapped in old blankets. Their dunnage-bags were kept by the crimp, and the contents sold for whatever they would bring. As a final step in this phase of shanghaiing, the sailors were driven or carried to the waterfront, loaded into boats, and rowed out to the ship. There they were hoisted aboard as if they had been so many sacks of meal. One of the ship's officers checked them as they came over the rail, and when the proper number lay about the deck, the captain appeared and paid to the crimp the advance wages which had been assigned by each man of the crew. The captain also paid the crimp a bonus, ranging from twenty-five dollars to a hundred dollars, for each man delivered on board. Sometimes he had to pay more. During the eighteen-fifties, when the rush for the gold-fields made it extremely difficult for outgoing ships to obtain crews, an able-bodied man was worth as much as three hundred dollars. Whatever sum was paid in bonuses was always, on one pretext or another, deducted from the sailor's pay.

There were plenty of state and city laws under which the activities of the runners and crimps could have been controlled or even prevented, one municipal ordinance in particular imposing a fine of a hundred dollars upon any person who boarded a vessel without the consent of the captain. But little or no attention was paid to these statutes. Few runners or boarding-house masters were ever arrested, and even fewer convicted, for the politicians and city officials protected them just as they did the purveyors of vice in other parts of the Barbary Coast. Consequently both runners and crimps waxed fat and sassy. In busy seasons, when the port of San Francisco was crowded with shipping, and sailors were both plentiful and much in demand, some of the runners earned as much as five hundred to eight hundred dollars a week, while many of the boarding-house masters banked fifty thousand dollars a year clear profit over a long period. There is no record, of course, of the number of sailors who passed through the hands of these villains, but the annual turnover must have been several thousand. Of British seamen alone it was estimated[1] that during the eighteen-nineties between eight hundred and eleven hundred deserted their ships each year and were immediately shanghaied out again by the crimps. The Britishers were easiest of all sailors to influence, for the standard wage out of English ports was two pounds and ten shillings a month, while out of San Francisco it was between four and five pounds. Most of the difference went into the pockets of the crimps, and in the long run the sailor actually earned little more out of one port than out of another.

In this more or less enlightened age it is difficult to understand why the sailors submitted with such docility to the fearful abuse meted out to them by both runners and crimps. The answer probably lies in the fact that in those early days the vast majority of seamen were great stupid, hulking brutes of scant sensitivity and little or no intelligence. Aboard ship they were held under iron discipline and were accustomed to brutality from their officers. They naturally expected the same sort of treatment from everyone else and were seldom disappointed. Moreover, they had no legal rights that anyone, including the authorities, recognized, and no knowledge of how to obtain justice, even if it had occurred to them that they were entitled to it. The practice of enslaving sailors began to decline only with the gradual disappearance of the tramp sailing-ship; the formation of the Seaman's Union, the Seamen's Institute, and other labor and welfare organizations; the enactment of additional legislation for the protection of sailors and the regulation of shipping; and the effective enforcement of laws which already existed, particularly "An Act to Prohibit Shanghaiing

[1] By the Reverend James Fell, an English clergyman who conducted a mission in San Francisco from 1892 to 1898 and wrote a book called *British Merchant Seamen in San Francisco* (London, 1899).

in the United States," passed by Congress in 1906, which imposed, upon conviction of the offense, a fine of a thousand dollars or one year in prison or both. During the past twenty-five or thirty years shanghaiing has seldom been heard of, although it probably still occurs occasionally in San Francisco and other American seaports.

4

IN the main the crimp who operated along the waterfront of San Francisco was so thoroughly a crook that he refused to play fair even with his confederate the shipmaster. Quite often the men who signed the articles in the presence of the ship's captain were strong, husky specimens, obviously sailors, while the ones actually shipped were just as obviously physical weaklings, puny little dock rats whom the crimp's runners had picked up along the waterfront. It was comparatively easy thus to impose upon a ship's captain, for all of the men delivered to his ship were invariably so sodden with drink or drugs that they appeared to be lifeless. Sometimes, also, the crimp included a dead man or two among the crew. The presence of a corpse was seldom discovered until the ship was at sea, and then the captain usually thought it that of a sailor who had died of acute alcoholism. The body was heaved overboard and nothing more thought of it. Nor did the captain report the matter to the police when, if ever, he again dropped anchor in the Bay of San Francisco, for the death of a sailor was a matter of little importance. Many murder mysteries in early San Francisco were never solved because of this practice of shipping the *corpus delicti* to sea as a live sailor; many crimps did a flourishing business in so disposing of the victims of criminals who had found that the easiest way to rob a man was to kill him first. Another way in which the crimp fleeced the shipmasters was to include a dummy among the sailors whom he delivered. A suit of clothes was stuffed with straw and properly weighted, while that part of the dummy which represented the head was swathed in mufflers or other heavy cloths. This fraud was not much easier to detect than the inclusion of a corpse, although when it was found out, the ship's captain didn't merely fling the dummy overboard and forget about it. The fact that he had paid a hundred dollars or more for a bundle of straw was usually enough to embitter him for years. But he had no recourse.

The first man to sell a dummy to an unsuspecting shipmaster is said to have been a wizened little Laplander known as Nikko, for many years runner and right-hand man for Miss Piggott, a ferocious old woman who operated a saloon and boarding-house in Davis Street during the eighteen-sixties and the eighteen-seventies. No one ever knew her first name; she insisted upon being addressed, with proper respect, as Miss Piggott. Her only rival of importance as a female crimp was Mother Bronson, whose establishment was in Steuart Street. Both these ladies were worthy compeers of Pigeon-Toed Sal and the Galloping Cow, who were then rising to fame elsewhere on the Barbary Coast. Like these celebrated personages, Miss Piggott and Mother Bronson were their own bouncers and chief bar-tenders, but neither enforced her edicts with a bludgeon or a slung shot, as did Sal and the Cow. Miss Piggott remained faithful to the bung-starter, and in the use of this implement as a weapon she developed amazing skill. On the other hand, Mother Bronson, who was nearly six feet tall and broad in proportion, scorned to use any other than Mother Nature's weapons. She possessed a fine and strong set of sharp teeth, which she was delighted to sink into the anatomy of an obstreperous customer; her enormous feet were encased in No. 12 brogans, and her fist was as hard as a rock and in size resembled a small ham. With the toe of her boot she once hoisted a Chinaman from the floor of her saloon to the top of the bar, and she often boasted that she could fell an ox with one blow of her fist, although no one ever saw her do it. Nor did anyone dispute the statement.

Sometimes Miss Piggott lacked enough sailors to round out an order, whereupon Nikko prowled through the Barbary Coast until he found a likely-looking prospect, and enticed him into the Davis Street saloon. There he was nudged along the bar until he stood upon a trapdoor built into the floor. Then Nikko called loudly for drinks, which were served by Miss Piggott in person. The Laplander received beer, while for the stranger Miss Piggott prepared a concoction much used in shanghaiing circles and called a Miss Piggott Special. It was composed of equal parts of whisky, brandy, and gin, with a goodly lacing of laudanum or opium. While the victim was shivering under the terrific impact of this beverage, Miss Piggott leaned across the bar and tapped him on the head with a bung-starter, while Nikko made matters certain with a blow from a slung shot. As the prospect began to crumple to the floor, Miss Piggott operated a lever behind the bar and dumped him into the basement, where he fell upon a mattress which Miss Piggott had thoughtfully provided, realizing that the man might receive an injury which would lessen his value. When the object of all these attentions awoke, he was usually in a ship bound for foreign climes, with no very clear idea as to how he got there. All of Miss Piggott's regular customers knew the exact location of the trapdoor and kept away from it, for it was an unwritten law of the establishment that any man who stood upon the fatal spot was fair game. The spectacle of Miss Piggott drugging and then slugging a stranger and dropping him into the basement excited no particular attention. The bystanders might comment judiciously upon the force and accuracy with which the old lady delivered the knock-out blow, but that was about all. It never occurred to anyone to go to the victim's assistance or to call the police. What happened to him was his own affair.

Nikko is said to have sold more than a score of dummies to shipmasters during his long and busy career as a runner for Miss Piggott. He devoted a great deal of time to building them and made them more lifelike by imprisoning a rat in each of the coat sleeves, so that when the dummy lay upon the deck of the ship the efforts of the rodents to escape produced very satisfactory twitchings, while their muffled squeaks passed muster as the groans of a very sick man. When, in the early eighteen-seventies, Miss Piggott passed to whatever reward awaited her, Nikko became a bartender for Olaf Frisson, who operated a saloon in Harrison Street which was much frequented by Norwegian sailors and ships' officers. Olaf's resort was an honest drinking place, with no shanghaiing done on the premises, and Nikko virtually had to begin life anew. He became, instead of a runner and a slugger, an oracle, and was soon known far and wide for the uncanny accuracy of his prophecies. For drinks to the assembled company, Nikko would predict in detail the happenings of any given year in any man's life. Olaf himself was seven feet tall in his socks and was a man of tremendous bulk besides, weighing more than three hundred pounds. He was healthy and popular and owner of a prosperous business; nevertheless he nursed a secret sorrow. He often complained that no woman had ever loved him for himself alone, and this distressing situation he attributed to the fact that he had practically no neck — his head jutted abruptly from between his shoulders, and he was never able to find a collar narrow enough for him. However, he had one great gift of which he was extremely proud and which made him famous all along the waterfront. He could, and frequently did, drink a gallon of whisky at one sitting — and a very short sitting, at that — and feel no ill effects.

While the unquestioned abilities of Miss Piggott and Mother Bronson were recognized and generously applauded by the critical population of the Barbary Coast, the ladies were more or less regarded as freaks because they were women. As a general rule, despite an occasional bold stroke and the unflagging industry of Nikko and their other runners, they were forced to content themselves with the leavings of the masculine shanghaiers. The dominant figure of the waterfront during the years in which Miss Piggott and Mother Bronson flourished, and perhaps the most successful and dangerous crimp who ever operated in San Francisco, was a short, thick-set Irishman, with flaming red hair, a bristling red beard, and an irascible disposition. Throughout the underworld, and wherever sailors gathered, he was known and feared as Shanghai Kelly. Of scarcely less renown were such crimps as Jimmy Laflin, who with Bob Pinner operated a place at No. 35 Pacific Street and specialized in crews for whaling vessels; George Reuben, who kept a boarding-house for German sailors; Horseshoe Brown, who at length killed his wife and himself in front of their resort in Kearny Street; Shanghai Brown, whose place was in Davis Street; Calico Jim, a Chileno who conducted a particularly low saloon and crimping joint at Battery Point; Johnny Fearem, Patsy Corrigan, and Michael Connor, who had saloons and boarding-houses in East Street, now the Embarcadero; and Billy Maitland, of Front Street. Some time during the eighteen-nineties Calico Jim is said to have shanghaied six policemen who were sent, one after another, to arrest him. Soon afterwards he left San Francisco. When his victims returned from their enforced cruise, they pooled their resources, chose one of their number by lot, and sent him to South America to search for the crimp. After several months the policeman came upon Calico Jim in the streets of Callao, Chile, and shot him six times, once for each shanghaied officer.[1]

---

[1] The story of Calico Jim has been current in San Francisco for many years, but I was unable to find any verification of it. The Police Department has no record of the shanghaiing of six policemen.

In his latter years, about 1880, Michael Connor abandoned East Street and opened the Chain Locker Saloon
and Boarding House at Main and Bryant streets. While
Connor was a crimp and a shanghaier, he was also a deeply
religious man, and his proudest boast was that he never told
a lie, though when in his cups he would admit that he sometimes stretched or garnished the truth. In those days a man
was not considered a real sailor until he had made the
perilous Cape Horn passage, and a shipmaster who could
be convinced that a seaman had been round the Horn was
usually willing to pay a few dollars more for him than for
an ordinary man who had not undergone this tremendous
experience. Whenever Connor assembled a crew, he always
swore upon the Bible that each man had been round the
Horn. In one sense this was true enough, for the first thing
Connor did when a sailor was brought into his house was
to lay a cow's horn upon the floor and make the seaman
walk round it. In his back yard Connor also installed a ship's
steering-wheel and a mast with flying jib, main halyards,
truck, and rigging, upon which he gave his landlubber victims a few lessons in seamanship before loading them aboard
a vessel.

Shanghai Kelly's saloon and boarding-house was a
three-storey frame structure at No. 33 Pacific Street, between Drum and Davis streets, under part of which tide-
water flowed. Kelly preferred to handle *bona fide* sailors,
partly because they were more docile and partly because
there was seldom any danger of reprisal, no matter how
they were treated. But, in common with his co-workers in
the crimping field, he would, if necessary to fill out a crew,
shanghai whoever fell into his hands. And for a price he
would shanghai any man whose enemies wanted him out of
the way. Kelly's runners and strong-arm men went into the
streets or the dives of the Barbary Coast and blackjacked
the men they wanted, or induced them to visit Kelly's saloon.

There they were drugged, blackjacked, and dropped through trapdoors, of which there were three in the floor in front of the bar, into a boat which was always tied up to a pillar of the house. In his drugging operations this prince of shanghaiers used the Miss Piggott Special and also gave his victims a concoction of his own invention, compounded of schnapps and beer and seasoned with opium or laudanum. Besides these quieting doses he used a cigar heavily doped with opium, which was known as "the Shanghai smoke" and was manufactured especially for him by a Chinese cigar-maker.

Kelly's boarding-house was usually filled with sailors, many of whom put themselves in his power of their own accord and with full knowledge of what would undoubtedly happen to them, because he provided free women as well as free liquor and permitted any sort of debauchery a man might fancy—and sometimes men who had been several years at sea came ashore with very exotic ideas. Once during the middle eighteen-seventies, however, Shanghai Kelly found his place practically bare of seamen at a time when three ships anchored off the Heads, outside the Golden Gate, wanted crews immediately. One of these vessels was the *Reefer*, a notorious hell-ship out of New York, which was commanded by a captain with whom no sailor in his right mind would ship if he could avoid it. Confronted by the necessity of shanghaiing strangers in wholesale lots, Kelly performed the exploit which set the cap-stone to his fame and which is still talked about along the San Francisco waterfront as the most daring job of crimping in the history of the city. He chartered the *Goliah*, an old paddle-wheel steamer which had wheezed about the Bay for many years, and announced that he would celebrate his forthcoming birthday with a picnic, at which there would be free liquor and other attractions. He issued a blanket invitation to the Barbary Coast, and the riff-raff of that quarter answered in droves.

As his guests came aboard, however, Shanghai Kelly counted them, and when ninety men stood on deck, he cast off, and the *Goliah* chugged down the Bay and outside the Golden Gate into the broad Pacific. Barrels of beer and whisky were broached, and the picnickers began to drink Kelly's health with great enthusiasm. But the liquor was heavily drugged, and within two hours every man on board, excepting Kelly and his henchmen, was asleep. Thereupon the *Goliah* steamed alongside the *Reefer* and the two other ships, and a crew for each vessel was hoisted aboard, although there was scarcely a man among the ninety who knew one end of a ship from the other. On her way back to San Francisco the *Goliah* took off the survivors of the ship *Yankee Blade,* which had been wrecked on a rock off Point Conception, west of Santa Barbara. The landing of the rescued men at the Market Street wharf caused great excitement, and no one seemed to notice that Shanghai Kelly had returned without his picnic guests.

5

T H E most celebrated of the runners who made the port of San Francisco a byword in all the Seven seas was Johnny Devine, better known as the Shanghai Chicken, who was described by the San Francisco *Call* in 1871 as " one of the most dangerous of the habitués of the Barbary Coast." Devine was a New Yorker, and no one in San Francisco, at least so far as the police ever learned, knew anything about his early life except that he had been shanghaied out of the metropolis in 1859, when he was twenty years old. About two years later, in 1861, he appeared in San Francisco and soon became one of the principal ornaments of the water-front and the Barbary Coast. He was a bold and industrious burglar, footpad, sneak-thief, pickpocket, and pimp. At one time he had seven women walking the streets for him or entertaining men whom he brought to their quarters.

He was a real artist with the blackjack, the slung shot, and brass knuckles and for a small sum would commit, upon whoever was pointed out as the proper recipient of his attention, any sort of physical outrage from mauling to mayhem. In nine months he was arrested twenty-seven times for as many different crimes, but the only punishment meted out to him by the courts during this period was fifty days in jail. He had been hired for fifty dollars to attack a man against whom another and more cautious man held a griev-ance, and had done his work so well that his victim was in a hospital for several months.

When he first came to San Francisco, the Shanghai Chicken fancied himself as a prize-fighter. He defeated Patsy Marley in a bout at Point Isabel, and a little later he fought Soapy McAlpine at San Mateo. Soapy was a much better pugilist than Devine, and a bit more imaginative. He introduced kicking, biting, and butting into the fray and soon stretched the Shanghai Chicken unconscious on the floor. When he was able to walk, Devine said with great firmness that he was through with the prize-ring. He became a runner for a crimp named Johnny Walker and later was a sort of chief of staff for Shanghai Kelly, on whose behalf he performed great deeds. He was particularly adept at hi-jacking sailors whom other runners had captured and were escorting to the boarding-houses of their employers. He once tried to take a drunken sailor away from Tommy Chandler, one of Shanghai Brown's runners, and Chandler promptly knocked him down with a hearty punch to the jaw. The Shanghai Chicken got to his feet, carefully felled the sailor with a slung shot so that he couldn't escape, and then drew an old pepper-box pistol and shot Chandler in the left breast and right hand. He then lugged his booty to Shanghai Kelly's boarding-house. The shooting ruined a promising career in the prize-ring, for Chandler had shown consider-able ability as a fighter and had already defeated Dooney

Harris, a well-known English pugilist, and Billy Dwyer, who was murdered by Happy Jack Harrington. Chandler never fully recovered the use of his right hand, and never again entered the ring. Nevertheless, he refused to appear as a witness against the Shanghai Chicken, and the latter escaped punishment.

On June 13, 1868 Devine went on a spree with Johnny Nyland, another of Shanghai Kelly's runners. Both had guns, and Nyland also carried a huge knife which he boasted had been stolen from the dead body of a waterfront policeman. They shot and knifed several men — none seriously, however — in Billy Lewis's saloon, on Battery Street, and then swaggered into the bar-room attached to Billy Maitland's boarding-house, in Front Street, near Vallejo Street. There Nyland cut two men with his knife, while the Shanghai Chicken fired half a dozen shots at the bottles behind the bar, and several at the bar-tender. Devine was thus engaged when Billy Maitland, a huge man of tremendous strength and with a wide reputation as a rough-and-tumble fighter, came into the saloon. Maitland took Nyland's knife away from him and kicked him into the street. With the knife in his hand he returned to the bar-room to find the Shanghai Chicken unsteadily aiming a pistol at him. Maitland lunged forward, Devine dropped the gun and raised his left arm to protect his throat, and the heavy knife sheared cleanly through the flesh and bone of his wrist. While the Shanghai Chicken screamed in pain, Maitland tossed him into the street beside Nyland and slammed the door. Devine struggled to his feet, shrieked curses at Maitland for a moment, and then cried:

"Hey, Billy, you dirty bastard! Chuck out me fin!"

Maitland opened the door of his saloon and threw Devine's severed hand onto the sidewalk. Supported by Nyland, the Shanghai Chicken carried it to Dr. Simpson's drug-store, at Pacific and Davis streets, where he flung the gory member on the counter.

"Say, Doc," he said, "stick that on again for me, will you?"

Before Simpson could tell him that such surgery was impossible, Devine collapsed. He was sent to a hospital, where his left arm was amputated a few inches above his wrist. When he recovered, he had a large iron hook attached to the stump and thereafter was more dangerous than ever. He sharpened the point of the hook to needle fineness, and in his fights used it as an offensive weapon, inflicting terrible wounds. He began to drink more and more after his injury, however, and soon became so unreliable that Shanghai Kelly not only discharged him, but tried to shanghai him. Several attempts failed, although once Kelly's strong-arm men captured him and got him as far as the boat-landing. There the Shanghai Chicken broke his bonds and went into action with his iron hook. He soon had Kelly's sluggers fleeing for their lives. Then Devine rowed Kelly's boat down the Bay and sold it to another crimp.

As a criminal, the Shanghai Chicken sank pretty low after his hand had been cut off by Billy Maitland. His women left him, and he managed to eke out an existence only by robbing drunken men and committing small thefts. About 1869 he served a year in the county jail for larceny and soon afterwards was imprisoned for thirty days for stealing three pigs' feet from a lunch-room. A few weeks after he had served this sentence, in May 1871, he committed the final crime of his career. He shot a German sailor at Bay View, in South San Francisco, and then threatened to kill a woman because she refused to hide him from the police. He was not caught until the next morning, however, when Patrolman John Coulter found him aboard the steamer *Wilson G. Hunt*, which was about to sail from

Meiggs Wharf. He was wearing his victim's cap, having left his own black sombrero at the scene of the crime. While Coulter was taking him to police headquarters, the Shanghai Chicken said:

"John, you're a damned good fellow, but I'm afraid you'll have me hung."

"Why so?" asked Coulter.

"Well," said Devine, "I shot a son of a bitch at Bay View yesterday, and I think they'll make me swing for it."

He was right. They did.

6

NOT every seaman who sailed into the Bay of San Francisco fell into the hands of the runners and crimps. There were many who were given shore leave by their captains and returned to their ships when it expired; many who deserted of their own accord and came in contact with the boarding-house masters only when their money was gone and they were ready to ship out again; and many who ended their voyage at San Francisco and were paid off there. These men, especially those in the last-named class, always came ashore with a little money, which they were anxious to spend. For many years they provided a large share of the revenue which flowed into the bar-rooms, dance-halls, concert saloons, and brothels of the Barbary Coast. They were always welcome in any of the resorts, while scores of places made special efforts to attract their custom. Some of the dives catered particularly to the Souwegians, as the Scandinavian sailors were called, and provided the sort of women and entertainment which these sons of the north were likely to prefer; others sought to entice the German or the Englishman or the Frenchman; while perhaps a score bent their energies to the amusement of the Negro. Curiously enough, a Negro sailor in San Francisco was always called Mister Peters, a queer bit of nomenclature which persisted for years, but of which no one appears to know the origin.

Large numbers of sailors could invariably be found in the audiences of the Bella Union on the Barbary Coast, and the Midway Plaisance in Market Street, particularly the latter after it had begun to feature hoochy-coochy dancers. Bottle Koenig's concert saloon, where the immortal Oofty Goofty made his theatrical début and which was noted for the beauty and amiability of its pretty waiter girls, was also a place of resort for sailors, although it probably would have been more popular if the bouncers had been a little less enthusiastic in their use of hickory bludgeons. There was no dancing at Bottle Koenig's or at any of the other resorts of that type; they strove to hold the sailors' interest with liquor and bawdy shows. Seamen who desired to dance went to the scores of dance-halls which flourished throughout the Barbary Coast. On the floor of any of these places, with a fair damsel clasped in his arms, the frolicsome sailor was encouraged to express himself in any manner which might seem to him best suited to the occasion; he was not molested, indeed, if he chose to execute dance movements which might with more propriety have been performed behind the closed doors of a sleeping-chamber.

When a sailor with money in his pockets had tired of women and entertainment and wanted to do some serious drinking, he was welcome in many famous saloons, among them the Balboa, the Foam, the Bowhead, the Grizzly Bear, and Sverdrup's, all on East Street; the Cowboy's Rest, in Pacific Street near Kearney; and the Whale, also in Pacific Street. Excepting the Cowboy's Rest and the Whale, these were decent enough drinking places. The Whale, which was run by Johnny McNear during its period of greatest renown, was as tough a bar-room as San Francisco ever harbored. Sailors were encouraged to come there and drink because they were notoriously free spenders and not over-captious about the quality of the liquor served them, but no one not a recognized criminal was permitted to make the place a regular haunt and rendezvous. Any murderer, burglar, or footpad whom the police might be seeking was almost sure to be found in the Whale, but it usually required several policemen to get him out. A list of the criminals who sought refuge there would be a roster of San Francisco's worst citizens during a period of some ten or fifteen years. One of the most notable of the Whale's habitués was Cod Wilcox, who in the late eighteen-seventies stole a sloop and enjoyed a brief but prosperous career as a pirate in the Bay of San Francisco before he was caught and sent to San Quentin Prison for twenty years. Another was Tip Thornton, a pickpocket, burglar, sneak-thief, and footpad, who usually worked with his brother, Mush Thornton. Although he was a slim, soft-spoken little man, Tip Thornton was acclaimed as one of the most ferocious fighters on the Barbary Coast and as a very dangerous man to annoy. He always carried a long knife with a narrow blade, but sharp as a razor, and when he became involved in an altercation, his sole idea was to slice off his opponent's nose. If he couldn't get a nose, he'd take an ear. He is said to have cut off at least a score of noses in the Whale and elsewhere on the Barbary Coast, and almost as many ears. But he finally sliced off one nose too many, and Patrolman Jack Cleary, one of the few policemen who dared enter the Whale alone, went to the saloon, fought off the bar-tender and half a dozen other men, and came out dragging Tip Thornton at the end of a pair of nippers. The nose-slicer was sent to San Quentin.

The Cowboy's Rest, the site of which is now a dairy lunch-room, was operated by Maggie Kelly, a large and voluptuous blonde who was variously known as Cowboy Mag and the Queen of the Barbary Coast. No women were regularly attached to her place, but she operated a rooming-house in connection with her saloon, and whoever rented one of her rooms was never asked any embarrassing questions. She flourished after Pigeon-Toed Sal, the Galloping Cow, Mother Bronson, and Miss Piggott had been gathered to their fathers, but she was in every way their equal. Like these ferocious females of an early day, she was her own bouncer, and whenever a customer became obstreperous, she relieved him of his weapons and ran him into the street. Her place was destroyed by the holocaust of 1906, and when the police searched the ruins, they found, behind the bar, a neat pile of some fifty revolvers and a score of knives, besides many slung shots, blackjacks, and brass knuckles. Cowboy Mag was arrested frequently and became the subject of critical comment in the newspapers because of the extreme excitement and irregularity of her love life — in the course of her somewhat hectic career she found it necessary to shoot one husband and one lover, to discipline with a club several other men who had enjoyed her favors, and to administer sound thrashings to various ladies who attempted to trespass upon her amorous preserves. Fortunately for her, the husband and the lovers were too gentlemanly to appear in court against her, and the other women dared not. Her greatest public renown came in 1898, when several Negro regiments were waiting in San Francisco for transports to take them to Manila. Other Barbary Coast dive-keepers welcomed the black soldiers, for they had money to spend, but Cowboy Mag remained true to her principles. Each morning until the regiments had embarked, she mounted guard at the door of her saloon with a revolver and remained there throughout the day, threatening to shoot every Negro who tried to enter. When a newspaper reporter suggested that she wasn't being very patriotic, she said, simply:

"I hate niggers! I'll blow the head off any nigger that comes into my place!"

7

THE commanders of the ships which anchored in the Bay of San Francisco seldom frequented the Whale, the Cowboy's Rest, and the other dives of that character at which the common sailors were such welcome guests. During their hours ashore the shipmasters were usually to be found spinning their yarns in the innumerable respectable bar-rooms, along the waterfront and elsewhere, which did much toward increasing and spreading the fame of San Francisco as a cosmopolitan and hospitable city. One of the most famous of these places was the Bank Exchange, in Montgomery Street near California Street, a magnificently appointed saloon paved with marble and decorated with oil paintings valued at a hundred thousand dollars. M. S. Latham, a San Francisco capitalist, eventually bought one of these pictures for $10,500. The Bank Exchange was especially noted for Pisco Punch, invented by Duncan Nichol, who was second only to Professor Jerry Thomas as bar-tender. During the eighteen-seventies it was by far the most popular drink in San Francisco, although it was sold for twenty-five cents a glass, a high price for those days. The secret of its preparation died with Nichol, for he would never divulge it. But descriptions of the San Francisco of the period abound with lyrical accounts of its flavor and potency, and it must have been the *crème de la crème* of beverages. Its base was Pisco brandy, which was distilled from the grape known as Italia, or La Rosa del Peru, and was named for the Peruvian port from which it was shipped. And the brandy itself, even without the other ingredients which made it into punch, must have been something to write home about. It was thus described by a writer who first tasted it in 1872:

"It is perfectly colourless, quite fragrant, very seductive, terribly strong, and has a flavour somewhat

226

resembling that of Scotch whiskey, but much more delicate, with a marked fruity taste. It comes in earthen jars, broad at the top and tapering down to a point, holding about five gallons each. We had some hot, with a bit of lemon and a dash of nutmeg in it. . . . The first glass satisfied me that San Francisco was, and is, a nice place to visit. . . . The second glass was sufficient, and I felt that I could face small-pox, all the fevers known to the faculty, and the Asiatic cholera, combined, if need be."[1]

Among other famous saloons wherein sea captains were wont to forgather and flavor the atmosphere with the tang of their salty reminiscences were the Cobweb Palace, on the northern end of Meiggs Wharf; the Cottage Bar, in Stevenson Street, then a dingy alley; the Martin and Horton saloon, in Clay Street near Montgomery; and John Denny's grocery and bar, at Salmon and Pacific streets, which was also a noted political rendezvous. In the alley behind Denny's place hung a large bell, which was rung by a push-button under the bar. Whenever a politician entered, particularly one who was running for office, Denny pressed the button, the bell rang, and everyone within hearing rushed into the saloon to drink the politician's health — at the politician's expense. The Cottage was run by Barney Schow, who was celebrated both for the length and luxuriance of his mus-

---

[1] *Underground, or Life Below the Surface*, by Thomas W. Knox, page 253. During my stay in San Francisco I tried industriously, even desperately, to find some of this rare liquor, but, so far as I could learn, no recognizable Pisco brandy has been seen there since Prohibition. The speakeasy bar-tenders had never heard of it.

Pisco brandy was also used in a drink called Button Punch, which Rudyard Kipling, in his *From Sea to Sea* (1899), described as the "highest and noblest product of the age. . . . I have a theory it is compounded of cherubs' wings, the glory of a tropical dawn, the red clouds of sunset, and fragments of lost epics by dead masters."

tache and for his great strength — he could juggle a thirty-gallon barrel of beer with one hand. His most prodigious feat was performed in 1898, when he lifted the anchor of the bark *Elsie Thurston,* after the vessel's donkey-engine had broken down. He saved the lives of six men who had been caught in the anchor chain, but injured his own back so seriously that thereafter he walked with a cane. Schow's saloon was popular at a time when one of the ambitions of every young man was to own a meerschaum pipe, although few were willing to do the almost continuous smoking required to color it properly. Barney Schow contracted to do this work and loaned the pipes to shipmasters bound for the Orient, who kept them burning to China and back.

The Cobweb Palace, a favorite resort of those who liked hot toddies concocted of boiling whisky, gin, and cloves, was opened in 1856 by Abe Warner and operated continuously by him until he retired, in 1897, at the age of eighty years. It was really an extraordinary place. Warner had a great liking for spiders and never interfered with one when it started to spin. As a result, the interior of his place was a mass of cobwebs; they hung in festoons from the walls and ceiling, covering the lighting fixtures and decorations and even extending to the row of bottles behind the bar. Set against the wall under the cobwebs were rows of cages containing monkeys, parrots, and other small animals and birds which Warner had purchased from sea captains and sailors. One parrot, which had the freedom of the saloon and frequently imbibed too much liquor, called Warner Grandfather and cursed in four languages. During the course of his career Warner also acquired one thousand garish paintings of nude women, a few of which were faintly visible beneath the masses of cobwebs on the walls; and a unique collection of walrus tusks and the teeth of the sperm whale, all handsomely carved with patriotic scenes, which is now in the Museum of Golden Gate Park. A frequent visitor to the

Cobweb Palace was William Walker, the famous Central American filibuster who, with his long, black cloak and big, floppy hat, was a familiar figure in San Francisco for several years. Once when Walker poked with his cane at a cobweb, Warner remarked: "That cobweb will be growing long after you've been cut down from the gibbet." It was only about three years later that Walker was shot by a firing squad in Honduras.

The Martin and Horton saloon was an unpretentious place with long, bare tables and sawdust-covered floors, but the liquor and free lunch were unexcelled anywhere in San Francisco, and prices were extremely low. Beer never cost more than a dime for a large glass, and whisky and other spirituous liquor sold for a bit, or twelve and one-half cents, a drink. This bar-room was the favorite loafing place of most of the queer characters who were seen about the streets of San Francisco during the two decades that followed the Civil War, but it was even more than that to Willie Coombs, who thought he was George Washington and always wore a Continental uniform of tanned buckskin. To Willie Coombs the saloon was both General Headquarters and the White House. He appeared there each night with his maps and his state papers and over a glass of beer planned his battles and composed messages to Congress and foreign nations. Once he almost starved himself to death before his friends could convince him that he was no longer at Valley Forge.

Old Orthodox and Hallelujah Cox, street preachers who sometimes descended from their soap-box pulpits long enough to absorb a sustaining ration of beer, were among the regulars at Martin and Horton's; and so was their nemesis, Crisis Hopkins. Although he wore a high clerical collar and a ministerial frock coat, Crisis Hopkins was a scornful free-thinker. He followed Old Orthodox and Hallelujah about the streets and heckled them, and when they had finished their stints, he mounted a soap-box and delivered a reply. He always began with: "The hell-fire and damnation preachers are gone, friends; now listen to reason." For a few months Crisis Hopkins strove unsuccessfully to convert to free-thinking a shy little man, calling himself Charles E. Bolton, who often came into Martin and Horton's and drank beer, retiring to the remotest corner of the room. This same shy little man was at length, in 1883, unmasked as Black Bart, a famous road-agent who prowled the Western highways for some seven years and held up innumerable stage-coaches with an unloaded shot-gun. At the scene of each robbery he left a bit of verse, signed "Black Bart, the PO8." Another habitue of Martin and Horton's, and an occasional visitor at the Cobweb Palace, was an itinerant healer who called himself the King of Pain. He was probably the most ornate personage in the San Francisco of his time — his customary attire was scarlet underwear, a heavy velour robe, a high hat bedecked with ostrich feathers, and a heavy sword. When he went abroad, he rode in a coal-black coach drawn by six snow-white horses. The King of Pain made a fortune selling aconite liniment from a pitch at Third and Mission streets, but he lost all his money at the gaming tables and finally committed suicide.

By far the best known of all San Francisco's queer characters, however, was the Emperor Norton, whose real name was Joshua A. Norton. He was born in England in 1819 and at the age of thirty came to San Francisco with forty thousand dollars, with which he established himself as a real-estate operator and broker. Within ten years he had increased his fortune to two hundred and fifty thousand dollars, all of which he lost in an unlucky investment. The financial disaster unbalanced his mind, and on September 17, 1859 he sent to the newspapers an announcement that the California Legislature had chosen him Emperor of the United States, and that henceforth he must be addressed by his proper title. For a while he also called himself Protector of Mexico. For nearly thirty years he was one of the best-known men in San Francisco. Each afternoon he promenaded the down-town streets, graciously greeting his subjects. He wore a blue military uniform with tarnished gold-plated epaulets, which had been given him by the officers at the United States Army post, the Presidio, and a beaver hat decorated with a feather and a rosette, and he always carried both a cane and an umbrella. When his uniform began to look shabby, the Board of Supervisors, with a great deal of ceremony, appropriated enough money to buy him another, for which the Emperor sent them a gracious note of thanks and a patent of nobility for each Supervisor. He ate without paying at whatever restaurant, lunch-room, or saloon took his fancy; and whenever he wanted cash, he issued bonds in the denomination of fifty cents and sold them to his subjects. He also drew an occasional check for that amount, and it was invariably honored by the San Francisco bankers and merchants. On January 8, 1880 the Emperor died, leaving an estate which consisted of a two-dollar-and-a-half gold piece, three dollars in silver, a franc piece of 1828, and 98,200 shares of stock in a worthless gold mine.

CHAPTER X

"COMPANY, GIRLS!"

THE FOUNDATION upon which the Barbary Coast reared its fantastic structure of crime and debauchery was a system of commercialized prostitution that occupied a semi-lawful status in San Francisco for more than sixty years. Throughout that period the harlot was the dive-keeper's greatest single asset and his most important attraction; whatever she did worked to his advantage, whether she labored as a streetwalker, as an inmate of the brothels, as a decoy in the deadfalls, or as a waiter girl and performer in the dance-halls, concert saloons, melodeons, and peepshows. Without the drawing power of the professional bawd it is doubtful if the Barbary Coast could have maintained, for more than a few years, a profitable existence as a so-called amusement center. In the final analysis a great majority of the men who visited the quarter did so because of the lewdness and depravity of the women who were to be found there; and when open prostitution was driven out of the shadow of the Golden Gate, the Barbary Coast soon followed it into oblivion.

The first bagnios in San Francisco were the tents and slab shanties of the Chileno harlots who, during the early days of the city, plied their ancient trade on the slopes of Telegraph Hill and at various points along the waterfront. To a very large extent these shabby dens vanished with the filling in of Yerba Buena Cove and the development of the

harbor, and during the final years of the gold rush the center
of prostitution shifted to Portsmouth Square. From there
the harlots were expelled by the encroachments of business — an unwilling exodus which was virtually completed
by the late eighteen-fifties. Thereafter, until the pressure
of public and journalistic opinion compelled the enforcement of laws which abolished the public bawdy-house, most
of San Francisco's brothels were to be found in or adjacent
to the Barbary Coast. The red-light district was thus more
or less confined within an area bounded, roughly, on the
north by Broadway, on the east by the waterfront, on the
west by Powell Street, and on the south by Commercial
Street, with a southwestward dip to Morton Street, later
called Union Square Avenue and Manila Street and now,
ironically enough, Maiden Lane. These boundaries encom-
passed portions of such main thoroughfares as Pacific,
Kearny, Sacramento, Clay, California, Jackson, Washington, Montgomery, and Stockton streets and Grant Avenue,
in all of which were many blocks containing nothing but
saloons and houses of prostitution. Innumerable alleys and
short passageways, among them Belden, Bacon, and Berry
Places and Hinckley, Pinckley, and Virginia alleys, were
almost entirely given over to vice.

In later years, especially after the great conflagration
of 1906, attempts were occasionally made to open bagnios
in the Western Addition and other residential sections, but
because of the strenuous opposition of indignant property-
owners, only a few met with even temporary success. A
woman known as Madame Labrodet opened a resort at
Turk and Steiner streets and operated it successfully for
several months in 1906, and long before that, for a few
years in the middle eighteen-seventies, Johanna Schriffin
considerably annoyed her neighbors and the police by the
manner in which she conducted the House of Blazes, a large
three-storey rookery in Chestnut Street between Mason and

Powell streets. This aptly named establishment contained two or three open brothels, and many rooms which were always available to streetwalkers. It was a refuge for criminals of every description and was so tough and dangerous that if it could have been transferred to the Barbary Coast, it would have added luster to the reputation of even that celebrated quarter. A policeman once went alone to the House of Blazes to arrest a thief, and before he could escape, his handcuffs, pistol, cap, and blackjack had been stolen. The place was finally raided and closed in November 1878.

About the beginning of the present century a comparatively small colony of prostitutes succeeded in gaining a foothold among the gambling houses, shady saloons, and cabarets of the Uptown Tenderloin — parts of Mason, Larkin, Eddy, Ellis, O'Farrell, Powell, Turk, and other streets leading northward or westward from Market Street, the principal business thoroughfare and traffic artery of San Francisco. In this region were also many important hotels and restaurants, and most of the theaters. It was the center of the city's more reputable night life, but was never a part of the Barbary Coast. The brothels of the Uptown Tenderloin were generally regarded as being of a higher class than those of the Barbary Coast, meaning that their prices were higher, that they were usually more elegantly furnished, and that as a rule they provided handsomer and more accomplished girls. The inmates of these resorts, too, considered themselves infinitely superior to the women who dragged out their miserable lives in the comparative squalor of the cheaper dives, a viewpoint in which the latter shared. The ambition of every Barbary Coast prostitute, unless she had sunk so far in sin and degradation that she no longer cared what happened to her, was to obtain a post in a fashionable uptown bordello; while the bagnio-keeper who had amassed sufficient money to abandon the Coast and open a place in the vicinity of Market Street felt that she had taken a distinct step upward.

The differences between the brothels of the Barbary Coast and those of the Uptown Tenderloin, however, were more apparent than real; precisely the same profession was practiced in the latter as in the former, and in much the same fashion. But in one particular the Uptown Tenderloin reached heights of distinction never attained by the Barbary Coast — soon after the earthquake and fire of 1906 it harbored, in a two-storey building in Mason Street, a house of prostitution which catered to women and offered a dozen handsome, stalwart young men for their amusement. The price was ten dollars, half of which went to the male harlot, although it was common gossip at the time that several had refused to accept any payment for their services, feeling that the experience was in itself sufficient compensation. The active management of the establishment was entirely in the hands of an old Negro woman known as Aunt Josie, who operated it as a call house; that is, the members of the — well, staff — were not actually resident upon the premises, but were chosen from photographs, and from charts which furnished all needful information as to color of the eyes and hair and other physical details. Once selected, the male Magdalen was summoned by telephone or messenger.

Aunt Josie took every possible precaution to prevent recognition of any women who might visit the house. All entrances and exits were so arranged that they might come and go with slight danger of detection, and the lower floor of the building was divided into small reception-rooms, hung with heavy curtains and opening into a darkened hallway, wherein the visitors inspected the photographs and selected their lovers. All the bedrooms were upstairs and could be securely bolted from the inside; and as an additional safeguard against any accidental disclosure of identity, Aunt

235

Josie furnished her customers with silk masks, so that not even a woman's partner could see her face unless she so desired. These elaborate arrangements, however, were wasted, for it is doubtful if any woman ever entered the resort except a few professional prostitutes who were intrigued by the idea of paying instead of being paid, and so embarked upon a sort of busman's holiday. The bagnio was closed within a few months, partly because of lack of business, and partly because of threats made by the macks, or pimps, who flourished in large numbers throughout the city. These gentry complained that the harlots were spending their money foolishly.

The name of the owner of this unique brothel was not generally known — even the police disclaimed knowledge of his, or her, identity — but the resort was popularly believed to be one of the many underworld properties of Jerome Bassity — his real name was Jere McGlane — who was once described by Pauline Jacobson in the San Francisco *Bulletin* as possessing a moral intelligence scarcely higher than that of a trained chimpanzee. Miss Jacobson also, in her article on Bassity, invited her readers to " look at the low, cunning lights in the small, rapacious, vulture-like eyes; look at that low, dull-comprehending brow; the small sensual mouth; the soft puffy fingers with the weak thumb, indicating how he seeks ever his own comfort before others, how his will works only in fits and starts." [1] Despite these undesirable characteristics, or rather, perhaps, because of them, Bassity was for more than a dozen years the veritable lord of the Barbary Coast and the red-light district — he probably owned more houses of prostitution than any other one person in San Francisco. He was by far the most powerful figure in the underworld during the three terms of Mayor Eugene Schmitz, from 1901 to 1907, when the city was at

---

[1] Miss Jacobson's article was called " Jerome Bassity, a Study in Depravity," and appeared in the *Bulletin* of May 14, 1910.

the mercy of the political machine created by Abe Ruef;[1]
and again during the régime of Mayor P. H. McCarthy,
one-time president of the Building Trades Council, who was
elected in 1909 on a platform of "make San Francisco the
Paris of America." To the realization of this more or less
laudable ambition Bassity gave freely of his peculiar talents;
he was manager of the McCarthy Non-Political Liberty
League, and throughout McCarthy's administration he was
one of a triumvirate which really ruled San Francisco. The
others were Harry P. Flannery, Police Commissioner and
owner of the Richelieu Bar, at the junction of Market,
Kearny, and Geary streets; and, of course, McCarthy
himself.[2]

At least two hundred prostitutes shared their earnings
with Bassity during the long period in which his star was
in the ascendancy, and in addition he derived a considerable
revenue from his interests in dance-halls and other dives;
and from his saloon in Market Street, which had a tamale
grotto in the basement, and a dance-hall and low variety
theater upstairs. For a year or so before the conflagration
of 1906 he also operated, very successfully, a Market Street
deadfall called the Haymarket, which was so low that it was
shunned even by the streetwalkers. For many years Bassity's
income probably averaged from six thousand to ten thousand dollars a month, trifling sums when compared to the
takings of modern racketeers, but a great deal in those days.
He kept very little of it, however. As he often boasted, his

---

[1] Abe Ruef was a lawyer and originally a Republican. He was active
in politics for several years, but his influence was slight until 1901, when he
took advantage of labor disturbances and formed the Workingmen's party,
which gave him control of the city by electing Mayor Schmitz and a new
Board of Supervisors.

[2] In 1917 Flannery was convicted of selling liquor to soldiers in uniform and was sentenced to a year in prison. Later he was adjudged incompe-
tent, and his saloon fixtures were sold at auction. A mahogany bar for which
he had paid ten thousand dollars sold for $127.

237

living-expenses alone exceeded fifteen hundred dollars a month, and he spent enormous sums for jewelry and clothing, particularly for diamond rings and fancy waistcoats. Of the latter he possessed no fewer than half a hundred, all made to his order and decorated with embroidered flowers and hunting scenes. He wore three diamond rings on each hand, and a great gem glistened from his shirt-front. It is also said, perhaps apocryphally, that when he retired for the night, a diamond ring encircled each of his big toes. Most of his jewelry, besides a great deal of his cash, eventually found its way into the hands of prostitutes, for he was an assiduous patron of the brothels as well as an owner. Curiously enough, he seldom looked with favor upon any of the women employed in his own bagnios, although he usually claimed seigniorial rights when one of his places acquired a virgin or a very young girl. In the main, however, he frequented the establishments of his competitors. In few of them was he welcome, despite his lavish spending and his gifts of jewelry, for he always carried a revolver and he was generally drunk. He customarily climaxed a night of debauchery by shooting out the lights, or by firing at the girls' toes to make them dance.

Bassity's power and influence in San Francisco were never better shown than during the autumn of 1906. Although indictments had already been returned against Ruef and Mayor Schmitz, and the newspapers, particularly the *Bulletin* under the editorship of Fremont Older, were daily exposing the corruption of the Ruef machine, Bassity, in partnership with a woman known as Madame Marcelle, began the erection of a huge brothel in Commercial Street with accommodations for one hundred women, who were to be housed in small, box-like rooms. Another woman, named Peterson, was appointed resident manager of the bagnio and began scurrying busily about the Barbary Coast, recruiting girls and dickering with the procurers. The Grand

Jury investigated Bassity's activities and recommended that the police prevent the opening of the resort, but Bassity publicly boasted that he had arranged everything with Abe Ruef and Mayor Schmitz.

"I don't care a snap for the Grand Jury," he said. "I'm going to open, and they can't stop me."

And open he did, on December 17, 1906, with a wild debauch at which everything, for that night only, was free. He operated the brothel profitably until September 1907, when it and several other places were closed by the reform administration, headed by Dr. Edward R. Taylor as Mayor, which had succeeded Mayor Schmitz and the Ruef machine. The closing, however, was only temporary. Bassity reopened some of his bagnios even before Mayor Taylor left office, and the remainder resumed operations as soon as McCarthy had been elected. Bassity continued to be an important underworld personage until 1916, although his political influence declined considerably with the election of Mayor James Rolph, Jr., now Governor of California, in 1911. About a year before the beginning of the crusade which finally closed the Barbary Coast, Bassity saw the handwriting on the wall and retired from business. He went to Mexico, where he spent several years trying unsuccessfully to wrest control of the Tia Juana race-track from J. W. Coffroth. His last public appearance in San Francisco was in January 1921, when he was arrested on a warrant which charged him with swindling the seventeen-year-old son of a New Orleans newspaper publisher out of seven hundred dollars at the Thirty-third Assembly District Club in Turk Street. Neither the boy nor his father appeared in court, however, and Bassity was released. He died in San Diego, California, on August 14, 1929, leaving an estate of less than ten thousand dollars.

ONLY a few blocks from the extraordinary brothel managed by Aunt Josie, in O'Farrell Street, was the popular establishment presided over by Miss Tessie, otherwise Tessie Wall, a flamboyant, well-upholstered blonde who was a familiar figure in the Uptown Tenderloin for many years. She was particularly noted for her ability to consume enormous quantities of wine, and her resort was celebrated for the beauty of its inmates, all of whom were young, blonde, and plump. Tessie Wall's early career is more or less cloaked in mystery, although she is believed to have spent several years, in one capacity or another, on the Barbary Coast. She first began to attract attention in the Uptown Tenderloin during the early part of 1907, when she opened a place in Larkin Street, between Ellis and Eddy. A year or so later she removed to O'Farrell Street and established the house which was much frequented by college boys and other roisterers of the younger set. In 1909 Tessie Wall became acquainted with Frank Daroux, a gambler who was interested in several so-called sporting houses, and at their first dinner together she fascinated him by drinking twenty-two bottles of wine without once leaving the table. They were married soon afterwards and gave a historic wedding feast at which one hundred guests consumed eighty cases of champagne, or 960 bottles, or about 240 gallons. Daroux could see nothing wrong in himself owning houses of bad repute, but he didn't want his wife to be engaged in the same business. He tried repeatedly to induce her to sell her properties and make her home in the country, on an estate which he had purchased for her in San Mateo County. But Tessie Wall flatly refused to leave the bright lights.

"I'd rather be an electric light pole on Powell Street," she said, "than own all the land in the sticks."

After a few years of wedded bliss Daroux procured a

divorce. He declined to return to Tessie Wall despite her anguished entreaties, whereupon that forthright lady armed herself with a twenty-two-caliber revolver and sent word to him that if she couldn't have him, she would fix him so no other woman would ever want him. Daroux laughed at her warning, but she did her best to carry out her threat. One day in the summer of 1916 she met him on the street and fired three bullets into his body. She stood weeping over him until the police came. When they arrested her, she cried: " I shot him because I love him — damn him! "

Daroux recovered, although the shooting permanently affected his health. He refused to appear as a prosecuting witness, and Tessie Wall was promptly released from custody. A year or so later, during the uproar of reform that ended with the abolition of the Barbary Coast and the more sordid features of the Uptown Tenderloin, Daroux went to New York, where he remained. He died there in December 1928. Tessie Wall closed her resort about the same time and retired with a modest fortune to a flat in Eighteenth Street, taking with her the enormous gilded bed in which she had slept for many years, and many other garish pieces of furniture from the O'Farrell Street establishment. There she lived until her death in April 1932, at the age of sixty-seven.[1] During her latter years San Francisco journalists invested her with a glamour which was noticeably absent during the heyday of her career, and customarily referred to her as the one-time Queen of the Barbary Coast. As a matter of fact, Tessie Wall had very little, if any, connection with the Barbary Coast, and was never a figure of importance in that hive of vice and violence. Whatever prominence she enjoyed was achieved in the Uptown Tenderloin.

---

[1] Tessie Wall's effects were sold at auction soon after her death. The huge bed was bought for $105 by Sheriff Ellis W. Jones of Sacramento.

3

IN that portion of the red-light district which formed a part of the Barbary Coast, there were three main types of brothel — the cow-yard, the crib, and the parlor house. The cow-yard was really just a group of cribs under one roof, usually a U-shaped structure or enclosure of from one to four storeys, divided into small cubicles on either side of long hallways. Some of these buildings provided accommodations for as many as three hundred women, and several were planned to accommodate even more, but all of the space was never rented. In addition to these establishments the Barbary Coast was crowded with call houses, and cheap hotels and lodging-houses to which streetwalkers took their customers. There were also the dens above and below the dance-halls and concert saloons, which were maintained for the convenience of the pretty waiter girls and female performers employed in the resorts, to whom prostitution was more or less of a side-line. Of all the so-called sporting houses, the cow-yard was probably the most profitable, while the crib was the lowest and most disreputable. The parlor house generally made a considerable pretense at refinement and a certain gentility and professed to cater to a higher-class clientele than did the others, although it is extremely doubtful if any man with money in his pockets was ever refused admittance. Prices in the cribs and cow-yards, over a long period of years, ranged from twenty-five cents to a dollar, while the inmates of the parlor houses received from two to ten dollars for their favors. Very young and handsome girls were sometimes paid as much as twenty dollars for entertaining visitors for a half-hour or so, as were a few older women who made up in skill and simulated passion what they lacked in youth and beauty. Only in a parlor house could a man remain throughout the night and have, during that time, the exclusive company of a particular girl. For this privilege he paid from five to thirty dollars, depending upon his own generosity and the standing and popularity of the bagnio.

The parlor-house girls were the aristocracy of San Francisco's red-light district — as a class they were much younger and handsomer than the streetwalkers or the inmates of the cribs and cow-yards. Many, perhaps a majority, were small-town girls, brought into the city by the procurers, who operated with great industry and success throughout California and up and down the Pacific Coast — prolific sources of supply were the villages and towns on the eastern shore of the Bay of San Francisco and in the southern part of the San Francisco peninsula. Sometimes these girls were sold to the brothel-keepers for cash, but more often the procurer received a small percentage of their earnings and so in time built up a regular and substantial income. Other parlor-house inmates were girls who had come to San Francisco to obtain jobs or otherwise to better their fortunes and had been forced into prostitution by economic stress. Still others were former dance-hall women who found life easier and more remunerative in the bagnios than in the dives of the Barbary Coast. And there were, of course, some who became harlots simply because they followed the line of least resistance, or surrendered to their natural inclinations, or fell in love with a man who seduced them and then set them to work earning money for him. Occasionally a girl of good family appeared in a brothel, but most of the inmates came from the middle and lower classes and were deficient in both education and intelligence. They held their places in the parlor houses only so long as they retained something of their youth and beauty, which was seldom more than half a dozen years. Then they became streetwalkers or went into the cribs or cow-yards — or committed suicide. A few — very few — abandoned the life entirely and either married or engaged in work upon which society looked with more respect.

A woman who practiced the arts of harlotry in a crib or a cow-yard kept for her own — or rather, in most cases, gave to her pimp — all the money she earned, and paid a nightly rental of from two to five dollars for the space she occupied. In the parlor houses, however, various methods of dividing the revenue of the establishments were employed. In some the girls paid from twenty to forty dollars a week for board, lodging, and laundry and retained for themselves whatever they earned above that amount. In others the inmates were paid from one-fourth to one-half of their total earnings, and in still others they received a weekly wage, ranging from twenty to sixty dollars, and no other remuneration. They usually paid nothing for board and lodging or for the scanty raiment which they wore during their working hours. The girl who was employed on a percentage basis was compelled to depend upon her mistress for the proper determination of the amount due her at the end of each week, and it is doubtful if she ever received a correct accounting until the cash register came into general use. Thereafter in many houses the brothel-keeper or a trusted servant sat enthroned behind a cash register at the foot of the stairs which led to the bedrooms. When a visitor had selected the harlot who most pleased him, he paid the regular fee to the mistress of the bagnio, for payment in advance was an unalterable rule in all except a very few of the houses. The amount was rung up on the cash register, and the girl received a brass check, which she kept until pay-day.

The number of girls in a parlor house varied, of course, according to the brothel's size and popularity, but it was seldom less than five or more than twenty. They were expected to be ready for work by noon of each day and remained on duty until dawn the following morning, unless excused for illness or other cause. Each girl had one day off a week, which she usually spent with her lover or drinking in the dives of the Barbary Coast. The income of a parlor-house prostitute was sometimes considerable; an occasional girl, if employed in a popular bagnio, earned as much as two hundred dollars a week, the greater part of which went to her pimp. As a rule the owners of the resorts made enormous sums; many retired with fortunes.

The parlor houses also derived a considerable income from the sale of beer in bottles and hard liquor by the half-pint and from music. Practically every resort was equipped with some sort of automatic — and in later years electrical — musical instrument, which played only when fed with nickels or quarters. A great deal of the revenue from the music and sale of liquor went to the police and politicians as graft, in addition to the regular payments, which were usually based on the number of girls in a house. Sometimes besides taking most of the coins which had been dropped into the machine, the greedy grafters levied a special unofficial tax upon each musical instrument; or ordered all music stopped and then permitted its resumption upon payment of another so-called tax or license fee. Again, they used a method similar to that which proved so successful in 1911. In the late spring of that year the police forbade all music in houses of prostitution and ordered the removal and destruction of every musical instrument in the red-light district. A month later, in July, the proprietors of the houses were told that they might provide music for the entertainment of their guests, but that it must be the music of the automatic harp. There wasn't such an instrument in the Barbary Coast, but the lack was soon remedied. A few days after the bagnio-keepers had been notified, a salesman for a Cincinnati piano house appeared in the district and offered automatic harps for sale at $750 each, about four times what they could have been bought for in the open market.

But he bore references from important politicians and experienced no difficulty in making sales.

The location of every brothel on the Barbary Coast, whether crib, cow-yard, or parlor house, was indicated at night by a red light which burned before its door from dusk to dawn, and during the day by a red shade behind at least one of the front windows. From some of the parlor houses also flapped signs, gaudily painted on wood or metal, which bore the name of the establishment and, sometimes, pertinent information about its inmates. Madame Gabrielle's bagnio in Dupont Street (Grant Avenue), which she rebuilt in Commercial Street after the fire of 1906, displayed an ornate sign which depicted a huge insect lying at ease in a bed of fragrant flowers, surrounded by sweet-faced, simpering Cupids. Her place was called the Lively Flea. Near-by, another and an equally flamboyant sign ornamented the entrance of the Parisian Mansion, which was owned by Jerome Bassity and Madame Marcelle. Also on Commercial Street, during the first year or so of the present century, was a very popular French bawdy-house before which swung the cast-iron figure of a rooster, painted a brilliant scarlet and with a red light burning in its beak. The talons of the metal bird clutched a placard on which was painted the legend: "At the Sign of the Red Rooster." In the hallway of this brothel was a smaller replica of the figure, and a sign similar to that outside except that it bore a shorter synonym for "rooster." The Red Rooster was the property of Madame Lazarene, who also owned several other resorts, some of which were in the name of her husband, Labrodet. Instead of using signs, some of the parlor-house proprietors in Commercial and other streets affixed to their front doors or walls brass or copper plates, on each of which was stamped the street number of the resort and the first name of the woman who operated it. One brothel-keeper in Sacramento Street, who had formerly conducted a tea-room, achieved undying

fame in the middle eighteen-nineties by nailing to her door
a copper plate on which had been engraved this startling
announcement:

MADAME LUCY
YE OLDE WHORE SHOPPE.

Not unnaturally, this sign attracted a great deal of attention, but Madame Lucy removed it within a few days
at the request of the police.

4

A FEW of the Barbary Coast parlor houses were managed
by men, who, for some reason which never was quite clear,
invariably wore pink or canary-colored silk shirts embellished with huge diamond studs. Most of the bagnios of this
type, however, were operated by women, the great majority
of whom were fat and—or had been—blonde. The mistress of such an establishment was always called Miss by the
inmates, but the customers addressed her—and with considerable respect, too—as Madame. In time this title became generally used as a common noun to designate any
brothel-keeper. When, as occasionally happened, one of
these women was arrested and asked her occupation, for the
purpose of the police record, she replied simply and with
pride: "I am a madame." Practically all of the parlor
houses were in two- or three-storey buildings which had once
been private residences. When they were transformed into
bagnios, the interior arrangements were usually altered to
provide additional bedrooms, and, if possible, the living-
room or parlor was enlarged. The sleeping-chambers were
each equipped with a dresser, a chair or two, and a strong
iron or brass bed, while the parlor was a potpourri of gaudy
rugs, erotic paintings or photographs, garish couches and
divans, and heavily gilded chairs and tables. In one corner
was the omnipresent automatic or electrical musical instru-

ment, and in some places a small section of the floor was
cleared for dancing.

When a man stepped across the threshold of a parlor
house, the subsequent procedure was much the same as if he
had gone into a store to buy a spool of thread. A Negro
maid escorted him into the parlor, where he was greeted by
the madame and immediately asked what type of girl he desired. If he intimated, as he usually did, that he preferred
to look at the stock before buying, the madame summoned
her harlots, who trooped into the parlor and were paraded
for inspection. Whether or not the visitor made his selection
immediately, he was importuned to purchase liquor or provide coins for the music. The dress of the prostitutes on
these important occasions varied with changing fashions, but
was always extremely scanty. In some houses they wore
flannel or cotton night-gowns; in others the parade costume
was a thin house-dress with nothing underneath; in still
others the prostitutes were clad only in flimsy underwear.
In a few resorts the girls wore no clothing whatever except
slippers and stockings. The traditional call by which the
harlots have been summoned into the parlors of American
houses of prostitution for more than fifty years is said to
have originated in a Sacramento Street bagnio kept by
Madame Bertha Kahn. When visitors entered her brothel,
Madame Bertha, who was a huge woman with a tremendous
contralto voice, strode to the foot of the stairs and shouted:
" Company, girls! "

Madame Bertha employed thirty girls, and dressed
them in red sandals, long, white night-gowns lavishly
trimmed with lace, and red velvet caps which perched pre-
cariously atop short, frizzed hair. During the middle
eighteen-seventies this bagnio was one of the most famous
houses in San Francisco and was especially popular with the
so-called higher classes because of the refined and genteel
manner in which it was conducted. Madame Bertha sold no

liquor, permitted no obscene talk or ruffianly conduct, and sternly forbade the punching and prodding and public caressing with which the girls of other houses were greeted. When her harlots were summoned to parade, they came into the parlor like ladies and were formally introduced to the gentlemen present, after which they sat demurely in a row on a long couch, across the room from the men who desired to purchase their favors. If one of the latter fancied a girl, he indicated the object of his desire to Madame Bertha, who made the necessary arrangements and informed the prostitute that the gentleman wished to speak to her in private. No money was paid until the pair had ascended the stairs, and sometimes not even then, for many of Madame Bertha's regular customers had charge accounts. Besides the automatic instrument which required nickels and quarters to burst forth into melody, Madame Bertha's house boasted an organ, upon which the mistress of the bagnio performed with rare skill. On Sunday afternoons she closed the resort for an hour or two, except to specially invited guests, and during that time, becomingly attired in black silk, she played sentimental airs on the organ, while the harlots and the guests sang. At these functions tea and cake were served. The policy of this unusual brothel was aptly expressed by the signs which were prominently posted in the parlor and in every bedroom:

NO VULGARITY

ALLOWED

IN THIS ESTABLISHMENT.

Madame Bertha's most important rival in the parlor-house field was Madame Johanna Werner, who also kept a place in Sacramento Street and prospered for some ten or fifteen years. The popularity of her resort began to decline in the late eighteen-seventies, however, when the police arrested the procurer who had kept her supplied with girls, and imprisoned him for sending a fourteen-year-old girl to a crib in Portland, Oregon. This human vulture was appropriately named Johnny Lawless. Madame Johanna specialized in girls between fourteen and seventeen years of age, and frequently offered her clients children whom she said were even younger. The services of the very young girls who fell into her hands were sometimes sold at auction, at which the bidding was usually very brisk. Besides these sales, the brothel was noted, about 1875, for the erotic exhibitions which were given there at regular intervals by three French girls known as the Three Lively Fleas, who also performed at other peep-shows on the Barbary Coast. A frequent spectator of these shows, and a customer of the bagnio on other occasions also, was Jeanne Bonnet, better known as the Little Frog Catcher, who wore men's clothing and for a few years earned an honest living catching frogs in the marshes of San Mateo County. Early in 1876, however, she abandoned the ways of integrity and organized a criminal gang, the membership of which comprised a dozen young girls whom Jeanne Bonnet had induced to leave Madame Johanna's and other brothels. They eschewed prostitution, had nothing to do with men, and eked out an uncertain living through shop-lifting and other forms of thievery. Their headquarters was a shack on an unfrequented part of the waterfront, south of Market Street. The life of the gang was short, for within a few months the Little Frog Catcher, then only twenty-five years old, was found dead with a bullet in her heart. She was believed by the police to have been murdered by the pimps whose girls she had taken.

Madame Johanna had still another claim to fame as the first bagnio-keeper who seriously attempted to publicize her resort outside of San Francisco, a practice which was soon adopted by other madames. The ordinary channels of advertising, of course, were closed to them, but they procured mailing-lists from various sources and sent to towns and cities throughout the West, and particularly to those along the Pacific Coast, circulars describing their girls and dwelling lyrically upon the delights of the brothel. Many offered reduced rates to parties from out of town. At first some of the circulars were extremely frank, and the illustrations were photographs of naked girls in various poses, but in later years both text and pictures were considerably changed to avoid prosecution by the Federal authorities under the laws which prohibited the sending of obscene literature through the mails.

Logical developments of this system of advertising were the custom of using business cards and the extensive use of wall mottoes and signs. From about the middle eighteen-eighties until the closing of the Barbary Coast, practically every prostitute in San Francisco, even those who occupied the lowest cribs and cow-yards, kept a supply of business cards on hand and distributed them whenever an opportunity offered. On most of them nothing more was printed than the name of the girl and the address of the bagnio to which she was attached, but some were more fanciful in design and offered information which, to say the least, was likely to be a bit startling. Few, however, aroused as much favorable comment as the card of a gigantic Negress who lived in a Hinckley Alley cow-yard. It was designed and written for her by a San Francisco newspaper reporter, and bore this inscription within a border of forget-me-nots:

BIG MATILDA
THREE HUNDRED POUNDS OF BLACK PASSION.
HOURS: ALL HOURS.
RATES: 50C EACH: THREE FOR ONE DOLLAR.

The wall mottoes and signs were particularly prevalent during the eighteen-nineties. Most of the former were handsomely done in embroidery, and many were the work

251

of the prostitutes, who made them in their hours of leisure. Others were burned in wood or leather, for in those days the art of pyrography was highly regarded in all strata of society. All were extremely sentimental in character; they extolled the virtues of home and mother, set forth highly moral precepts, or advised whole-hearted participation in various aspects of the good life. In each room of a Pacific Street brothel was a framed motto saying: "God Bless Our Home," while in another place, in California Street, was a great profusion of burnt leather masterpieces asking: "What Is Home Without Mother?" A great favorite, found in many parlors, offered this good advice: "If At First You Don't Succeed, Try, Try Again." In some of the brothels hung printed signs offering to refund whatever money a man had spent in the event that illness resulted from the visit, while in others this was prominently displayed:

SATISFACTION GUARANTEED

OR

MONEY REFUNDED.

The man who asked for his money back on the ground of dissatisfaction, however, did not receive actual cash. Instead he was given a sort of due bill — a metal disk on which had been stamped: "Good for One." Attached to the disk by a fine wire was a pointed, flat-topped sliver of steel in which circular threads had been cut.

A few years before the abolition of open prostitution in San Francisco a bitter price war raged among the cheaper parlor houses, and in most of the establishments which had previously maintained a standard fee of two dollars appeared this sign:

UNION HOUSE

PRICE: $1.50.

The French parlor houses in Commercial Street and Grant Avenue (Dupont Street) were at the height of their prosperity and popularity during the late eighteen-nineties and for some ten or twelve years after the turn of the present century. They were by far the lowest brothels of this type in San Francisco; it is doubtful, indeed, if viler dens were ever operated anywhere in the United States than Madame Gabrielle's Lively Flea, Madame Lazarene's Red Rooster, and the Parisian Mansion, owned by Madame Marcelle and Jerome Bassity. In each of these places, and in other Commercial Street bagnios as well, was a special chamber called the Virgin's Room, the walls and ceiling of which were covered with mirrors, while the furniture, except for a huge brass bed decorated with rosettes and streamers of ribbon, was upholstered in gaudy plush and velvet. Between the mirrors were cleverly concealed peep-holes. Whenever a visitor entered who seemed to be sufficiently gullible — usually a countryman or a sailor with his wages in his pocket — he was offered a virgin at double or triple the usual fee. If he accepted, he was escorted into the Virgin's Room, and places at the peep-holes were sold at from five to ten dollars each. Occasionally a real virgin was available, but more often this *rara avis* was impersonated by an inmate of the brothel who had retained, despite the ravages of her profession, an appearance of youth and demureness and who was enough of an actress to simulate fright and bewilderment. In every bagnio there was always at least one such girl, and as the official virgin of the establishment she was usually paid slightly more than the customary percentage of her earnings.

The Virgin's Room was also the scene of most of the erotic exhibitions, called circuses, for which the Commercial Street resorts were particularly celebrated, although in some resorts they were staged in a large cabinet which was wheeled into the parlor. Both men and women participated in these shows, and sometimes, instead of men, dogs, goats, and other animals were used. Perhaps the most extraordinary performance of this character ever seen in San Francisco, or, for that matter, anywhere else, was that given about 1900 in Madame Gabrielle's Lively Flea, then in Dupont Street — an exhibition in which a woman and a Shetland pony took part.[1] This spectacle was shown every ten days or two weeks for several months, and the admission charge was twenty-five dollars. In another bagnio owned by Madame Gabrielle, at Geary and Stockton streets, a weekly show was presented in which the actors were Negro men and white women. The Commercial Street houses were much frequented by degenerates, largely because of the so-called circuses, and also because they were encouraged to do whatever their erotic fancies might dictate. Perhaps the most noted of these was Theodore Durrant, San Francisco's most celebrated murderer, who in his saner moments was a medical student and an assistant superintendent of a Sunday school, prominent in the work of the Christian Endeavor Society. For a year or so during the early eighteen-nineties Durrant visited the brothels in Commercial Street several times a week. He always brought with him, in a sack or a small crate, a pigeon or a chicken, and at a certain time during the evening's debauch he cut the bird's throat and let the blood trickle over his body.[2] Another Commercial Street character of this period, about whom there was considerable mystery, was a middle-aged man who appeared each morning at the Parisian Mansion, carrying a bundle which contained a complete outfit of women's clothing. These garments he donned, and then he swept and dusted the brothel

---

[1] This exhibition is said to have been first seen in the United States on the Midway at the Chicago World's Fair in 1893.

[2] In April 1895 Durrant murdered and mutilated two young girls — Minnie Williams and Blanche Lamont — and hid their bodies in the library and belfry of Emanuel Baptist Church. He was hanged January 7, 1898.

from cellar to garret. His work completed, he resumed his proper attire and departed, leaving a silver dollar on the parlor table. No one but Madame Marcelle knew his name, and she kept the secret.

5

THE cribs and cow-yard cubicles occupied by white women and Negresses were very similar, in design and general construction, to the dens in which the Chinese slave girls were imprisoned. The single crib was simply a shanty with a narrow door, on one side of which were small double casement-windows, usually with padded ledges. It was divided into two small chambers, one of which, about six feet square, was used as a reception-room, while the other was known as the "workshop." In the former there was seldom any furniture except a built-in window-seat and a chair or a couch, although the Mexican and Spanish harlots usually added a small altar with a figure of the Holy Virgin and other religious images. The "workshop" was just large enough for a three-quarter-size iron bed, a wash-stand with a marble top, and a kerosene stove on which always bubbled a kettle of hot water. Otherwise the room contained a tin wash-basin, a large bottle of lysol or carbolic acid, and a small chest or trunk, in which the prostitute kept her street attire. During her hours in the crib she wore nothing but a white night-gown, a gaudy kimono, or a short skirt. The walls of both the reception-room and the "workshop" were decorated with sentimental mottoes, calendars, and chromos, while above the bed hung a framed placard on which had been painted or printed, usually within a border of flowers, a woman's name, supposed to be that of the occupant of the crib. If these identifications were accurate, however, the cribs of San Francisco must have been largely populated by girls named Rose, Daisy, Martha, or Leah. The bed itself was always dirty and usually rickety and dilapidated. It was covered by coarse sheets and a bright-colored spread, and across the foot was thrown a piece of red or brown oilcloth. This was to prevent the spread's being soiled by the boots or shoes of the customers, for in the twenty-five- and fifty-cent cribs, and in the others on busy nights, a man was not permitted to remove his foot-wear, or, for that matter, any of his garments except his hat. He was always requested to take off his hat. No self-respecting prostitute would entertain a man while he had his hat on.

The only exceptions to the rule which forbade the removal of clothing were to be found in a type of crib known as a " creep joint." In the " workshops " of these places were small closets, the back walls of which were really doors which could be opened from the outside. A visitor was encouraged to hang his clothing, particularly his coat, waistcoat, and trousers, in the closet, and when his attention was otherwise engaged, as it usually was, an accomplice of the harlot opened the door and removed all money and valuables from the garments, leaving in their stead a shiny new dime. The origin of the custom of putting a dime in a pocket of the rifled raiment is unknown in present-day San Francisco, although the coin was obviously meant for car-fare home. Men who had been robbed in these places seldom made a complaint, for it was widely known that most of the cribs were connected by push-button with the nearest barroom. When trouble arose, the alarm was answered by the saloon bouncer, and a man who demanded the return of his stolen property was fortunate if he managed to keep the dime. Many of the cribs and other brothels were also protected by special watchmen, who received five dollars a month from each inmate.

The cribs were not confined to any particular section of the Barbary Coast, but were scattered throughout the red-light district. From the early eighteen-seventies until the abolition of open prostitution they were to be found in large numbers in Pacific, Jackson, Washington, Kearny,

Montgomery, Stockton, Commercial and many other streets, in Broadway and Grant Avenue, and in scores of alleys which opened into these thoroughfares. In Hinckley and Pinckley alleys, and in Broadway between Grant Avenue and Stockton Street, were most of the Negro cribs, as well as many such dens filled with Spanish and Mexican women. French harlots occupied a row of cribs in Commercial Street, and in order to meet the competition offered by the Parisian Mansion and other parlor houses many of them employed barkers, who stood before their doors and cried: "Only fifty cents for a French girl, gents!" Some of the women did their own ballyhooing, leaning from their windows and shrilly enumerating the variety of amorous entertainment which was to be found within. French women also predominated in the cribs of Bacon and Belden Places, in the southwestern part of the Barbary Coast, each of which was entered through heavy iron gates which stretched across the street. During the eighteen-nineties and for some three years of the present century both of these thoroughfares were entirely devoted to prostitution. In Bacon Place alone there were fifty-four cribs, for each of which the owner of the property received a daily rental of four dollars, and almost as many in Belden Place. A crusade against these dens was begun early in 1898 by the Reverend Father Otis of the Paulist Community and the Reverend R. C. Foute of the Grace Episcopal Church. They were soon joined by the Society for the Prevention of Vice and the St. Mary's Square Association, and in December 1898 the embattled crusaders made a mass attack against Bacon Place, tearing down the iron gates and wrecking several cribs. A similar onslaught was made upon Belden Place, and the prostitutes were driven out of both thoroughfares. They soon returned, and were again expelled in 1903. Once more they came back to their old haunts, however, and were not finally dispersed until the cribs were destroyed by fire in 1906.

The worst cribs in San Francisco were probably those which lined both sides of Morton Street (Maiden Lane), a short thoroughfare of only two blocks running from Union Square at Stockton Street across Grant Avenue to Kearny Street, and now in the heart of the retail shopping district. These dens were occupied by women of all colors and nationalities; there were even a few Chinese and Japanese girls. And not only were the Morton Street cribs the lowest in San Francisco's red-light district; they were also the most popular, partly because of the great variety and extraordinary depravity of the women to be found there, and partly because the police seldom entered the street unless compelled to do so by a murder or a serious shooting or stabbing affray. Ordinary fights and assaults were ignored. Occasionally a respectable woman came through Morton Street on a slumming tour, but she seldom made a second visit, for the prostitutes greeted her with ribald jeers and curses, and cries of "Look out, girls, here's some charity competition!" and "Get some sense and quit giving it away!"

Every night, and especially every Saturday night, this dismal bedlam of obscenity, lighted only by the red lamps above the doors of the cribs, was thronged by a tumultuous mob of half-drunken men, who stumbled from crib to crib, greedily inspecting the women as if they had been so many wild animals in cages. From the casement-windows leaned the harlots, naked to the waist, adding their shrill cries of invitation to the uproar, while their pimps haggled with passing men and tried to drag them inside the dens. If business was dull, the pimps sold the privilege of touching the breasts of the prostitutes at the standard rate of ten cents each or two for fifteen cents. But on Saturday nights some of the more popular women, who had built up a more or less regular clientele, remained in their "workshops" from dusk to dawn, while the pimps kept the men standing in line outside, their hats in one hand and money in the other. It was not uncommon for a Morton Street prostitute to entertain as many as eighty to a hundred men in one night.

Prices in Morton Street ranged from twenty-five cents for a Mexican woman to one dollar for an American girl. The regular rate in the cribs occupied by Negresses or by Chinese or Japanese girls was fifty cents, while the Frenchwomen sold their favors for seventy-five cents. Even higher prices than any of these, however, were sometimes obtained by prostitutes of unusual youth and attractiveness, and particularly by red-haired girls. It was a popular superstition in San Francisco for many years that a woman with auburn tresses was exceedingly amorous, and that a red-haired Jewess was the most passionate of all. A pimp who owned two or three such girls was on the highroad to fortune. Curiously enough, the principal owner of red-haired Jewish girls in San Francisco's red-light district was an extraordinary woman known as Iodoform Kate, who flourished in the eighteen-nineties. She was herself a prostitute for several years, during which time she gained considerable renown by refusing to have any dealings with the pimps. Instead Iodoform Kate saved her money, and about 1895 she was able to purchase a dozen or more Morton Street cribs. In each of them she installed a red-haired Jewess, and after a few years she retired with a comfortable fortune.

Another noted Morton Street prostitute was a young woman known as Rotary Rosie, an appellation which perhaps sufficiently described her. Rotary Rosie, like Iodoform Kate, maintained no pimp and was also distinguished among the crib women for her erudition; she read books and appeared to have the rudiments of an education. A year or so before the fire of 1906 she fell in love with a student at the University of California, and he introduced her to several of his fraternity brothers. For a few months thereafter she entertained these young gentlemen without expense to them, requiring only that they read poetry to her for half an hour.

Her ambition was to quit the brothel and attend college, but after a few years she became discouraged and committed suicide.

Except for a brief period in 1892, when they were closed as a result of a crusade by the Civic Federation, the unholy dens in Morton Street maintained a continuous existence for more than forty years. They were finally destroyed in the conflagration of 1906 and were not rebuilt, principally because the land on which they had stood was too valuable for business purposes.

6

FOR at least forty of the more than sixty years in which open prostitution flourished in San Francisco, cow-yards were to be found in all parts of the Barbary Coast and the red-light district; they were probably as numerous as the parlor houses and the single cribs. Three of these monstrous kennels stood out among the others like veritable sore thumbs upon the hands of the body politic — the Nymphia, in Pacific Street near Stockton; the Marsicania, in Dupont Street (Grant Avenue) near Broadway; and the celebrated Municipal Brothel, also called the Municipal Crib, in Jackson Street near Kearny. The last-named lingered for several years under the protection of the politicians and city officials and finally died a more or less natural death; but the Nymphia and the Marsicania succumbed, after comparatively brief periods of prosperity, to the crusading prowess of the Reverend Terence Caraher, pastor of the Roman Catholic Church of St. Francis and chairman of the Committee on Morals of the North Beach Promotion Association. Father Caraher was an Irishman who came to the United States in 1873. After nine months at the Mission San Rafael he was sent to the Church of St. Francis, and except for fifteen years at the Mission San Jose — from about 1885 to 1900 — he remained in San Francisco until a

few months before his death, which occurred in October
1914, at a sanatorium in San Jose.

Throughout his San Francisco pastorate Father Caraher waged incessant warfare against the red-light district
and the Barbary Coast. He blockaded the brothels and the
dives, particularly the former, with volunteer pickets; he
exerted religious and political pressure upon the real owners
of the property used for prostitution; he haled the operators
and inmates of the bagnios into court and otherwise harried
them in every possible fashion. In common with most reformers, however, he was not long content to confine his
activities to the special field in which the value of his work
was unquestioned and in which he had the support of every
right-thinking citizen; he was soon heavily engaged in what
might best be described as a general denouncing business.
Scarcely a week passed in which the newspapers did not contain at least one statement of violent protest signed by him,
and scarcely a sermon did he deliver in which something or
someone was not denounced in language which left no doubt
as to his meaning. He inveighed against public dancing as
vicious and immoral and against the nickelodeons as possessing the same undesirable attributes; he condemned most
of San Francisco's trolley cars, and especially those which
traversed Kearny Street, as "dance halls on wheels . . .
full of lewd women and beastly men"; and during his latter
years he fell into the habit of fulminating against practically
every public amusement and pastime which threatened to
obtain a foothold in San Francisco. At mass on January
27, 1907 he delivered this typical attack upon roller-skating
rinks, which were then becoming popular throughout the
city:

"While I approve of athletic sports and games in
general, I have only words of condemnation to utter
against skating rinks. I condemn public skating because
it is dangerous both to body and soul. Many receive

261

injuries at the skating rinks from which they never re-
cover. In skating the bones are oftentimes broken,
limbs are twisted, and the body severely bruised. While
the danger to the body in the skating rink is great, the
danger to the soul is greater. Skating rinks are frequented by the worst elements of society. Some of the
male skaters speak to one another afterwards of their
experiences and their conquests of young women in the
rinks, and where do the skaters go after they leave the
rinks? I answer, some of them go to perdition. Skating
is not only a foolish, silly exercise, but it is most dangerous to body and soul. I request you to avoid the skating
rinks and thereby show a good example to the rest of
the community." [1]

The Nymphia, the first important brothel to feel the
weight of Father Caraher's wrathful hand, was a flimsy
U-shaped building, three storeys in height, with about a
hundred and fifty cubicles on each floor. It was erected early
in 1899 by the Twinkling Star Corporation and soon after
its completion was leased to a syndicate composed of four
gifted impresarios of vice — Emil and Valentine Kehrlein,
Sam Blumenberg, and a man known on the Barbary Coast
only as Mr. Frey. It was opened about the middle of the
summer of 1899, with three hundred cubicles occupied by
as many women, each of whom paid a daily rental of five
dollars. Had everything gone well with this enterprise, it
would within a short time have become by far the largest
brothel on the Pacific Coast, for the syndicate planned not
only to fill the remaining cubicles with girls, but to erect an
annex with accommodations for five hundred more. The

---

[1] The San Francisco *Call*, January 29, 1907. So great was Father
Caraher's influence that the Board of Supervisors promptly adopted an ordinance prohibiting anyone under sixteen years of age to enter a skating rink.

original intention of the Kehrlein brothers and their associates was to call their cow-yard the Hotel Nymphomania and to people it with women suffering from that condition. The police, however, refused to permit the use of the name, so the syndicate compromised by calling it the Nymphia and filling the cubicles of only one floor with nymphomaniacs, or, at any rate, with harlots who were advertised as such. Each inmate of the Nymphia was required to remain naked all the time she was in her crib; she was obliged to entertain every man who applied, regardless of race or color, or lose her place in the brothel; and she was subject to constant inspection through a long, narrow window cut in the door. A shade covered each of these windows, but it was automatically raised for a few moments by a dime dropped into a slot outside the door, so that anyone with the necessary coin could see what was taking place in any of the cubicles at any time. This novel feature was immensely popular, but it was abandoned after a few months. Instead of dimes, too many customers used slugs, which were sold for a few cents each by venders on the Barbary Coast.

The Nymphia had been in operation only a short time when Father Caraher returned to San Francisco from his fifteen-year sojourn at the Mission San Jose. He found the cow-yard running full blast, with two uniformed policemen mounting guard at the entrance. They were there to maintain a semblance of order, however, and not to interfere with the operation of the resort. After a Saturday-night inspection of the brothel, when he found the hallways swarming with drunken men and saw things which he had supposed went out of fashion with the destruction of Sodom and Gomorrah, Father Caraher immediately launched a vigorous offensive. He found the heads of the police department and other city officials in a somewhat sympathetic mood, for the blatant depravity on exhibition at the Nymphia

had caused considerable talk even among the hardened de-
bauchees of the Barbary Coast. The priest finally succeeded
in enlisting active police support, and in January 1900 the
Nymphia was raided. Thirty-three women were arrested,
and the four members of the operating syndicate. Some of
the women were convicted in police court and fined, and
others were released, while the Kehrleins, Blumenberg, and
Frey were found guilty of maintaining a nuisance and operating an immoral resort. Each was sentenced to six months
in prison, but on appeal a higher court reduced the penalty
and directed their release on payment of a fine of two hundred and fifty dollars.

One of the prostitutes arrested in this raid was a nine-
teen-year-old girl named Polly Knight, who called herself
Reine Adams. She was released, but was again arrested on
August 25, 1900, for shooting Billy Abbott, who owned a
brothel in Grant Avenue and a small cow-yard and saloon
in Pacific Street, in the rear of which was a garden in which
erotic exhibitions were staged. The girl told the police that
when she was eighteen years old, Billy Abbott had induced
her to leave her parents and live with him, and that after a
few months he had compelled her to become a streetwalker.
But she was too shy to be successful in this exacting profession, and Abbott put her in his brothel in Grant Avenue,
which catered principally to Chinamen. When the Nymphia
was opened, he sent her there with several other girls whom
he had sold to the Nymphia operating syndicate. The Adams
girl finally realized that Abbott's treatment of her had not
been of the best, and she determined to kill him. She shot
him with a twenty-two-caliber revolver, but he was not seriously wounded, and soon recovered. He refused to prosecute
her, however, and she was released. What became of her
afterwards the police never knew. When she was brought
into police court for dismissal from custody, Judge Conlan
remarked: " This case resembles that of Kitty Turner, who

stabbed a member of the same class of men recently. . . .
It is to be regretted that in neither instance was the wound
fatal."

The Nymphia syndicate reopened the cow-yard as soon
as its members had paid their fines, but Father Caraher and
the police harassed them so successfully that they abandoned
it in disgust early in 1901. It was again in operation, under
new management, in August 1902, and the police immediately began to arrest the inmates, all of whom demanded
jury trials. One or two convictions were obtained and
promptly appealed to higher courts, and for the next year
or so, pending the final outcome of these cases, the police
contented themselves with blockading the resort. Uniformed
police were once again stationed at the entrance, but they
now had orders to take the name of every man who entered,
and to keep him out if possible to do so without using force.
Judging from the lists of names these policemen turned in
to their superior officers, no one except John Smith ever
visited the Nymphia. In the early spring of 1903 Judge
J. C. B. Hebard of the Superior Court, who had heard one
of the appeals in an early case against the Nymphia, handed
down a decision in which he said that Chief of Police George
Wittman could send policemen into the Nymphia to make
arrests if he had reason to believe that the law was being
violated, but that he could not legally blockade the resort.
Chief Wittman thereupon began a series of raids, and
within a few weeks the doors of the Nymphia once more
were closed. They never opened again, although in July
1903 B. Ferner and F. J. Drake announced that they had
leased the place for five years at a rental of $18,000 for the
first year, $36,000 for the second year, and $48,000 for
each of the next three years and would operate it as a
"high-class" bagnio, whatever that might mean. But Chief
Wittman told them that he would raid the brothel the moment it reopened, and when the Superior Court refused to

grant an injunction against the police, Ferner and Drake abandoned the project.

Much the same plan of campaign that had proved so successful against the Nymphia was followed by Father Caraher in his attack upon the Marsicania, which the San Francisco *Call* described as "one of the vilest dens ever operated in San Francisco." This was a smaller cow-yard than the Nymphia, with only thirty-three cribs, in a stable-like enclosure at the end of a long passageway which opened into Grant Avenue less than two blocks from Father Caraher's church. Some of the cribs were larger than ordinary dens of the sort, however, and were occupied by from two to five women, so that the population of the brothel was usually about one hundred prostitutes. Each paid five dollars nightly rental. While the Marsicania appears to have been a resort of singular depravity, catering especially to the riff-raff of the Barbary Coast, it possessed none of the special features which distinguished the Nymphia and other bagnios of the same type. It was opened about the middle of 1902, while Father Caraher was in Europe on a vacation, on property owned by P. Marsicano, but leased to P. Vincent and subleased to George Sellinger. According to the *Call*, the brothel was actually operated by Auguste Houges and Emil Kehrlein, the latter of whom had been one of the owners of the Nymphia, with Sellinger as manager and figure-head.

Also, while Father Caraher was away, several parlor houses had been established in the immediate vicinity of his church. A blockade by volunteer pickets soon compelled these bagnios to close their doors, but this sort of systematic annoyance failed to daunt the frequenters of the Marsicania; on the contrary, they seemed delighted to divulge their names to whoever asked for them, and many even insisted upon giving the names of their friends. They became frightened, however, when the priest induced Chief of Police George Wittman to post uniformed policemen before the brothel as pickets, and the operators of the Marsicania appealed to the courts, many of which had already shown a friendly attitude toward various brothels. In February 1903 George D. Collins, attorney for Sellinger, obtained a temporary injunction from Judge Carroll Cook of the Superior Court, restraining the police from blockading the Marsicania or from entering the premises except in serious emergencies. The brothel thus operated under judicial protection and enjoyed a period of great prosperity until May 28, 1903, when Judge Cook, having heard arguments and testimony in April, dissolved the injunction. He held that Sellinger had not come into court with clean hands and so was not entitled to relief. Attorney Collins at once filed notice of appeal, whereupon Judge Cook issued an interlocutory injunction pending a decision by the California Supreme Court. It imposed the same restrictions upon the police as had the temporary writ.

The Marsicania was now safe from molestation, either by the police or by Father Caraher, for at least two years, for a decision by the Supreme Court could not be expected in less than that time. The night the injunction was granted, there was a great celebration at the Marsicania, and several women were badly beaten by drunken customers. Next day Emil Kehrlein and his associates began the erection of additional cribs. But such a storm of protest arose, not only from Father Caraher and clergymen of other denominations, but from the newspapers and various civic societies as well, that Attorney Collins arranged another series of legal shenanigans. Jean Pon, who was cook and housekeeper for the inmates of the Marsicania, installed a stove, a dozen chairs, and two or three tables in the passageway leading to the brothel, and set himself up as a restaurant-keeper. Then Attorney Collins appeared before Judge Cook on behalf of Pon, and in June 1903, without publicity, obtained an injunction restraining the police from interfering with the business of Pon's restaurant. The court held that any sort of surveillance over the Marsicania would have that effect. Judge Cook then dissolved the interlocutory injunction, whereupon Chief of Police Wittman, knowing nothing of the writ which had been granted to Pon, ordered a raid upon the brothel. Twenty-eight women were arrested. They were all released upon arraignment in police court, and Chief Wittman and Father Caraher, who was accused of being responsible for the raid, were cited to appear before Judge Cook on charges of contempt of court.

The priest was purged of contempt when he said that he had no knowledge of the raid, but Chief Wittman was found guilty. An appeal was immediately taken, and in July 1905, after two years in which the Marsicania was the most thoroughly protected brothel in San Francisco, the Supreme Court handed down a decision reversing Judge Cook and dissolving Pon's injunction. Justice Lorigan, who wrote the opinion, said: "It would be preposterous to say that where the public may freely enter to violate the law a police officer is excluded from entering to enforce it." The decision also characterized the Marsicania as "the scene of bestial and unnatural crimes" and found that Pon and his so-called restaurant were being used as a subterfuge to prevent police interference. With the way thus cleared, Chief Wittman began a vigorous offensive which soon closed the bagnio and so added another scalp to Father Caraher's collection of trophies.

7

THE famous cow-yard in Jackson Street, variously called the Municipal Brothel and the Municipal Crib, was erected in 1904 on the site of an underground Chinese tenement known as the Devil's Kitchen and the Palace Hotel, which was condemned by the Board of Health. When originally opened, the Municipal Crib was a three-storey structure with ninety cubicles, but it was destroyed by the earthquake and fire of 1906 and was replaced by a four-storey building and basement, containing 133 cribs and a saloon. The basement cubicles were occupied by Mexican prostitutes, and those on the fourth floor by Negresses, while on the other floors were representatives of various nationalities, with American and French girls predominating. The women were more or less graded by floors and sections according to their youth and beauty, and prices varied accordingly. The standard rates were twenty-five cents in the Mexican basement cribs, fifty cents on the first floor, seventy-five on the second, and one dollar on the third, which was occupied entirely by French prostitutes. The Negresses on the top floor charged fifty cents, with the customary reduction for parties of two or more.

Billy Finnegan, a well-known character in the Barbary Coast dives, recruited for the original crib, and promised immunity from arrest to all harlots who rented space in the building, at from two to five dollars a day for each crib. The brothel was then known simply as 620 Jackson Street, but within a short time it was popularly called the Municipal Crib, for it was soon common knowledge that most if not all of the profits flowed into the pockets of city officials and prominent politicians. Saloon-keepers and others who wished to curry favor with the political powers advertised the brothel whenever possible; strangers who asked policemen where women could be found were directed to it, and it was a regular stop for the Jackson Street cars. If there were no women on the trolleys, the conductors usually shouted: "All out for the whore house!" Several parlor houses and cow-yards in the immediate neighborhood were closed because they attracted men who might otherwise have gone to the Municipal Crib. Among them was a cow-yard in Pacific Street near Grant Avenue, which was operated by A. Andrien, Jerry Driscoll, Dick Creighton, and three others. Driscoll was a cousin by marriage of Mayor Eugene Schmitz and had been a lieutenant of Christopher A. Buckley's during the height of the latter's power as the political boss of the city. Each of the six men interested in the project had invested twenty-five hundred dollars, and the Pacific Street brothel was opened a few weeks after the fire of 1906, with forty-eight women in as many cribs. Some seven months later Andrien testified before the Grand Jury that he had regularly paid a city official $440 a week for protection, and Creighton told the jurors that Abe Ruef had personally received $250 a week.

As Billy Finnegan had promised, the Municipal Crib was protected for more than two years, until the Grand Jury began its inquiry into the corruption of the Ruef political machine and Mayor Schmitz's administration. The crib was investigated by the Grand Jury and was frequently in the limelight during the graft prosecution that followed the indictment of Ruef, Mayor Schmitz, and several members of the Board of Supervisors, who were described by Ruef himself as "being so greedy for plunder that they'd eat the paint off a house." [1] On December 4, 1906, while the Grand Jury was trying to determine the source of the unusual protection accorded the Municipal Crib, one Paul Hendiara testified that the profits of the brothel since the fire had averaged $3,830 a week, and that Herbert Schmitz, the Mayor's brother, owned a one-quarter interest in the place and received one-fourth of the earnings. According to Hendiara, the other owners were James Finnegan, Emilio

---

[1] The Grand Jury returned 383 indictments, of which 129 were against Ruef and 47 against Mayor Schmitz. Most of the others were against various members of the Board of Supervisors. Few of the indictments were tried, and only one conviction was obtained, that of Ruef, who in December 1908 was found guilty of bribing Supervisor John J. Furey to vote for a trolley franchise. Ruef was sentenced to fourteen years in San Quentin Prison. When he was released, he returned to San Francisco, where he is now engaged in the real-estate business.

Lastreto, and Joseph Michel. Herbert Schmitz denied Hendiara's testimony *in toto,* and Mayor Schmitz and Abe Ruef likewise disclaimed any connection with the bagnio.

In November 1906 the members of the Grand Jury visited the crib and were greeted by the inmates with jeers and curses. The jurors were told by the manager, Louis Peterson, that the real owner of the cow-yard was Joseph Alexander, a traveling salesman who had no permanent address and whom Peterson admitted he had never seen. A few days later, on November 23, the first raid was made upon the resort, and six women were arrested. They were immediately released when arraigned in police court. On January 28, 1907 the police again invaded the crib and locked the doors. They were reopened in February, and the place was raided once more on February 20 by order of the Grand Jury. Eighty-two women were driven from the cubicles, but no arrests were made. In March the crib resumed operations, and five raids during that month, upon this and another brothel in Pacific Street, resulted in the arrest of fifty-seven women. They were all released on bail of twenty dollars each, which they forfeited. Despite these frequent attacks by the police and the Grand Jury, the cubicles of the Municipal Crib were again filled with prostitutes during the summer of 1907. It was finally closed in September of that year, a few days after Chief of Police William J. Biggy had visited the resort and found the halls and cribs swarming with boys from fourteen to eighteen years of age. During the summer of 1910 Louis Michel attempted to open the place as a brothel, but the police compelled him to close after the crib had been in operation for less than a week. About a year after his visit of inspection Chief of Police Biggy was ordered removed from office for reasons which were not divulged. He refused to accept dismissal and on the night of November 30, 1908 crossed the Bay of San Francisco in a police launch for a conference with Hugo

Keil, a member of the Board of Police Commissioners and one of his supporters. He left Keil's residence in a cheerful mood and was seen by several people to embark in the launch for the return trip to the city. But when the boat reached San Francisco, Chief Biggy had disappeared. His body, with no marks of violence upon it, was found floating in the Bay about a week later. What happened to him was never known, although it was common gossip in San Francisco for several years — the story is still heard occasionally — that the truth about the tragedy was contained in a police report which was suppressed by the authorities. In June 1911, three years after Chief Biggy's death, the engineer of the launch, William Murphy, went insane, and in his ravings frequently cried: "I don't know who did it, but I swear to God I didn't!"

The Municipal Crib was the last cow-yard of any considerable size to operate openly in San Francisco, although only the interference of Father Caraher and the San Francisco *Globe*, the unsympathetic attitude of Chief of Police Jesse B. Cook,[1] and the unusual position assumed by a property-owner prevented the opening of one in Pacific Street, near Montgomery Street, in the early spring of 1909. The men who conceived this project were Tom Magee and Ed Pincus, both of whom were widely known in red-light and Barbary Coast circles. Magee had been a blacksmith, a pugilist, and a saloon-keeper; Pincus had been about everything that it was possible for one man to be on the Barbary Coast. Both had at various times owned interests in brothels and deadfalls, and in partnership with Billy Harrington had operated the Seattle Dance Hall in Pacific Street for a year or so after the fire. Pincus was also renowned as a very dangerous man in a rough-and-tumble fight. One of his eyes

---

[1] Before Chief Cook became a policeman, he was a tumbler and an acrobat, with the troupe of Renaldo, Cook, and Orr. He also played in the first road company of *The Black Crook*, in 1875.

was gouged out in a saloon brawl in Vancouver, B. C., whither he had gone after being expelled from Los Angeles and Seattle by the police of those cities. When he came to San Francisco, he was asked what had happened to his opponent. Pincus replied: "He'll never blow his nose again."

Early in 1909 Pincus and Magee obtained a sub-lease on a brick building in Pacific Street which had housed, successively, a brothel and a low variety theater, and began remodeling it into a cow-yard at an estimated cost of thirty-five hundred dollars. They installed sixty cubicles — tiny plastered cells some six feet wide and eight feet long — and rented them to prostitutes at thirty-five dollars a week each. By the first of April 1909 the brothel was almost ready for occupancy, and Pincus and Magee let it be known that they would open for business within two weeks. Up to this time their plans had attracted little or no attention, but they now made two serious mistakes, which brought the wrath of the entire city down upon them. Next door to the proposed cow-yard was a branch of the Whosoever-Will Mission, of which J. C. Westenberg was secretary. Pincus brazenly offered to pay Westenberg fifteen hundred dollars in cash if he would move the mission to another part of the Barbary Coast, and promised to send him enough fallen women to keep the mission busy. Then Pincus called on Father Caraher and tried to enlist the aid of the priest in a campaign to move all brothels and deadfalls east of Montgomery Street and concentrate them in a comparatively small area. He mentioned casually that he planned to open a little place of his own, which he hoped would start the exodus. Father Caraher not only refused to have anything to do with Pincus's transparent scheme, but both he and Westenberg complained to Chief Cook, who sent for Pincus and Magee and told them that so long as he was head of the Police Department the cow-yard would not be permitted to open. Father Caraher also obtained the support of the San Francisco

Globe in his campaign against the brothel, and the newspaper at once began a vigorous crusade, with editorials,
front-page articles, and streamer headlines. The great clerical and journalistic uproar which ensued was increased when
Tom Magee slugged S. Fred Hogue, publisher of the *Globe,*
in a corridor of the Hall of Justice. Next day work on the
new crib stopped, and the site swarmed with souvenir-
hunters, who carried away everything that was loose or that
they could detach from the building. Pincus and Magee
were compelled to abandon their project entirely when they
were informed by Henry C. Breeden, manager of the Butler
estate, which owned the building, that all leases and sub-
leases had been voided by their attempt to use the property
for immoral purposes.

Both Pincus and Magee left San Francisco soon afterwards, but Pincus returned in about four months and approached William Maxwell, manager of the Zelle estate,
with a scheme to erect a cow-yard on a vacant lot in Pacific
Street near Sansome Street, which the estate owned. Maxwell refused to listen, and Pincus began following him about
the streets, cursing and berating him. On August 20, 1909
the two men met at Market and Mason streets, and Pincus's
attitude became so threatening that Maxwell drew a revolver and killed him. Maxwell's statement that he had acted
in self-defense was accepted by the police.

8

WHILE San Francisco's reformers tolerated the red-light
district and the Barbary Coast for almost three-quarters of
a century, with only sporadic and usually ineffectual outbursts of opposition, they fiercely combated every effort to
control or prevent the spread of diseases that are always
rampant in a city which permits open but unregulated prostitution. For many years the reform element, particularly
the clergy, successfully advanced the curious argument that

since the brothels could not be abolished, fear of disease would keep men from frequenting them; they never seemed capable of realizing that vice regulated, even to a slight extent, is vice in retreat. They ignored the frequent warnings of reputable physicians and medical societies that venereal diseases were becoming alarmingly prevalent in all classes of San Francisco's population. With equal obtuseness, they greeted with frenzied trumpetings of righteous denunciation and unbelief the publication of such unpleasant facts as were brought to light during the survey of Chinatown by the Board of Supervisors in 1885, when a member of the Board of Health and other physicians testified that they had found young boys, scarcely in their teens, suffering from diseases contracted in the Chinese cribs, and that they knew of no city in the world which harbored as many diseased children as San Francisco.

It was not until 1911, more than sixty years after the first Chileno harlot had set up her tent on the southern slope of Telegraph Hill, that a proper agency was formed to deal with a situation which competent medical men believed to be a serious menace to the health of the city. In March of that year, under the authority of ordinances adopted by the Board of Supervisors, the Municipal Clinic was established by the Board of Health and an auxiliary committee of physicians and business men. It was empowered to compel every prostitute in the city to submit to examination and, if necessary, treatment; and the police were instructed to enforce its regulations. No woman was permitted to enter a brothel without a medical certificate, and all harlots were required to report at the clinic every fourth day for medical inspection, which included a blood test. For this they paid fifty cents, but treatment in case of disease was free. Each prostitute received a booklet containing her photograph and a record of her examinations, and if she failed to produce this identification upon demand of a policeman or a member of the clinic's staff, she was liable to arrest for vagrancy. If a girl was found to be diseased, her booklet was surrendered to the clinic, and she was ordered to refrain from prostitution until she had been cured. Not all obeyed this last regulation, of course, but those who didn't ran a considerable risk of imprisonment.

The clinic opened its doors on March 21, 1911, with Dr. O. B. Spalding as supervising inspector, and existed for two years and one month. In that brief time it succeeded in reducing the prevalence of venereal disease in the red-light district sixty-six per cent, or from 148 per thousand prostitutes to about 40 a thousand. In the first month of its operation 14.69 per cent of the women examined were diseased; in its last month, May 1913, the percentage was 4.66. The daily average of women who reported for inspection was 125. In addition to this work, the clinic staff rehabilitated at least two hundred harlots and found respectable jobs for 140. Fifty girls who asked for permits to enter brothels were persuaded to abandon their intentions and seek other means of livelihood. Many minors were rescued from the bagnios and turned over to the Juvenile Court, and convicting evidence was furnished to the police in twenty-five white-slave cases.[1]

Despite this record, the Municipal Clinic had to fight for its existence from the day of its establishment. Practically every clergyman of prominence in San Francisco, with the notable exception of the Reverend Dr. Charles F. Aked of the First Congregational Church, was violently opposed to it; the Reverend Terence Caraher denounced it as "a blow at marriage," although the logic by which he reached this extraordinary conclusion was not divulged. Early in 1913 a large number of ministers held a meeting and de-

---

[1] A full account of the work of the clinic may be found in *Our Nation's Health; the Protective Work of the Municipal Clinic of San Francisco and Its Fight for Existence;* by Dr. Julius Rosenstirn (San Francisco, 1913).

manded that Mayor James Rolph, Jr., abolish the clinic, and a little later a committee of preachers issued a long and violent attack in which they charged the clinic with operating a cow-yard containing one hundred women. At the conclusion of its statement the committee admitted that it had no proof whatever to support the accusation, which was immediately denied by Dr. George L. Eaton, president of the Board of Health.

The clergymen next brought political pressure to bear, and on February 13, 1913 the Board of Supervisors adopted a resolution forbidding the further use of the word "Municipal," although nothing was said about the Municipal Bar, some fifty yards from the Hall of Justice. On May 20, 1913 the Board of Police Commissioners ordered police protection withdrawn from the clinic. Later the commissioners admitted that the order had been issued at the command of Mayor Rolph, who had previously been quoted as favoring the continuance of the clinic's work. But, whoever was responsible, the order effectually destroyed the clinic's usefulness; it retained the authority to compel prostitutes to report for examination and treatment, but lacked the means of enforcing its regulations. Soon thereafter it was closed and the work abandoned. Thus the clergymen were victorious —and disease again raged unchecked throughout the red-light district.

SLUMMERS' PARADISE

AT TWELVE minutes and six seconds past five o'clock on the morning of April 18, 1906, the San Francisco peninsula began to shiver in the grip of an earthquake which, when its ultimate consequences are considered, was the most disastrous in the recorded history of the North American continent. The shocks continued for one minute and five seconds, and while the actual damage done to property by the temblor was comparatively slight, it made possible the greater calamity of fire by shaking down chimneys and breaking water-mains and electrical connections throughout San Francisco. Within a few minutes after the earth had ceased to rock, sixteen fires were throwing their menacing glare against the morning sky from as many sections of the city south of Market Street. No water was available except a relatively small quantity found in a few abandoned cisterns, and the Fire Department was practically helpless. By noon a square mile had been devastated, and during the early afternoon the conflagration crossed Market Street at Third and Kearny Streets. Driven by a strong southeast wind, it spread rapidly northward and westward, through the business and financial districts, the Barbary Coast, and Chinatown. For two days the holocaust raged unchecked, while the trains and ferries, and the roads throughout the countryside, were crowded with frightened and unhappy refugees. The fire finally burned itself out, but not until it had destroyed 28,188 buildings in 522 blocks, covering an area of more than four square miles, or 2,593 acres, of which 1,088 acres were north of Market Street. The property loss was estimated at about four hundred million dollars, while 315 persons were known to have lost their lives, and 352 had been reported to the police as missing. Only a few were ever found.

The destruction of Sodom and Gomorrah by fire and brimstone from heaven was scarcely more complete than the devastation of Chinatown and the Barbary Coast by fire and earthquake from, perhaps, the same source. On the morning of April 20, 1906, the opium dives and slave dens, the cow-yards and parlor houses, the cribs and deadfalls, the dance-halls and bar-rooms, the melodeons and concert saloons — all the abode and paraphernalia of vice, from the waterfront to Grant Avenue and from Morton Street to Telegraph Hill, lay a mass of smoking ruins. Only an occasional dive or brothel remained, looming stark and solitary in the cloud of murky smoke which overhung the whole of San Francisco, and they were immediately closed by the police and the troops of the United States Army, who patrolled the burned area to protect the city from looters. At the request of the San Francisco authorities, the bagnios in Oakland, across the Bay, were likewise compelled to shut their doors. But they were reopened almost at once. As Walter J. Peterson, Chief of the Oakland Police Department, told Pauline Jacobson of the San Francisco *Bulletin* in an interview seven years later:

> "San Francisco was still smoldering, the earth still rocking, and we didn't know when the Almighty might send another visitation, yet on the incessant demand the authorities [of Oakland] had to open up the houses of prostitution. All day long and at night men were lined up for blocks waiting in front of the houses, like at a box office at a theatre on a popular night."

As an organized center of vice and crime Chinatown virtually came to an end on that catastrophic spring day; the underworld of the Oriental quarter was never able fully to overcome the cleansing effect of the fire and earthquake, and very few of the opium resorts and slave cribs were rebuilt. But unlike Chinatown and its own Biblical prototypes, the Barbary Coast immediately rose, phœnix-like, from its ashes. While the municipal and military authorities, aided by committees of reputable citizens, struggled with the vast problems of reconstruction and rehabilitation which the disaster had created, the overlords of vice loosened their purse-strings and devoted their ill-gotten treasure to the erection of a new and bigger Barbary Coast upon the ruins of the old. Within three months after the flames had subsided, half a dozen brothels and as many deadfalls and dance-halls were in prosperous operation in Pacific and adjacent streets, and by the beginning of 1907 the Barbary Coast was once more roaring in full blast. The final cycle of its career of vice and crime had begun.

The distinction of being the first important resort to flaunt its iniquities after the fire — and the further glory of being perhaps the lowest dive in all the post-earthquake period — belongs to the Seattle Saloon and Dance Hall, which was opened in Pacific Street, near Kearny Street, during the early summer of 1906 by Ed Pincus and Tom Magee, with Billy Harrington as manager. The Seattle was not as pretentious a place as the old Bull Run of more or less hallowed memory, but otherwise it suffered little by comparison with that celebrated dive of an earlier day. The Pincus-Magee enterprise was housed in a large, two-storey frame building, with a U-shaped entrance lobby decorated by framed panels containing gaudy paintings of women in varying stages of undress. The upper floor was occupied by an assignation house, and the saloon and dance-hall were downstairs in a long, rectangular room, at one end of which was a small stage whereon bawdy shows and hoochy-coochy dances were presented. Behind the stage were a few small dressing-rooms hung with curtains, where the performers changed their costumes and into which drunken men were enticed and robbed. Rough tables, chairs and benches were scattered about the dance-floor.

Pincus and Magee employed twenty girls, who were paid, as wages, from fifteen to twenty dollars a week, according to their beauty and popularity. They wore thin blouses cut very low, skirts cut very high, and black silk stockings held in place by fancy garters. Mindful of the success of the notorious deadfall and dance house at Kearny and California streets, which in pre-earthquake days had aroused a considerable commotion throughout the Barbary Coast by its rule forbidding underwear, Pincus and Magee enforced a similar fashion in their establishment and advertised the fact by cards discreetly distributed in saloons and other places where men were wont to gather. In general, duties of the women employed in the Seattle were the same as those of the pretty waiter girls, but in one respect Pincus and Magee introduced an innovation which was soon adopted by most of the other Barbary Coast resorts. They employed men to serve drinks to customers at the tables and benches on the dance-floor and thus gave their girls more time to dance with and otherwise entertain the men who succumbed to their charms. Drinks could be purchased over the bar of the Seattle at the prices which prevailed in ordinary saloons, but if a man seated himself at a bench or table with one of the dive's female attachées and ordered liquor, he paid a dollar for a pony of whisky, the same for a pint of beer, three dollars for a small bottle of bitter wine known as Dago red, and five dollars a bottle for a beverage labeled champagne, which was in reality aerated cider. The girls were paid a small percentage on drinks sold in the dance-hall and were also entitled to half of whatever they managed to

281

abstract from their partners' pockets during the close contact of the dance. Pincus often complained, however, that most of his female employees were dishonest and failed to render true accounts of their stealings.

Another and even more important source of income was developed by the girls in the Seattle and was their own particular racket; it was practically the only activity of which they were not supposed to share the proceeds with their employers. A woman employed in the dive was not permitted to leave the premises for purposes of prostitution, but if a man expressed a desire for her company in ways other than dancing, she would immediately promise so to arrange matters that she might spend the night with him, or rather what remained of the night after the Seattle had closed its doors, which was usually about three o'clock in the morning. She would point out, however, that there were great difficulties to overcome, and that they must proceed shrewdly and with caution. It was impossible, she would explain, for her to meet him anywhere or for him to wait for her at the back door of the resort, for her lover was extremely jealous and always walked home with her to make certain she didn't get into mischief. But after much discussion and many drinks she would evolve a plan whereby they might hope to circumvent the watchful sweetheart. She offered to sell, for a dollar or two dollars or whatever she thought the traffic would bear, a key to her room, so that the enamored visitor might join her there an hour or so after she had finished her work at the dance-hall. If he objected to thus buying a pig in a poke, she would indignantly retort that, after all, she didn't know him, and that if he failed to appear with the key she would have to employ a locksmith to make another. To a man befogged by bad liquor and confused by the joys of propinquity, all this sounded very reasonable. Nearly always he bought the key and carefully noted the address she gave him, which was usually a street number of a near-by tenement, but never that of the house where she actually lived. Some of the more popular girls sometimes sold as many as a dozen keys a night, at prices ranging from one to five dollars each, and for several hours after the Seattle had closed, furtive figures could be seen flitting through the streets searching hopelessly for doors which their keys would open. This lucrative scheme was practiced for more than a year, not only by the girls of the Seattle, but by those of other dives also. It was finally stopped by the police. They received too many complaints from honest householders who had been annoyed by drunken men trying to unlock their doors.

Pincus and Magee operated the Seattle until the early spring of 1908, when they sold the property to a syndicate headed by their manager, Billy Harrington, and thereafter confined their activities to brothels, in several of which they owned large interests. The names of Harrington's partners were not generally known until October 1908, when the San Francisco *Call*, during one of its periodic crusades against Judge Carroll Cook, revealed that they were two officers of Judge Cook's branch of the Superior Court. Harrington and his associates changed the name of the resort to the Dash, and remodeled the interior, installing a row of curtained booths on either side of the dance-floor. They also discharged most of the dancing girls and in their places employed male degenerates who wore women's clothing. From one to three of these creatures were always to be found sitting in each of the booths, and for a dollar they would perform in a manner which may be imagined, but which may not be described. It was with good reason that the *Call* described the Dash as " one of the vilest saloons and dance halls ever maintained in San Francisco." The place was not very successful under the new régime, however, and was closed late in 1908, soon after Judge Cook had been defeated for re-election by the narrow margin of two thousand votes.

2

T H E most vicious dives of the new Barbary Coast were the
wine dumps — dismal cellar dens in the alleys and along the
waterfront which catered to the very dregs of Barbary Coast
humanity, where the floors were covered with damp sawdust, where wine was sold for five cents a pint, and where
the bars were rough boards laid atop kegs. They provided
neither dancing nor entertainment — nothing but a few hard
benches on which men and women sat and guzzled wine.
And the wine, as often as not, was simply raw alcohol colored and flavored. These places were the particular rendezvous of the bums, the oldest and most hopeless of the
streetwalkers, the sneak-thieves and pickpockets, and the
many Fagins who took street boys and girls under their
wings and taught them to steal. Most of the wine dumps had
been closed by the middle of 1913, principally because of
the viciousness of their habitués — who, of course, were
utterly without political or other influence — and the innumerable serious brawls which occurred in them. In one
place known as the Morgue (no connection with the saloon
of that name in the old Devil's Acre) the police averaged
twenty-seven arrests a night over a period of almost a year.

The early traditions of the Barbary Coast were ef-
fectively maintained by the wine dumps, by the Seattle and
similar establishments, and by the houses of prostitution;
but as a whole the district underwent a radical change after
the earthquake and fire. The decade that followed the rebuilding and reopening of the Barbary Coast was an era of
glamour and spectacularity, of hullabaloo and ballyhoo, of
bright lights and feverish gayety, of synthetic sin and imita-
tion iniquity. Practically everything that occurred in the
dives of this period was deliberately planned to startle and
impress, and if possible to shock, the tourist and sightseer;
in its last incarnation, particularly from about 1910 to the

end of its existence, the Barbary Coast was a veritable slummers' paradise, although underneath there still flowed the same old current of vice and corruption which had been the life-blood of the quarter since the days of the Sydney Ducks. In earlier years visitors from the upper strata of society had been both infrequent and unwelcome, but virtually every dance-hall on the new Barbary Coast provided, as a special and very remunerative feature, a " slummers' balcony," which was filled each night by palpitant, wide-eyed spectators. They were firmly convinced that they were watching the underworld at its revels, and seeing life stripped to its elementals, and so they submitted meekly to exorbitant charges for admission and liquor. Beer was never less than a dollar a pint in the sightseeing galleries, and a highball, which might or might not contain a trace of whisky, was likewise a dollar, and sometimes even more. During this same period the maximum price of any mixed drink at the best bars in San Francisco was twenty-five cents, and of beer, except the finest imported brews, a dime. In the manner of the modern moving-picture cathedral, most of the better-known resorts on the Barbary Coast employed gaudily uniformed sidewalk barkers and doormen, who bellowed the glad tidings of glamour and excitement almost without cessation from early afternoon until long past midnight. They were usually fellows of little or no imagination, and their patter was fairly well standardized after this fashion:

" Right this way to the visitors' gallery, folks! Everybody happy! Everybody welcome! Everybody safe! The hottest show and the prettiest girls on the Coast! Watch 'em wiggle, gents; watch 'em wiggle! Don't talk about what you see in here, folks! It'll shock you, but it's worth seeing! "

While most of San Francisco's reputable citizens publicly bemoaned the iniquities of the Barbary Coast and performed lip-service in the many campaigns designed to elimi-

nate its more objectionable features, secretly they were, for
the most part, enormously proud of their city's reputation
as the Paris of America and the wickedest town on the continent. A tour of the district, under proper police supervision,
was usually a part of the itinerary of the distinguished
visitor to San Francisco, and if through some oversight it
wasn't, the distinguished visitor very frequently included it
on his own account, for no area of similar size in the
Western Hemisphere had been so widely publicized or was
so universally known. And since comment upon the evils of
the quarter was eagerly sought by the newspapers, few
celebrities set foot in San Francisco without seeing it. Sarah
Bernhardt always visited the Barbary Coast when she
played in San Francisco on her frequent tours, and pleased
local journalists immensely by declaring that she had found
it more fascinatingly wicked than Montmartre. Anna Pav-
lowa, the famous dancer, often visited the dance-halls, and
avowed that she had obtained many ideas for her own dance
creations by watching the gyrations of the light-footed Barbary Coasters. And when John Masefield, now Poet Lau-
reate of England, arrived in San Francisco some sixteen
years ago, the first thing he said when he disembarked from
a ferry-boat at Market Street was: " Take me to see the
Barbary Coast."

Although prostitution and robbery remained the basic
industries of the Barbary Coast, the resort features which
brought thousands of sightseers into the district after the
earthquake and fire were the dance-floors and the low variety shows. The latter usually consisted in skits, songs, and
exhibition dancing, all carefully designed to shock, but not
disgust. They were undeniably bawdy, coarse, and vulgar, for
otherwise they would not have interested the slummers; but
they were not nearly so obscene as the shows which were
given as a matter of course in the old-time concert saloons.
And, of course, in comparison with the peep-shows which

were extremely popular features of San Francisco's brothels until the red-light district was abolished, they were as innocuous as so many Sunday-school tableaux. The *pièce de résistance* of a Barbary Coast variety program was the lewd cavorting of a hoochy-coochy artiste, or the Dance of the Seven Veils as interpreted by a fat and clumsy Salome dancer, who simply wiggled a muscle dance to semi-classical music. Occasionally a few of the veils were omitted, and the dancer squirmed and twisted in very scanty raiment indeed. For some curious reason, perhaps to show that her strength and agility were not confined entirely to her abdominal muscles, the Salome dancer almost invariably concluded her performance by gripping a chair between her teeth and swinging it about her head.

The variety shows, particularly those which included hoochy-coochy or Salome dancing, were very well liked, but it is doubtful if they alone could have made the Barbary Coast the extraordinarily popular place that it became during the last ten years of its existence. The principal attraction was dancing. The whole Barbary Coast was dance-crazy, and practically every dive of any pretentiousness was a combination dance-hall and concert saloon, offering both theatrical entertainment and an opportunity to trip the light fantastic or to watch it being tripped. The number of resorts which sprang up after the earthquake and fire and enjoyed their comparatively brief flurries of success and prosperity was really extraordinary — by 1910, four years after the disaster, there were no fewer than three hundred saloons and dance-halls crowded into six blocks, centering, of course, in Pacific Street, which was more than ever intrenched in its position as the main thoroughfare of the Barbary Coast. Throughout the quarter, rentals soared to amazing heights; basement and street-level store-rooms, which if rented to legitimate businesses would never have brought more than thirty to a hundred dollars a month, were let for ten times

287

those amounts to be used as saloons and dance-halls — one dive-operator paid nine hundred dollars a month on a ten-year lease for a cellar about sixty feet long and thirty feet wide. Many of these places were still in operation, though the names of some had been changed and they were under different managements, when the Barbary Coast was finally closed in 1917. The most important, or at any rate the best-known, were the Hippodrome, the U. S. Café, the Jupiter, Coppa's, the Golden City, the Folies Cabaret, the White House, the House of All Nations, the Dragon, the Bella Union, the Thalia, the Cave, the Comstock, the Golden Star, the Turkish Café, the O. K. Café, the Ivy Café, the Moulin Rouge; the California Dance Hall, which was the first place in San Francisco where Filipinos were permitted to dance with white girls; Spider Kelly's, the Red Mill, the Bohemian Café, the Diana Hall, the Bear, the Manila, the Queen Dance Hall, the So Different, the Olympia Café, the Frisco, the Old California, the Scandinavian Dance Hall, Thorne's, the Criterion, the Headlight; the Belvidere, also called the Old Ladies' Home because it employed women who were more than thirty-five years old; Lombardi's, Dew Drop Inn, Purcell's, Dutch Emma's, Squeeze Inn, the Owl Dance Hall; the Admiral, owned by Billy Finnegan of Municipal Crib fame; the Cascade, Menio's, the Palms, Marconi's, the Elko, and the Neptune Palace.

The House of All Nations was operated by a Portuguese named Louis Gomez, who boasted that among his dancing girls were to be found women of all civilized nations. Purcell's, the Dew Drop Inn, the Squeeze Inn, and the So Different were Negro places, employing Negro women, but catering to white men and particularly to white slummers. For a year or so the Owl Dance Hall was the property of one of the Barbary Coast's most celebrated characters, Black Tony Parmagin. As a boy Black Tony learned the ways of crime under the tutelage of Buzzard Maloney, a well-known

sneak-thief and lush-worker of the eighteen-nineties. Later
he left the protecting wing of the Buzzard and organized a
gang of juvenile pickpockets, who varied their arduous
labors in this field by robbing drunken men as they staggered
from the dives in the early hours of the morning. In the late
autumn of 1906 Black Tony acquired control of the Owl
Dance Hall, but the venture was not very successful, and a
year or so later he sold the property to Irish Annie Davis.
Black Tony joined the bunco gang headed by Mike Gallo
and is said to have acted as a go-between in the payment of
graft to the police and politicians. Another of Gallo's workers was Jim Le Strange, who was interested in the Cave, the
Cascade, Menlo's, and the Bella Union. When Gallo's gang
was finally smashed, Black Tony Parmagin entered the bail-
bond business, but this was a comparatively honest occupation and held little attraction for him. He soon abandoned
it to sell dope and operated with fair success until 1931,
when he was arrested and sent to prison for seventeen years.

The number of girls employed in the dives during the
final ten years of the Barbary Coast varied as the tide of
prosperity ebbed and flowed, but ranged from about eight
hundred to three thousand. Their principal duties were to
dance and drink with the customers and to appear in the
ensemble and chorus numbers of the shows. They received
as wages from twelve to twenty-five dollars a week and were
also paid a small commission on all liquor sold through
their efforts. Many of the girls took beer when their dancing
partners bought them a drink, but most of them ordered
whisky — and were served the usual jigger of cold tea or
colored water, called in this period a Kelly. It is doubtful
if there were as many prostitutes in the dance-halls as in the
early days of the Barbary Coast, and most of those who
dabbled in the ancient profession of harlotry did so after
they had finished their work in the dives. They were required to remain on or near the dance-floor during their

hours of duty, from about one o'clock in the afternoon until closing-time. Legally this was one a.m., for the law prohibited music and dancing in saloons and public dance-halls between that hour and six a.m., but actually it depended upon the temper of the police, the political influence of the dive-keeper, and, to some extent, whether the city's reform element was quiescent or on a rampage. In many of the resorts the girls wore their regular street dresses, and in others evening gowns were compulsory, while in a few, notably the Midway, the Turkish Café, the Cave, and the Tivoli, they were clad in silk stockings, short skirts, and low-necked blouses or shirt-waists. The manager of the Tivoli prescribed blue skirts and black stockings, but the operators of the other places permitted their girls to wear whatever color they preferred. Even these special costumes, however, do not appear to have been particularly seductive. The San Francisco *Call* described them in the summer of 1911 as " of the cheapest fabric, many of them torn and stained, none reaching below the knees, and here and there hooks missing and bodices yawning in the back, but always the silk stockings as the inevitable mark of caste."

During this period the Midway, on the south side of Pacific Street near Montgomery Street, was one of the shabbiest dives on the Barbary Coast, but early in 1913 it came under the management of George Kelley, better known as Red Kelley, and for several years thereafter it was one of the most pretentious resorts in the district. It was also a favorite haunt of the sightseers, for Kelley was an accomplished showman and could always be depended upon to provide entertainment calculated to thrill and to shock the outlander. For a considerable period the bright particular star of his variety programs was a fat Salome dancer appropriately called Gyp. She performed the sensual twistings and writhings of a muscle dance in a very lascivious manner, but the effect of her contortions was less exhilarating than it might have been because from start to finish of the dance her face was wreathed in a sweet, infantile smile. In later years the name of the Midway was changed to Hippodrome, and finally it was called the U. S. Café, while another Hippodrome was opened directly across the street by Frank Scivio. It was during the Midway's days as the Hippodrome that new decorations, by far the finest and most celebrated ever seen on the Barbary Coast, were installed in its entrance lobby — six bas-relief panels in plaster, depicting a group of satyrs happily and purposefully pursuing as many nymphs, with anatomical details all complete. These details, however, aroused such a storm of shocked comment that they were eventually removed, and the areas in dispute were covered by bands of ribbon, done in reddish plaster, which trailed upward over the shoulders of both nymphs and satyrs. The figures were the work of Arthur Putnam, who later became one of America's most noted sculptors. According to one story, his only compensation was a few drinks, but according to another — and probably the correct one — he was paid $175 for the job.[1]

The operators of most of the large resorts of the post-earthquake period, in direct violation of the ancient code of the Barbary Coast, did their best to protect their sightseeing customers, and casual visitors were safer than at any other time in the history of the quarter, as long as they kept out of the alleys and avoided the wine dumps, the deadfalls, and the brothels. Thieves and other criminals continued to frequent the dance-halls and, as of old, made them their headquarters, wherein they planned their depredations and spent their gains on wine and women; but actual robbery on the

---

[1] Putnam died in Paris in 1930. Examples of his later work may be seen in the Paris Salon, the Boston Museum, and the Metropolitan Museum of Art in New York. He was awarded a gold medal at the Panama Pacific Exposition in San Francisco in 1915. He also designed the Sloat monument at Monterey, California.

premises was frowned upon as tending to frighten away the slummers and so kill the geese that laid so many golden eggs. The revenue of the better-known places was derived almost entirely from the dancing (for a dance of two minutes they charged from ten to twenty-five cents) and from the sales of liquor and tickets of admission. The prices of the latter ranged from a quarter to a dollar, although sometimes on gala nights the tariff was boosted to two dollars. For the benefit of the sightseers, who looked on from the slummers' balconies, fake fights were staged on the dance-floors, with occasionally the flash of a knife-blade or the dull gleam of a pistol-barrel; and each night several couples were ceremoniously ejected for indecent dancing. In many of the dives, of course, especially the Negro joints, it was seldom necessary to fake a row, for plenty of real fracases occurred in the natural course of events. And as far as indecent dancing was concerned, if a man bought a dance ticket and ventured upon the floor with one of the high yallers employed in these places, his conduct was determined only by his conscience and the amiability of his partner. The best-known of the Negro dance-halls, and the most turbulent, was Purcell's, which occupied a long, narrow room on the north side of Pacific Street between Montgomery and Kearny streets. It was furnished only with a bar, a few rough tables and chairs, and a score or more of wooden benches which faced a splintery dance-floor. No nonsense about buying liquor was permitted in Purcell's; a visitor either drank, and drank frequently, or he was thrown into the street by several husky bouncers who patrolled the dive. The bar in Purcell's was at the left of the entrance and was set against a thin wooden partition which separated the resort from the saloon and dance-hall operated by Spider Kelly, who in his earlier years had acquired considerable renown as a light-weight prize-fighter. Kelly's bar was also against the partition, at the right of his entrance. Shooting affrays were of frequent oc-

currence in Purcell's, and bullets often ripped through the
flimsy wall and endangered Kelly's bar-tenders. To protect
them Kelly lined his "back-bar" and mirror with sheet-iron
boiler plate. And to safeguard them against stray bullets in
his own place, where life was also uncertain and filled with
surprises, he likewise covered the front of his bar. Captain
Meagher of the Chicago Police Department, who made a
tour of the Barbary Coast in December 1912, described
Spider Kelly's saloon and dance-hall as "undoubtedly the
worst dive in the world." Captain Meagher also expressed
his dismay at the great number of young girls whom he found
in the Coast resorts as members of slumming parties, and
declared that "compared to San Francisco, Chicago's vice
districts are as nothing."

3

NOT only did the dance-halls of the Barbary Coast attract
enormous crowds, but they exercised a tremendous influence
upon the dancing habits of the whole United States. In these
dives originated dance steps which practically every dancing
young man and woman in America strove to master. For the
turkey trot, the bunny hug, the chicken glide, the Texas
Tommy, the pony prance, the grizzly bear, and many other
varieties of close and semi-acrobatic dancing, which swept
the country during the half-dozen years that preceded the
World War despite the scandalized roaring of the nation's
pastors, were first performed in the dance-halls of San
Francisco's Barbary Coast for the delectation of the slummer. The birthplace of the best-known of these terpsichorean
masterpieces — the turkey trot and the Texas Tommy —
and of several others also, was the Thalia, which for many
years was the largest dance-hall on the Pacific Coast. From
eighty to one hundred girls were employed there during its
heyday, and double shifts of bar-tenders, with from four
to six men in a shift, worked like beavers behind the long

bar. The original dive of that name was a cheap saloon and dance-hall in the Uptown Tenderloin at Mason and Turk streets, about where both thoroughfares run into Market Street. It catered particularly to sailors and was a worthy rival of the Midway Plaisance, a few blocks farther east. But the old Thalia fell on evil days a few years before the earthquake and fire of 1906 and passed out of existence. When the Barbary Coast was rebuilt, a new Thalia was erected on the north side of Pacific Street, about half-way between Kearny and Montgomery streets. Throughout its existence the new Thalia always seemed to be especially favored by the police and the political powers and almost invariably led the way in tilting the lid which, for various reasons, was occasionally clapped upon the Barbary Coast. Such a period of comparative quietude was imposed upon the district in the late spring of 1911, during a reorganization of the police force undertaken, as the Police Commission announced, "for the good of the department." Early in July, however, the Thalia came under the management of Eddie Englehart and Louis Parente, who was one of the owners of Parente Brothers' Saloon on the northeast corner of Kearny and Pacific streets. They immediately made the necessary political arrangements for removing the disabilities under which the Barbary Coast was then languishing, and distributed handbills announcing the " grand opening " of the Thalia on Thursday, July 6, 1911, with " entertainment and dancing all night." All the other resorts, the disgruntled managers of which had been reluctantly closing their doors at one a.m., followed the Thalia's example and arranged special all-night programs. But by far the most important of the " grand openings " was that of the Thalia, for the guests of honor were Joseph Sullivan, president of the Board of Police Commissioners, and Chief Jailer Walter McCauley of the county jail. The San

Francisco *Call* thus described the dive on this memorable occasion:

" Different from all the others is the Thalia, where early Thursday evening the president of the police commission and a party of friends were made guests of honor at the ' opening.' It is a great barnlike structure, with the dance floor in the center fenced off at each end, and at either side the drinking places raised in double tiers of low balconies. To the extreme right from the entrance lobby is the higher section whither the ' slumming' parties are directed and where the habitués of the place are scarce. Below, on the same side, are the tables for the dancers and their companions. Opposite, in the lower balcony, just a few feet from the dance floor, are long rows of wooden benches, where beer may be had for five cents a glass, and where women of the place seldom go.

" Above the ' nickel a glass' section is the real money getting section of the hall. Here, in half open booths, the women of the dance hall ply their trade. Here are invited the sailors who drift into the place. Here men are plied with liquor and urged to part with their cash. In these booths Thursday night were many sailors, drunk or nearly drunk, each with a woman at his elbow. Others were there, too — men showing signs of labor and young fellows in good clothing and bearing evidence of coming from decent homes. Below, in the cheaper section, were many men sprawled asleep or in a drunken stupor. On the dance hall floor a few couples cavorted and displayed the fancy steps of the newest tenderloin dances.

" The lobby of the Thalia is a great open space before the bar, and here the women congregate and at-

295

tempt to entrap every patron who enters. Hesitation
means a dozen groping hands and a dozen voices
clamoring for drinks. ' Be a sport; buy just one.' . . .
The Thalia provided a ' Salome dance ' just before one
o'clock as the final ' big ' attraction of the night. The
' Salomes ' danced and strained and twisted, received
a faint spattering of applause, and then, throwing
coats or loose gowns over their scant costumes, joined
the throngs of dancers in the comparatively conserva-
tive steps of the Grizzly Bear, the Bunny Hug, and the
Texas Tommy.

"Three o'clock in the morning, and the dancing at
the Thalia was beginning to lag. An hour later, and the
place was half deserted. The few remaining were men
and women listless in appearance, with bloodshot eyes
and pasty faces. Still the piano strummed on for an
hour."

Red Kelley acquired control of the Thalia about a year
or so after the president of the Board of Police Commissioners had honored it with his presence, but after operating
the dive successfully for a few years, he transferred it to his
floor manager, Terry Mustain, a former pugilist. During
the Mustain régime a frequent visitor to the Thalia was an
old man of whom attachés of the resort knew nothing except
that his name was Frank Mulkey and that he lived in Portland, Oregon. Every few weeks Mulkey spent several eve-
nings at the Thalia, sitting always in the same corner, buying
many drinks, which he never touched, watching the shows,
and talking to the girls and waiters. When he was especially
pleased with one of the girls, or when a waiter showed unusual courtesy, he entered his or her name in a note-book
and said, benignly: "I'll remember you in my will. I'm a rich
man, you know."

The employees of the Thalia regarded Mulkey as a

harmless old coot, and not until he died in Portland, in 1927, did they learn that he was a lumber and real-estate operator and as wealthy as he had claimed to be. He was as good as his word and bequeathed a considerable sum of money to Terry Mustain and to each Thalia girl and waiter whom he had promised to remember.

4

BESIDES the Thalia, the Midway, and other elaborate dance-halls on the Barbary Coast property, there were at least fifty cheap resorts on the outskirts of the quarter, principally toward North Beach, where five minutes of dancing cost only five cents. These places sold no liquor, provided no entertainment, and employed no women, depending entirely upon those who came in from the streets, most of whom were of the factory-girl class. Admission was free to the women, but men paid a nickel each. The managers of the five-cent dance-halls professed to require very circumspect conduct from their customers, and the walls of most of the resorts of this type bore large signs thus inscribed:

ADMISSION

ONLY ON THE FOLLOWING
RULES AND CONDITIONS:

Turkey Trots, Couples
With Their Heads
Together, Walking,
Bowerying, Dipping,
Or Gentlemen Introducing
Themselves to Ladies in the Hall

STRICTLY
PROHIBITED!
Introducers on the Floor.

Under proper supervision the nickel dance-halls might have filled a very real need in San Francisco and provided opportunities for amusement and recreation to hundreds of poor but honest working girls. But all of the elaborate rules in which the operators of the resorts took such apparent pride were more honored in the breach than in the observance. No man, regardless of his appearance or what might be known of his character, was denied admittance, and the doors were likewise flung wide to young girls scarcely in their teens, who were easily led astray by the experienced pimps and recruiting agents for the dives and brothels of the Barbary Coast. In consequence, these dance-halls soon became little more than supply depots for the red-light district. Nevertheless, they were permitted to operate without effective interference for several years. But late in 1908 the Reverend Terence Caraher, unfavorably known to the Barbary Coast as Terrible Terry, turned his attention to them and began an energetic campaign to drive them out of existence, complaining that the children of the parish had to pass many of them on their way to church. He was supported in his crusade by Charles F. Skelly, secretary of the Board of Police Commissioners, who on February 9, 1909 told the Downtown Association that the nickel dance-halls should be abolished as soon as possible.

"Little girls fifteen and sixteen years old frequent these places," said Mr. Skelly, "and often it leads to their ruin. Unfortunately these nickel dance halls do not come under the jurisdiction of the Police Commission, and we are powerless to prevent the spread of these dens of vice."

Under pressure exerted by the Reverend Father Caraher and several business men whom he and Mr. Skelly had interested, the Board of Supervisors finally enacted regulations which enabled the police to proceed against the nickel dance-establishments. Within another year or so the last of them had been closed.

CHAPTER XII

THE END OF THE BARBARY COAST

THE HANDWRITING on the wall for the Barbary Coast, though dim and almost undecipherable for several years, was the decisive defeat of the remnants of Abe Ruef's Workingmen's party in the autumn of 1911, when James Rolph, Jr., was elected to the first of his ten terms as Mayor of San Francisco. Rolph's impressive triumph, which was followed immediately by the election of a Board of Supervisors committed to his policies and leadership, was the first actual repudiation by the voters of the evils which had marked the conduct of municipal affairs during the Ruef-Schmitz régime and, to a lesser extent, throughout the administration of Mayor P. H. McCarthy. But, even more important to the Barbary Coast, the downfall of the Ruef machine presaged the eventual abandonment of the gold-rush tradition which decreed that San Francisco must be a wide-open town. From the fall elections of 1911 until it was abolished half a dozen years later, the Barbary Coast was on the defensive and waged a losing fight for existence; it faced an unfriendly if not actively hostile administration, and also arrayed against it was a rapidly growing sentiment, even among those who professed to take great pride in the city's reputation for wickedness, that there was no place for mining-camp amusement features in the new and greater San Francisco which had arisen from the devastation wrought by the earthquake and fire of 1906. Business men, especially, were beginning to realize that obtrusive and spectacular vice was more likely to harm than to benefit an American city.

The first intimation that a new order of things impended came late in January 1912, when Police Commissioner Jesse B. Cook, who as Chief of Police a few years before had risked his official head by interfering with the schemes of the underworld, publicly complained of conditions in Pacific Street and in other thoroughfares of the Barbary Coast. He intimated that unless the dive-keepers cleaned their own Augean stables, the city authorities would eventually be compelled to undertake the task. A few weeks later, on February 12, 1912, before the Barbary Coast had recovered from the astonishment caused by Commissioner Cook's attack, the Police Commission announced to the newspapers that the following plans were under consideration for the ultimate cleansing and better regulation of the district:

1. All dance-halls and resorts patronized by women in Montgomery Avenue (now Columbus Avenue) west of Kearny Street, and on both sides of Kearny Street, to be abolished.

2. Barkers in front of the dance-halls in Pacific Street to be done away with and glaring electric signs forbidden.

3. No new saloon licenses to be issued until the number had been reduced to 1,500, which was to be the limit in future. There were more than 2,800 places in San Francisco where liquor was legally sold.

4. Raids to be made against the blind pigs. It was estimated that more than 2,500 were in operation throughout the city.

Not until a year after the announcement of these plans did the Police Commissioners cast another straw into the wind and throw another scare into the ranks of the dive-keepers. Then, in February 1913, they adopted a resolution aimed to discourage slumming, which had grown to such proportions that most of the dance-halls and other resorts depended upon it for a large part of their revenues:

"Resolved, That no female shall be employed to sell or solicit the sale of liquor in any premises where liquor is sold at retail to which female visitors or patrons are allowed admittance."

If this resolution had been enforced and if the announced plans of the Police Commission had been carried out, the Barbary Coast would have been dealt a blow from which it would never have recovered; ninety per cent of the dance-halls and other resorts would have been compelled to close their doors immediately, and the remainder would have been concentrated in the two blocks of Pacific Street between Kearny and Sansome streets. And most of the glamour of the quarter would have been dissipated, for it was born of the union of bright lights and noise. But while Mayor Rolph's election had deprived the dive-keepers of much of the political power which for more than sixty years had enabled them to operate their places without regard for public decency and the law, they retained enough influence to combat successfully the anti-slumming resolution and to prevent the transformation of the Commission's plans into enforceable regulations. Consequently both resolution and plans were, so far as immediate and visible effect were concerned, futile gestures which hampered the Barbary Coast not at all. Nevertheless, they were extremely significant, for the mere fact that such radical measures had even been considered showed that the city government no longer looked upon the district with a paternal and indulgent eye. A further indication of this change of attitude appeared in June 1913, when the Police Commission suspended the license of the Moulin Rouge for three weeks and found the manager guilty of contributing to the delinquency of two young girls whom he had employed to dance and entertain his customers. Hitherto the authorities had, except on rare occasions, ignored the well-known and obvious fact that scores of the girls who worked in the dives of the Barbary Coast were scarcely more than children.

2

To William Randolph Hearst's San Francisco *Examiner* goes the distinction of starting the first crusade which really succeeded in making any considerable headway against the political and other intrenchments of the Barbary Coast. On September 12, 1913, only a few weeks before James Rolph, Jr., was elected to his second term as Mayor, the *Examiner* launched its campaign with the fanfare of furious excitement which has always characterized Hearst's journalistic wars — a full-page editorial demanded that the district be wiped out, and carefully prepared news stories vividly described the wickedness to be found within its borders. The newspaper's attack came at the psychological moment toward which San Francisco had been slowly progressing since the Reverend William Taylor had preached against the iniquities of the city from the steps of the old adobe house in Portsmouth Square in the fall of 1849. Many churches, and practically every civic and social welfare organization of importance in San Francisco, immediately endorsed the *Examiner's* righteous warfare and offered their services. Within a week, one of the most formidable packs of reformers that ever hunted sin on the Pacific Coast was in full cry at the heels of the Barbary Coast and was, in particular, harrying the dive-keepers. And on September 22, 1913, ten days after the *Examiner* had loosed its first editorial blast, the Police Commission rang the death-knell of the quarter with this resolution:

"Resolved, That after September 30, 1913, no dancing shall be permitted in any café, restaurant, or saloon where liquor is sold within the district bounded on the north and east by the Bay, on the south by Clay Street, and on the west by Stockton Street.

"Further Resolved, That no women patrons or women employees shall be permitted in any saloon in the said district.

"Further Resolved, That no license shall hereafter be renewed upon Pacific Street between Kearny and Sansome Streets, excepting for a straight saloon."

The *Examiner*, which had entered the fight with very exalted ideas as to the future of the Barbary Coast, gave due credit to the Police Commission for promulgating the resolution, which was by far the most drastic measure ever enacted against the district, but declared vigorously that the crusade must not end with the elimination of dancing and the barring of women employees and visitors from the resorts. To make its meaning clearer and indicate the nature of its plans, the newspaper published a large cartoon which showed a dainty feminine figure, labeled "Spirit of Wholesome Fun," rising happily and proudly into the heavens from a smoking quagmire of corruption labeled "The Barbary Coast." Editorially the *Examiner* said in its issue of September 23, 1913: "If the campaign against the Barbary Coast ends with the destruction of the open market for commercialized vice, the good done will not be permanent. Because the purposes of this campaign are constructive as well as destructive. The purpose is to shut up the market of immoral and vulgar pleasure, and to replace that market with a great market for the sale of wholesome and decent fun."

The action of the Police Commission aroused nothing less than consternation throughout the Barbary Coast, for not even the traditional stupidity of the habitués and dive-

303

keepers of the district could prevent them from realizing that here at last was an enactment which would be devastating in its effects. Moreover, it was quite obvious that the Commission was prepared to enforce its decrees, and that the resolution was not, like so many measures of similar import in the past, designed merely as a temporary sop to the reformers. The owners of several resorts immediately discharged their dancing girls and female entertainers and turned their properties into straight saloons, while others said gloomily that they would have to go out of business when the new ordinance went into effect.[1] Forty dance-hall proprietors, however, formed an association and announced that they would obey the orders of the Police Commission to the letter by serving nothing but soft drinks. This plan was strenuously opposed by Frank Scivio, of the Hippodrome, who proposed that each dive be divided into two sections, one to be devoted to dancing and the consumption of non-intoxicating beverages, and the other to the sale of liquor, without dancing, entertaining, or the uplifting cajolery of the ladies. Scivio's scheme, however, was not only rejected by the Police Commission as impracticable, but an audible snickering arose when it was read to them. Apparently they did not feel that the business men of the Barbary Coast could be relied on to prevent the mingling of the virtuous and sinful sections. The Thalia, then the largest and most popular dance-hall in the district, sought to ward off the inevitable by protestations of purity. On the night of

---

[1] On September 26, 1913 the police issued a report on the results of a questionnaire which had been submitted to 303 dance-hall women. Most of them gave their ages as between twenty-one and twenty-nine, although a few confessed to being forty and said they had been on the Barbary Coast for twenty years. One hundred and sixty-one wanted respectable work if the dance-halls were closed, twenty-nine said they would enter houses of prostitution, and eleven said they wanted no work at all. The remainder either refused to answer the questions, or were non-committal. It is interesting to note that only one — a former chorus girl — had ever been on the stage.

September 30, 1913 this unusual sign appeared over the entrance to the dive:

> THIS IS A CLEAN PLACE FOR CLEAN PEOPLE.
> NO MINORS ALLOWED.

A few days after the new regulations had become effective the police added to the troubles of the Barbary Coast by ordering the elimination of the sidewalk barkers and the glaring electric signs. Thereupon the district became, almost immediately, what it had been before the slumming era — a region of dark and dangerous streets frequented principally by habitués of the quarter, with no visible gayety or excitement to attract sightseers from the upper ranks of society. By the middle of October the Barbary Coast lay, as the San Francisco *Bulletin* said, "harmless as a serpent bereft of its fangs." In most of the dance-halls, even in such well-known resorts as the Thalia and the Midway, scarcely a dozen dancing girls or entertainers remained, while the ancient traditions of the Bella Union, the oldest and most famous of all the Barbary Coast dives, were sturdily upheld by an old-time dance-hall woman known as Steam-Schooner Ruby, who was so called because of her extraordinary capacity for steam beer. Within another month the dive-keepers had become so desperate that they resorted to advertising — an aged and decrepit horse plodded painfully through the downtown business section drawing a wagon on which was mounted a four-sided sign, thus inscribed:

> BARBARY COAST STILL OPEN
> OPENED IN '49
> DANCING AT THE COAST
> EVERYBODY WELCOME.

But this pathetic appeal failed to bring back the vanished crowds or to revive the ancient glories of the district, for not even the most naïve slummer could thrill to the spec-

tacle of the denizens of the underworld gloomily and dis-
tastefully imbibing soda pop. By occasionally presenting obscene entertainments, by selling bootleg liquor whenever the
opportunity occurred, and by closing and reopening with
such rapidity that even the police could scarcely keep account
of their changes in management and ownership, a few of
the larger dance-halls managed to survive for several years;
but they never regained their lost privileges and powers, and
gave the authorities comparatively little trouble. The Grand
Jury of San Francisco County, indeed, after an exhaustive
survey of the resorts in April 1915, insulted the memory of
the quarter by describing them as law-abiding and harmless
to morals. The backbone of the Barbary Coast had been
broken by the *Examiner's* crusade and the action of the
Police Commission in the autumn of 1913. In the language
of the prize-ring, the Coast was punch-drunk; it could do
nothing but wait hopelessly for the knock-out blow.

3

THE final attack upon the Barbary Coast, directed principally against the traffic which had always been the life-blood
of the district, was begun in the late winter of 1914, when
the California Legislature enacted the Red-light Abatement
Act, which empowered the San Francisco authorities to proceed in the civil courts against the owners of any property
which was used for the purposes of prostitution. The law
became effective on December 18, 1914, and three days later
the police raided a building at Grant Avenue and Bartlett
Alley, which they alleged was occupied by Chinese harlots,
while the District Attorney began a test case against the
owner of the property, a Chinaman named Woo Sam. Supported by a hastily formed organization called the Property
Owners' Protective Association, which had raised a fund of
$37,500 by assessing each madame in the red-light district
three hundred dollars and each prostitute five dollars, Woo

Sam applied to the United States District Court for an injunction restraining the police from interfering with his tenants. In refusing to grant the writ the District Court held that while the city's procedure under the Red-light Abatement Act was limited to civil actions against property-owners, the police possessed the power under existing state and municipal statutes to make raids and arrest inmates of brothels. The test suit brought by the District Attorney had been appealed to the California Supreme Court, but not until early in 1917 did that tribunal hand down an opinion. It then decided unanimously that the Abatement Act was constitutional, and so put into the hands of San Francisco's reform element their first really effective weapon against open prostitution. Under its provisions property-owners could be held liable if their premises were used for prostitution or for other immoral purposes. And a great many of the buildings used by harlots were owned by very prominent citizens.

Meanwhile there had come to San Francisco, by way of Iowa and Los Angeles, a young Methodist clergyman, the Rev. Paul Smith, who combined an extraordinarily developed sense of the dramatic with a passion for reform. He became pastor of the Central Methodist Church and later president of the Federation of Churches, and after that an automobile salesman, but he made his mark in San Francisco as the instrument chosen by Providence to deliver the *coup de grâce* not only to the Barbary Coast, but to the Uptown Tenderloin as well. The Reverend Mr. Smith had no sooner assumed the duties of his pastorate than he launched into a crusade against vice in all of its innumerable forms and manifestations; whenever sin appeared, he deluged it with a flood of denunciation and expository facts. He began his campaign by giving to the newspapers copies of a letter to the president of the Police Commission, in which he declared that twenty-five thousand persons made a livelihood from vice in San Francisco, that brothels were in operation throughout the Barbary Coast and within a stone's throw of his church at O'Farrell and Leavenworth streets, and that streetwalkers made overtures to men on the very steps of the edifice. "Young men have told me," he wrote, "that they have been approached by women while on their way to church from the Y.M.C.A. Others have been approached almost before they left the doorsteps of the church after Sunday evening services." Reporters assigned by the *Examiner* to inquire into these charges were told by friendly streetwalkers that what the minister had said about them was quite true. They were, indeed, rather grateful to the Reverend Mr. Smith for coming to San Francisco; he preached such racy sermons that the vicinity of his church after services was one of the best places in the city in which to ply their trade.

On the Sunday following his letter to the head of the Police Commission, the Reverend Mr. Smith delivered a rousing sermon against prostitution, and next day the newspapers began the publication of a series of interviews in which he amplified his accusation that San Francisco was a moral cesspool, divulging information which he had obtained by venturing incognito into brothels, dance-halls, cafés, restaurants, and other resorts. He described a café in Ellis Street which with every private dining-room provided an equally private bedchamber, and told of visiting the Mason Street parlor house operated by Pearl Morton, one of the many aspirants to the title of "Queen of the Underworld." There a dozen handsome girls were paraded for his inspection, and when he declined to purchase, he was told that any type of woman he desired could be obtained within a few hours. He was also offered a fifteen-year-old girl at slightly higher than the usual rate. On the Barbary Coast, the Reverend Mr. Smith declared, conditions in the cribs, the cow-yards, and the parlor houses were so bad as to defy description. Again the *Examiner* sent its investigators into the field, and their reports more than verified the Reverend Mr. Smith's statements, as, of course, everyone who was at all familiar with San Francisco had known they would. The adventures of the investigators included being accosted by streetwalkers and dancing with strange women in cafés; they appeared to have been very much impressed by the fact that most of the café girls were young, and that they all smoked cigarettes and told dirty stories. One of the investigating parties went to a café at Mason and Geary streets and arranged with the manager of the floor show to meet a few girls in one of the curtained booths which lined each side of the room. In a few minutes the manager appeared with six girls who wore short skirts and sleeveless blouses cut very low at the throat.

" Here, boys," he said, " is a fine flock of chickens."

No further details of the investigators' experiences in this resort were given, but it was intimated that the girls displayed an embarrassing willingness to conduct themselves in a very improper manner.

The Reverend Mr. Smith's disclosures, together with the vivid reports of the newspaper investigators, aroused an even greater sensation than had been created by the *Examiner's* campaign against the Barbary Coast in 1913. The Chamber of Commerce officially demanded a thorough clean-up of the city, as did a group of influential citizens headed by Rudolph Spreckels, while clergymen, religious and civic organizations, and all of the newspapers announced that they would support the Reverend Mr. Smith's crusade. On January 15, 1917 Mayor Rolph said that he would order an inquiry and promised to close every brothel and disreputable resort in San Francisco. Six days later, on Sunday, January 21, thirty-nine clergymen delivered sermons against open prostitution and other forms of vice, and that afternoon committees of citizens assembled in various parts of the city to make arrangements for a mass meeting which had been called for January 25 at Dreamland Rink. On the appointed day seven thousand persons crowded into the Rink, where they listened to speeches and then adopted resolutions demanding that the city government proceed immediately against all places of ill repute.

On the morning of January 25, only a few hours before the great mass meeting was called to order, occurred the most dramatic incident of the entire crusade. More than three hundred prostitutes, dressed in their gayest finery and reeking with the noisome perfume so beloved of the harlot, left their quarters in the cribs, the cow-yards, and the parlor houses and, escorted by two policemen, marched to the Central Methodist Church to call upon the Reverend Mr. Smith. Although most of the women were from the alleys of the Barbary Coast, they were under the command of Mrs. M. R. Gamble, better known as Reggie Gamble, who with Maude Spencer operated a parlor house in Mason Street, in the heart of the Uptown Tenderloin. The prostitutes were admitted to the church by the pastor, who had been notified by newspaper reporters that the women were on their way. A dozen men who followed them inside were ejected by the police escort, but otherwise there was no disorder. The harlots sat quietly in the pews, hitherto occupied only by virtuous worshippers of the Christian God, until the Reverend Mr. Smith stepped into the pulpit and faced them. Then they rose and shouted as one woman:

" What are you going to do with us? "

The clergyman was nonplussed, but only for a moment. He urged them to seek refuge in the church.

" Can we eat that? " asked one woman.

" Will your congregation let us sit among their daughters? " asked another.

" Come and see," invited the Reverend Mr. Smith.

" You mean come and be snubbed."

" I've been running a house in San Francisco for eight

years," said Mrs. Gamble, "and I know something about women. And about men, too. How many patrons of your church would accept a woman out of this life into their homes? You would cast these women out of the city. Where to? Where would they drift?" [1]

"Can't they establish homes?" asked the Reverend Mr. Smith. "How many have children?"

By actual count, three-fourths of the harlots raised their hands.

"There isn't a woman here," said Mrs. Gamble, "who would be a prostitute if she could make a decent living in any other way. They've all tried it, and none could earn more than eight dollars a week. They became prostitutes because they didn't have enough to live on."

The Reverend Mr. Smith said that he would pledge himself to work for the enactment of a minimum-wage law, and that arrangements were already being made to assist the women after the brothels had been closed. A great shout of derisive laughter went up from the harlots when he declared that a woman could remain virtuous on an income of ten dollars a week. Several shouted that the minimum weekly wage should not be less than twenty dollars.

"Statistics show," said the Reverend Mr. Smith, "that families all over the country receive less."

"That's why there's prostitution," retorted Mrs. Gamble. "Come on, girls, there's nothing for us here."

As quietly as they had come, the harlots left the church.

4

THE climax of the warfare against the Barbary Coast and the Uptown Tenderloin, which by this time had become

---

[1] Where they did go remains one of the mysteries of the crusade. The San Francisco Federation of Women's Clubs opened a rehabilitation office in Montgomery Street and offered to provide assistance and, if possible, a job for every prostitute who applied. But only five appeared, although more than a thousand women were turned out of the brothels.

311

city-wide, came during the last week in January 1917, when
the Supreme Court made public its decision on the Red-light
Abatement Act. On January 30 James F. Brennan, assistant
District Attorney, announced that he was preparing to file
civil actions under the Act against every brothel in the city,
and at the same time the Police Commission issued new regulations for the control of the Uptown Tenderloin and
warned the few remaining Barbary Coast dive-keepers that
any violation of the law would be severely punished. Dancing
was prohibited in all cafés, restaurants, and other resorts
in the area bounded by Larkin, O'Farrell, Mason, and Market streets; managers of the places were instructed to bar
unescorted women from the premises; all curtains, boxes,
and booths were ordered removed from all places wherein
liquor was sold, and the license of the Lambs Club, a notorious café in Ellis Street, was revoked. Chief of Police David
A. White formed a special squad, consisting of a sergeant
and three policemen, to patrol the district and see that the
orders were obeyed. These regulations effectually disposed
of the Uptown Tenderloin, and within a week practically
every resort in the district either had been turned into a
straight restaurant or saloon or had closed its doors. Among
the famous places which thus passed from the San Francisco
scene were the Black Cat, the Panama, the Pup, Stack's,
Maxim's, the Portola, the Louvre, the Odeon, and the
Bucket of Blood.

Early in February 1917 the police raided and closed
every brothel in the uptown area, and on February 14 a
blockade was instituted against the Barbary Coast. The entire quarter was surrounded by policemen, no man was permitted to enter unless he could prove that he was engaged
in legitimate business, and the prostitutes were ordered to
vacate the cribs, cow-yards, and parlor houses. They were
allowed a few hours in which to pack and remove their belongings, but by midnight the red-light district was deserted;

eighty-three brothels had been closed and 1,073 women had been driven from their quarters. A hundred Chinese girls were evicted from the few bagnios which remained in operation on Grant Avenue. Two days later forty Barbary Coast saloons and dives closed their doors through lack of business, and within a week the remainder of the resorts had likewise abandoned the field.

The Barbary Coast was as dead as the proverbial door-nail until the summer of 1921, when a resurrection was attempted with the opening of the Thalia, the Neptune Palace, the Elko, and the Olympia. They sold near beer, employed a few dancing girls, and offered bawdy theatrical entertainment, the degree of obscenity depending upon whether or not the audience was composed of tourists. But the serpent of vice had scarcely reared its venomous head when it was scotched by Mrs. W. B. Hamilton, chairman of the Clubwomen's Vigilance Committee. Having heard rumors that immoral exhibitions were on display at the Barbary Coast, Mrs. Hamilton gathered a group of her friends and visited the district in a sightseeing bus, which they boarded at Market Street. The driver was told that the party was from out of town. When the bus stopped in front of the Neptune Palace, he said: "Now, ladies, if you are squeamish about entering this place, stay outside. But if you are good sports and want to see the sights, go in and keep your mouths shut afterwards."

Mrs. Hamilton went in, but immediately afterwards she called upon the police and the newspapers. In an interview she said:

"I have visited dancing places in Honolulu, Tahiti and various islands of the South Pacific, but I saw nothing in those places more obscene and morally degrading than I saw at the Neptune Palace."

The police took immediate action upon Mrs. Hamilton's complaint. They ordered the owners of sightseeing buses not to send their vehicles into the Barbary Coast and notified the dance-hall proprietors that not even the slightest infraction of the law would be tolerated. Within a week the dives were closed.

And that was the end of the Barbary Coast. Of its ancient glories nothing remains excepting a few battered façades, the tattered remains of signs, and the plaster nymphs and satyrs in the entrance lobby of the old Hippodrome, now befouled by dirt and penciled obscenities.

INDEX

318

CPSIA information can be obtained
at www.ICGtesting.com
Printed in the USA
LVHW030245271119
638639LV00004B/27/P